Parenting today is not easy. Teaching children to follow Christ in today's culture is even more difficult. *Raising Kingdom Kids* provides parents with sound biblical principles to help their children listen to God as they grow and mature. This is a tremendous resource for any parent who is committed to bringing up godly children.

> TONY DUNGY
> Super Bowl-winning coach and *New York Times*
> best-selling author

Dr. Evans has been a great friend to me, and a role model to many as a man of God, a husband, and a father. The Bible has a lot to say to parents, and Tony is a fantastic guide. This book will help you stay focused on the high goal of parenting: raising the next generation who will continue seeking to change the world for Christ.

> CAREY CASEY
> CEO, National Center for Fathering

This book is full of wisdom and practical guidance! What I love even more is how Dr. Evans encourages us as parents to discover and honor individual gifts and talents in each child as we are teaching them to use those strengths to bring honor and glory to their Creator and Designer.

> CYNTHIA TOBIAS
> Author of *The Way They Learn*

If you want to raise kids who will have an eternal impact, then *Raising Kingdom Kids* is for you. As Dr. Tony Evans so powerfully reminds us, kingdom parenting isn't perfect parenting, it is purposeful parenting. I highly recommend this book to all parents who want to intentionally instill in their children virtues such as wisdom, integrity, service, and love.

> MARK MERRILL
> President, Family First, and author of *All Pro Dad:*
> *Seven Essentials to Be a Hero to Your Kids*

RAISING KINGDOM KIDS

TONY EVANS
RAISING
KINGDOM
KIDS

 GIVING YOUR CHILD
A LIVING FAITH

TYNDALE HOUSE PUBLISHERS, INC.
CAROL STREAM, ILLINOIS

Library of Congress Cataloging-in-Publication Data
Evans, Tony 1949-
  Raising kingdom kids / by Tony Evans.
    pages cm
  "A Focus on the Family book."
  Includes bibliographical references and index.
  ISBN 978-1-58997-784-6 (hc)
  1. Parenting—Religious aspects—Christianity. 2. Child rearing—Religious acpects—Christianity. I. Title.
  BV4529.E93 2014
  248.8'45—dc23
                                  2014020857
ISBN 978-1-58997-880-5 (sc)

Printed in the United States of America

22 21 20 19 18 17 16
7   6   5   4   3   2   1

Let our sons in their youth be as grown-up plants,
And our daughters as corner pillars fashioned as for a palace.

—PSALM 144:12

To my four wonderful children: Chrystal, Priscilla, Anthony Jr., and Jonathan. I am deeply grateful to God for the honor and privilege of raising you and calling you my own. Your mother and I love you.

—Dad

CONTENTS

FOREWORD

Are you a mom or a dad? If so, you've probably noticed—parenting isn't as simple as it used to be.

Once upon a time, having and raising kids was an experience that most people sort of "fell into" as a matter of course. It was part of the natural order. "First comes love, then comes marriage, then comes baby in the baby carriage." That's what our grandparents used to say.

In those days, husbands and wives didn't always devote a lot of conscious thought to the challenge of becoming effective parents. They just did what came naturally. That may have been good enough in the past, but it isn't going to wash in today's high-tech, fast-paced, morally mixed-up society. Nowadays, mothers and fathers need a strategy, a plan—*especially* if they're the kind of parents interested in raising children who can be described as true kids of the kingdom.

If you fall into that category, this book is for you.

"Kingdom parenting," says Tony Evans, "involves intentionally overseeing the generational transfer of the faith in such a way that children learn to consistently live all of life under God's divine authority." That's something we care about deeply here at Focus on the Family. In fact, Tony's ideas on this topic dovetail perfectly with the objectives of our GEN3 initiative, a campaign designed to encourage folks to build marriages and families worth repeating *over three generations*. It's a goal we can all get enthused about.

How can parents create a home environment that fosters and facilitates that process? Dr. Evans offers a detailed response in the pages that follow. Not surprisingly, his parenting strategies go hand in hand with the time-honored, biblically based principles we've been promoting at Focus for more than thirty years—principles we've summarized and delineated as the Twelve Traits of a Healthy Family.

The first of these traits is a *strong marriage*. Matrimony deserves special attention in its own right, of course, but a solid marriage also has a direct impact on the development of healthy kids.

Next, thriving families are *committed* to one another. They take steps to develop a deeply rooted sense of "we-ness" among themselves. They emphasize loyalty, unity, and interdependency, and they develop traditions and rituals that become the basis of lasting bonds.

These households are also built upon a *shared spiritual foundation* that includes church attendance, family devotions, and moral discipline. After all, parents can't pass on a faith they don't possess.

Good *communication*—the open and frequent sharing of feelings—is another important characteristic of kingdom families. So is a strong sense of *connectedness*. Kids experience a high degree of warmth and closeness at home when their relationships with Mom and Dad are distinguished by play, fun, humor, shared meals, and a high level of parental involvement. Connected and communicating family members learn to *honor* one another with practical demonstrations of unconditional love, which in turn equip them with a *resiliency* that can weather any storm. By bending and flexing with circumstances, they're enabled to meet the challenges of life in a positive way.

It's important to add that loving, grace-based households are characterized by *consistent expectations and discipline*. Clearly expressed rules tend to produce secure and responsible kids. And when children are secure and responsible, they're ready to *share responsibility* with other members of the family by working together toward common goals.

Put it all together and what you have is an intergenerational group of *healthy individuals* who understand who they are, where their blessings come from, and what it means to be autonomous and interdependent at the same time. People like this have a unique capacity to reach out to others. They're *community-minded* in their approach to the outside world. Their relationships with folks beyond the front door bear the marks of strong *social skills*.

That's what a truly *thriving family* looks like. And that's what *Raising Kingdom Kids* is all about.

Want to know more? Then you've come to the right place! Dr. Tony Evans knows this subject inside and out. He's mapped out the course, and he's ready to guide you to a whole new level of parenting and family interaction.

The journey begins when you turn the page.

—Jim Daly, president of Focus on the Family

INTRODUCTION

I was raised to love memorizing Scripture. As Tony and I raised our own children, we agreed to place a priority on teaching our kids the Word in the spirit of Deuteronomy 6. It was our goal to make God's Word a topic of conversation, a symbol of our family culture, and a message that permeated every room in our house.

One of the ways that we did this was by hanging wall art with Scripture verses. I bought 'em; Tony hung 'em. Still adorning the walls of our home today are signs with verses such as "As for me and my house, we will serve the Lord," "By grace are you saved," and, my favorite, "I am the vine, you are the branches, He who abides in Me and I in him bears much fruit."

In addition to the Word, I also purchased décor that emphasized the importance of home and family. Words such as "The Gathering Place" and "Family Matters" communicated the high value we placed on our home. Hanging in our kitchen is a framed print that reads, "Write it on your heart that the ones you love are life's most precious gifts." That's exactly what we sought to help our kids do—love life, love God, and love each other.

Not only did we communicate the value of God and His Word to our children, but we also sought to help them understand their individual and unique importance to us and to God's kingdom.

There is a special set of signs vertically aligned right next to the doorway that divides our den from the hallway that leads to the bedrooms. Each sign has the name of one of our children. They read as follows: Anthony, *Priceless one*—"How blessed is the man who has made the LORD his trust" (Psalm 40:4); Chrystal, *Follower of Christ*—"For to God we are Christ's fragrance for those who are being saved and for those who are perishing" (2 Corinthians 2:15, paraphrase); Priscilla, *Full of honor*—"I will look to the LORD, I will wait for the God of my salvation, my God will hear me" (Micah 2:7, ESV); Jonathan, *God's gracious gift*—"The LORD will give grace and glory, no good thing will He withhold from those who walk uprightly" (Psalm 84:11, paraphrase).

We are now collecting meaningful art with messages that matter for our grandchildren.

Life-giving messages from the Word were not only presented in art form. We also purchased Scripture memory cards to use with our children as we sat at the table for dinner. Both Tony and I led our children as we read, discussed, and memorized quite a few of them.

Even now, on a monthly basis, our grandchildren recite memory verses they have learned as we gather together as a family.

Our desire was and still is rehearsing God's Word so we fulfill the commands of Deuteronomy 6 to keep God's words before our children and even our grandchildren. Our hope is to continually encourage them to experience God as a natural part of being in our home. Even as I write this brief reflection, I'm staring at the art resting on our fireplace mantle which reads, "The Spirit of Favor is on the Evans' home—Zechariah 12:10."

—Lois Evans

PART I

ESTABLISHING A KINGDOM MINDSET

1

THIS ISN'T THE
MAGIC KINGDOM

It began as a typical Evans vacation. My wife, Lois, and I piled our four ever-growing kids into the car and took off on a road adventure. Our car held sounds of cheerful anticipation because our destination offered promises of adventure, fantasy, and amusement. This was our first of many trips to Disneyland, but it stands out in my memory because our fairy-tale story nearly turned into a tragedy.

It was August—my vacation time—so the winding streets and pathways at Disneyland were packed with other people on summer break. The sheer volume of visitors pressed us in on all sides, and we were herded along with the masses. I felt as though I waddled more than actually walked.

Being forced to walk closely together, we chatted amicably. (This was before cell phones had become ubiquitous, so my family still had the easy freedom of actually talking to one another.) Cheerful conversations bounced back and forth among Lois, me, and our four children: Chrystal, Priscilla, Anthony Jr., and Jonathan.

Because all the kids were tall enough to get on most of the fast rides, we were thoroughly enjoying our time together, myself included. But the joy diminished somewhere between Adventureland and Tomorrowland when we realized that one of our kids had stopped participating in the conversation. Jonathan, our youngest, was missing.

Right around seven years old, Jonathan had never given us much cause for alarm. He rarely acted up or required any special attention to get him to obey the family rules. Jonathan had—and still has to this day—a strong yet gentle demeanor. Because he was so compliant, no one kept an especially keen eye on him—not even me. With each step inside the Magic Kingdom, I had become more and more captivated by the smell of good food and the sounds of the rides and the music. The promise of adventure consumed me.

I'm not sure who noticed it first, but soon the questions starting coming: "Where is Jonathan?" "Where do you think he went?" "Where was the last place anyone saw him?"

Concern rose to panic as the frightening reality settled in: Jonathan was nowhere to be found. We quickly divided up into groups and began to retrace our steps as best as possible. We decided to reconvene at a chosen location after a set amount of time. Ten minutes passed, and then twenty. Still no Jonathan. We gathered, divided, and searched again.

This time I informed a security officer, and the Disney staff began searching as well. Thirty minutes passed, and then forty. No Jonathan.

My heart raced faster than I ever knew it could. My eyes scoured the crowds as I looked for my son. *Where do all these people come from?* I wondered as I politely yet quickly wove in and out of them. Fifty minutes had passed, and then sixty. Still no sign of Jonathan.

> *Concern rose to panic as the frightening reality settled in: Jonathan was nowhere to be found.*

The sounds of the rides suddenly became an annoyance. The smell of food made me feel ill. What had been a place of pleasure just over an hour before had devolved into a locus of anguish. I realized that without my son, this was no magic kingdom.

And then . . . there he stood in the distance. When I first noticed him, Jonathan was looking at some baubles in a gift shop, unaware of the grief he had just put us all through. Jonathan had become caught up by the sights, sounds, and souvenirs that Disneyland had placed so invitingly for him to see. He was so engrossed that he had wandered off to enjoy them all by himself, not even realizing he was lost.

Jonathan smiled at me, and I rushed toward him, simultaneously wanting to hug him and spank him right there. I was grateful he was alive—yet also disappointed that he had wandered off from us. With mixed emotions I wrapped my arms around him. The story of the prodigal son became all too real in my mind at that moment. Sure, the similarities between Jonathan's actions and the rebellious son in the parable didn't entirely line up, but the concept of finding a child who was once lost and rushing to that child with a heart full of both frustration and elation seemed far more plausible than ever before. While Jonathan was lost, I would have given anything I had in order to find him. I felt that way despite the fact that he was the one who had chosen to wander off. I felt that way despite the nagging regret I had for becoming so engaged in the activities around me that I lost track of him. We both contributed to the problem in our own way, but, as the father, I was ultimately responsible.

The Journey of Kingdom Parenting

Parents, some of you are just beginning your journey in raising kingdom kids, and your eyes are filled with the bliss of those parents standing in line to board an enjoyable ride at Disneyland. Others of you have teenagers who are walking with the Lord and on the right path, but you are seeking wisdom on how to guide them through the transition from the youthful innocence of Fantasyland to the more turbulent times waiting in Tomorrowland. Still others may have children who have walked away from the Lord. Their fairy tales have morphed into tragedies, and you want to know how to point your kids back home. And others are facing the challenges of a blended family whose members may not even want to be at the park at all.

This book will meet each of you in a different place on your parenting path. Regardless of where you are, if you apply the principles we are about to explore, you will experience their fruits in your home. By intentionally applying these principles, you will reinforce one of the primary traits of a healthy home: honor. You will honor your kids by placing a high enough value on them to warrant the time and energy needed to parent well.

We're Not Perfect

by Priscilla Shirer

My family wasn't perfect. (I'm certain my dad and mom would agree.) But my parents made sure that our family was extremely purposeful. They worked hard to intentionally and deliberately create an environment where they could transfer the principles they believed in to my siblings and me.

And yet it's often only with the hindsight of age that a child can truly begin to appreciate and understand the effort and initiative involved in a process like that. The more the years gather behind me, the more easily I can recognize the sacrifice and diligence that such intentional parenting requires, not to mention how critical it is to giving a child any chance at maturing into a successful adult. I didn't really get it at the time. I found the boundaries and discipline of our upbringing to be strict. But I get it now.

I get it.

Daddy and Mommy constructed a bubble of sorts for us to live in. Home life was padded with instruction in God's Word, discipline in life lessons (such as saving and tithing our money), manners ("No elbows on the table!"), and good work ethics. We had lots of fun with our friends, but we played mostly at our home instead of theirs because my parents were so careful about the kinds of influences we might encounter somewhere else. Sure, that meant taking on the exhausting work of having a dozen sweaty kids track muddy prints in and out of the kitchen for snacks and Kool-Aid during games of basketball and Ping-Pong. But our parents did it for a reason. And they did it for us.

When we weren't at home, we were at church or at school—a simple, quaint, Christian school that reinforced the lessons taught at home. Public school came during our high school years. But even then, my parents were very involved in our studies and our friendships. They were watching, stewarding, shepherding.

They just seemed to have this *knowing* inside—a deep, inner consciousness about the culture. They knew their job as parents couldn't be passive. They knew they needed to fight aggressively against the low values and standards of the common crowd, the crude lasciviousness that was trying to seep into our minds and hearts, our attitudes and opinions, our actions and emotions.

So they put on their gloves . . . and fought.

And now that I'm older, I'm grateful for it. I can see it all more clearly. I recognize the wrinkles around the eyes that were whittled out of long nights and loving discipline.

In fact, I never thought I'd say this, but . . . I want those wrinkles, too. And I'm working on them as hard as I can.

That's why I'm sitting these three sons of mine around a dinner table tonight, just as my parents did, and teaching them God's Word. I won't allow myself to be lulled to sleep and disengage from their education, their friendships, their influences. And together with their father, I'll be intentional and purposeful in their lives every precious day that God gives us to share with them under our roof, until they spread their wings and fly out of this nest—off to their own where, hopefully, the cycle will continue.

Wherever you are on this pathway of parenting, God has a word for you. It's never too early nor is it ever too late to start applying biblical principles to parenting and watch God bring about the growth and the fruit. You may have regrets about the past and poor decisions you have made, but this is not the time to stop trying. As the saying goes, only a fool trips on what is behind him. Seize today, and start now if you haven't yet done so. I regretted not keeping a closer eye on our youngest child that day at Disneyland, but that didn't mean I didn't do everything I could to find him.

Just as Jonathan got so caught up in the sights, sounds, and smells of the park, it is easy for kids to get caught up in what our world so tantalizingly sets before them: social media, television, gaming, and peer groups. They may not even realize they have strayed off the family path. As a parent, it is your responsibility to locate them, guide them, and bring them back.

Kingdom Parenting in a Fallen World

It is easy for parents to get so caught up in the sights, sounds, and smells of their careers, entertainment, social lives, and even church commitments that they lose track of their kids as I did with Jonathan. Because parents have neglected their responsibilities to their children, there is chaos in the kingdom (see Isaiah 3:12).

Thankfully our story of losing Jonathan at Disneyland had a happy ending. But not all stories at Disneyland end that way. These stories don't normally hit the headlines because they are frequently swept under the carpet by the public-relations police, but the Magic Kingdom has had its own share of tragic endings.

Over the years, there have been people who have actually lost their lives at Disneyland or Disney World. One visitor died when a cable holding back an enormous anchor broke on the pirate ship. A registered nurse witnessed the scene and rushed to try and save the victim. Later, a colleague of mine who knows the nurse told me she said, "It came as such a shock. One minute everyone was happy and life seemed perfect, and the next minute a lady was dying before me. You just never think when you wake up to go to Disneyland that you might be going there to watch someone die."[1]

Tragedy hasn't struck just those within the park, though. Due to Walt Disney's enormous success, he was able to buy a new home for his parents in North Hollywood near the Disney studios. Yet less than a month after moving in, Disney's mom died of asphyxiation due to an improperly installed leaking furnace.

Clearly, the Magic Kingdom isn't always so magical after all.

Neither is the kingdom of the world that we are born into—a kingdom that surrounds us every day (see Ephesians 2:1-4; Matthew 12:25-26). While the world holds the glitter of success and the lure of the flesh, it also comes with the promise of death (see Proverbs 14:12; 16:25; Matthew 7:13; 1 Corinthians 15:21-22). Yet despite this reality, in so many ways it is easy to get caught up in and distracted by that which appeals to our sinful nature. Not only can we get lost and thus drop the baton of kingdom parenting, but our kids can get snared as well (see 2 Timothy 2:26), particularly if we as parents lack the tools and skills necessary to parent well because we didn't have good parenting strategies modeled for us.

It is difficult for a parent to pass on a faith that he or she does not possess. The best way for you to inspire your kids to have their own faith is for them to witness your faith—not only in your words, but also in your actions.

It is also difficult to pass on life skills you have not yet applied in your own situations. To parent well requires intentional personal growth in the art of living well, since much of parenting revolves around a child's innate ability to pattern the thoughts and actions of his or her parents. The first responsibility in parenting well is that you yourself are growing and developing as a healthy individual spiritually, physically, mentally, and socially.

Clearly, the Magic Kingdom isn't always so magical after all.

I witnessed the damage of young people parenting prematurely not long ago when I went to Baltimore to visit my own parents. As I sat on the porch and looked at the neighborhood I had grown up in, I grew saddened by what I saw. No longer did the homes contain two-parent families. Windows had been boarded up throughout, a tangible symbol of the state within.

Not too far from my parents' home sat two young women, talking loudly enough for me to hear. Each was a single parent, and each was complaining about how rough life was raising kids while also trying to survive.

Midway through their conversation, one of the ladies turned my way and said something; I don't remember what. I answered and then joined their discussion by asking them their names. I asked them to tell me their stories. As they began to talk, despair registered in their words. Phrases such as, "I'm not," "I can't," and "I don't know," punctuated their sentences.

"How do you make it?" I asked, curious if public assistance was actually enough.

"Me and my two kids live with my grandma," one woman replied. She paused and then added in a whisper, "And I sell drugs. That's the only way I know how to make it."

Her friend chimed in, perhaps trying to cover for her, "We don't have anyone to help us."

In other words, they didn't have any hope of a brighter tomorrow for themselves, let alone for their kids. At the heart of both of these ladies' troubles—as well as in the hearts of people throughout our country—is the hopelessness that comes as a result of poor parenting. We are witnessing a generation of parentless people who, either through neglect, abuse, or simple absence, are becoming parents themselves. And so the cycle continues.

You know the statistics. Nearly 50 percent of all the children in America are being raised in single-parent homes. Over three million kids drop out of school each year. High school dropouts commit 75 percent of all crimes in our nation.[2] Nearly one million teen girls get pregnant every year, burdening our already fragile economy through taxation expenses of nearly ten billion dollars annually,[3] not to mention the high emotional, physical, and spiritual cost on young mothers and their children. Churches no longer hold the appeal for our young people as they did in the past. As a result, churches are closing their doors at an alarming rate with somewhere around eight to ten thousand shutting down each year.[4]

Either through neglect, abuse, or simple absence, we are witnessing a generation of parentless people who are becoming parents themselves.

Urban problems now burden suburban centers with many of these same issues as well; drug use in suburbia more than doubled in the last decade.[5] Homicide is now the second leading cause of death for young people between the ages of fifteen to twenty-four.[6] Bullying has become an epidemic. Hopelessness is at an all-time high. Antidepressants are taken at nearly the same rate as vitamins, with over four million teenagers on some form of medication for the mind.[7]

I don't need to go over more statistics because you've already seen the alarming trends on the evening news, online, or in the papers. The culture in which we are seeking to raise our kids is clearly not a magic kingdom at all, although it declares itself as just that on the marquee of life.

Let me illustrate what I mean with a story. Long ago, there lived a man who sold pork as a butcher. He had never bought any pigs, rather he slaughtered wild pigs by the hundreds. A man from a neighboring town asked him one day, "How do you catch all of these wild pigs?"

The man replied, "It's easy. I just stick a big trough of food out there down low enough for the piglets. Then when the piglets come to eat, the parents follow. While they are getting used to it each day, I start putting up a fence at night. Just one side. I do another side every night until all I have left is a gate. Eventually they come in, distracted by the sweetness of the food, and I close the gate without their ever knowing what had happened."

In order to raise our kids with the skills to not only survive but also to thrive in the world, we need to raise children with the ability to discern what the world puts in front of them to lure them into bondage—whether that be emotional, spiritual, financial, or relational. We need to teach our kids how to look for the fences Satan seeks to erect in their minds and in their hearts (2 Corinthians 10:5). We need to raise them in a discerning environment. Because even though we live within the demonic influences of the prince of the power of this air in a world smoldering with strife, tantalizing temptations, and rebellion, we do not belong to this kingdom, and we have been given the ability to overcome. For Christ has "rescued us from the domain of darkness, and transferred us to the kingdom of His beloved Son" (Colossians 1:13).

The Kingdom Mindset

Parents, you have been called to raise kingdom kids—in *God's* kingdom. And His kingdom functions according to His rules and under His authority. In God's kingdom, He gives the agenda, and we are to advance it. In God's kingdom, the glory is His, and we are to reflect it. In God's kingdom, He provides the covenantal covering under which we are to submit and flourish.

Kingdom parenting involves intentionally overseeing the generational transfer of the faith in such a way that children learn to consistently live all of life under God's divine authority.

The command to "be fruitful and multiply" (Genesis 1:28) wasn't given simply so parents would have look-alikes. Rather, it was given so *God* would have look-alikes. The creation of humankind was established so man would be an image bearer of God Himself. This concept is captured in Genesis 1:26—"Let us make man in our image." Therefore, the goal of people in general—and the family in particular—is to mirror God in the visible realm predicated on His reality in the invisible realm. This obviously doesn't mean to mirror what God looks like, since none of us know what He truly looks like. It means we are to mirror His nature, character, values, and principles.

> *Kingdom parenting involves intentionally overseeing the generational transfer of the faith in such a way that children learn to consistently live all of life under God's divine authority.*

It is essential that parents teach their children the importance of submitting to God's legitimate authority in their lives. Through that submission to Him comes their greatest influence and impact for Him. Adam and Eve were meant to bring their children under divine rule as a reflection of their own submission to God, and we as parents are to do the same. The family is to be the replication of the image of God in history. Children are image bearers of our great God and King who seeks to promote His kingdom agenda, which is the visible manifestation of His comprehensive rule over every area of life.

Kingdom isn't a word we hear much about in Christian circles, and so before moving on, let me quickly set the stage. God has one agenda: To glorify Himself through the advancement of His kingdom. The Greek word the Bible uses for kingdom is *basileia*, which translates as "rule" or "authority."[8] Intrinsic within this rule or authority is power. So when we discuss the kingdom, we are also discussing a king and a ruler with power.

Now, if there's a ruler, there also have to be
- rulees (those ruled);
- a realm (the sphere over which the ruler rules); and
- regulations (guidelines that govern the relationship between the ruler and the rulees).

God's kingdom includes these three elements. He is the absolute Ruler of all creation, and His authority is final.

At the heart of the kingdom agenda is the reality that there is no separation between the sacred and the secular. All of life is spiritual because all of life comes under God's rule. Therefore, every issue mirrors God's nature and principles related to that specific area and thus reflects and promotes His agenda in history.

God has made Jesus Christ the sovereign over all of humankind's kingdoms (see Matthew 28:18; Colossians 1:13–18). His rule is to be represented in history by those who are a part of His kingdom (see Matthew 28:19; Ephesians 1:22–23).

And just in case you are wondering, there are no in-between kingdoms. There are only two realms in creation: the kingdom of God and the kingdom of Satan. You are subject to one or the other. Raising kingdom kids includes orienting them to God's kingdom, His principles, and the reality of His agenda on earth.

God Blessed Them

It is also important to note that prior to the day when God gave the command to "be fruitful and multiply," we read that "God blessed them" (Genesis 1:28). In other words, He provided Adam and Eve with all they needed to carry out His command. After all, the true definition of a blessing is that God provides the resources for what He asks you to do. It involves both enjoying and extending His provision in your life. The blessing is not only for the parents; it is also for the benefit of the children who would then bring about the expansion of God's image in His people. This blessing enabled Adam and Eve to fill the earth and also to extend God's blessing throughout the land to those who came after them as they established families of their own. That same blessing is there for you, too, in your parenting role.

God established the family as a conduit of blessing, providing both the opportunity and framework for individuals to collectively carry out His plan in history. In particular, that plan includes the implementation of His kingdom rule, or dominion, on earth. My definition of *dominion* means ruling on God's behalf so that all of life comes under His authority. Children are the divinely ordained means of bringing the world under the dominion of Jesus Christ.

The reason Satan continually attacks the family is that the family was specifically created as the channel through which God's kingdom would be reproduced, as kingdom kids were raised to become kingdom parents in their own homes. This is precisely why childbearing and parenting are so critical to the program of God. God foretold that it would be the woman's seed that would destroy the serpent (see Genesis 3:15). And Paul wrote in the New Testament that women would be preserved through childbearing (see 1 Timothy 2:15). In bearing and raising godly children, women participate in the kingdom of God, which overrules the kingdom of Satan. In this way a kingdom woman has the privilege of symbolically reversing what happened to Eve in the garden as a woman bears and raises new lives committed to God's truth (1 Timothy 2:14).

Through parenting, each of us raises kingdom kids to be kingdom men and women so that God's purposes are fully manifested on earth, and countless more are ushered into a saving knowledge of Jesus Christ. So then, kingdom parenting is more than a social enterprise; it is at its core a spiritual and theological imperative. Kingdom parents raise kingdom kids to fulfill God's plans and purposes for families, not what the culture intends. Our culture is seeking to redefine marriage and family in such a way that it no longer reflects how our Lord designed it. It is critical that we model godly parenting and marriages to our kids so they have the opportunity to see firsthand what kingdom families look like.

Yet unfortunately today, our Christian culture has bought into the secular culture in redefining children as burdens rather than blessings. Reducing the sizes of our families by reducing the number of children we bring into the world also reduces our capacity to be blessed. Scripture tells us that children are a gift from God. We read in the book of Psalms, "Behold, children are a gift of the LORD, the fruit of the womb is a reward" (127:3). Children are a blessing and yet ironically they are the one blessing we often seek to limit in our lives. But if we were to view children through the lens of kingdom dominion and influence—as God views them—I think we would have a different attitude about how many children we bring into our homes, as well as the priority we place on them once they are there.

Yet in order to raise kids equipped to fulfill their roles in God's kingdom, we are going to have to be intentional about our parenting. After all, it is far easier to shape a child than to repair an adult. And that's true even if you find yourself approaching this monumental task alone. Numbers of you reading this book are raising your kids without the help of another parent. Maybe you have been widowed, divorced, not ever married, or you are married to a spouse who doesn't share the same values as you or is not involved in the development of your kids. Whatever the case, let the Scriptures encourage you that you can do this well. Never underestimate the power of God when He is called upon and looked to as the source of strength, wisdom, and provision (Philippians 4:13).

Kingdom parenting is more than a social enterprise; it is at its core a spiritual and theological imperative.

The Bible tells us that Timothy, one of the great leaders in the early church, had a Greek father, who had apparently rejected God. His dad had never read *Kingdom Man*, and he certainly wasn't living up to the title. Yet Timothy still wound up faithfully serving God due to his mom and his grandmother's impact.

If you are raising your kids alone, remember Timothy. Keep him and what God did through him at the forefront of your mind. Even if you are a single parent, God has a plan for your kids. Commit your way to Him in all you do, and your kids will reap the benefits of having a parent who models biblical discipleship.

Kingdom kids don't need perfect parents. Kingdom kids need purposeful parents who seek to understand and apply God's principles in their homes. I applaud you for picking up this book and making use of other resources in order to better equip yourselves as parents under God.

It is far easier to shape a child than to repair an adult.

May God guide and bless your journey of raising kingdom kids so you will experience the great joy of seeing your children and grandchildren walking in His truth (see Proverbs 17:6; 3 John 1:4) and making a kingdom impact. No matter what your successes or failures have been up to this point, it is my desire that this book helps take you to the next level on your quest to raise kingdom kids.

2

ASHER AND THE ELEPHANT

Remember Mayzie, the lazy bird from Dr. Seuss's *Horton Hatches the Egg*? She lamented:

> I'm tired and I'm bored
> And I've kinks in my leg
> From sitting, just sitting here day after day.
> It's *work*! How I hate it!
> I'd *much* rather play!
> I'd take a vacation, fly off for a rest
> If I could find *someone* to stay on my nest![1]

If you've ever had toddlers in your home, you have probably read more than your share of Dr. Seuss's books to them. You might have even inadvertently memorized some by now.

Dr. Seuss artfully combines silliness with language finesse, but he's not typically known for moral instruction. One exception is *Horton Hatches the Egg*. This clever tale of parenting invites readers to look at the more essential components of being a parent. Commitment, connectedness, gentleness, resiliency, strength, character, and kindness show up in the pages of this book. Those traits subsequently transfer the likeness of the parent to the child.

Horton Hatches the Egg is the tale of a blended family. The story begins with

Mayzie, who gives up on the hard work of parenting and finds an elephant to take her place. Horton, an elephant of his word, sits on the egg for months on end, repeating the now famous line,

I meant what I said
And I said what I meant . . .
An elephant's faithful
One hundred percent![2]

Horton's home life with Mayzie's egg ends up challenging him in multiple ways. The job also takes him to many unexpected places that usher in hardships and even criticism from his friends. Ultimately captured by hunters, stuck on a boat for a treacherous sea adventure, and finally placed in a traveling circus—Horton remains nested on the egg.

When the circus winds up in Florida, Mayzie, who has been selfishly vacationing there all along, spots her egg and decides to reclaim it now that all the hard work has been done.

However, when the life in the egg emerges from the cracked shell, what it has grown into resembles Horton. It has developed into an elephant-bird. Thus, Horton and his new baby are promptly returned to the jungle to happily live out their days, while Mayzie is punished for her laziness and irresponsibility.

It is a child's story, yet it carries an overtly adult message: Successful parenting comes through commitment, dedication, love, and hard work. Successful parenting also ushers in a lifetime of reward.

Blended Families

The family unit in our nation today is no longer largely comprised of biological children in the home. We often have "blended families," where one or both parents are raising children they did not originally produce. I'm very familiar with this concept because our daughter Chrystal has a blended family of her own. Yet while two biological parents may be ideal, the underlying traits found in a healthy home aren't merely tied to genetics. Rather, they are tied to the kingdom principles of parenting, illustrated for us through an elephant named

Horton—commitment, connectedness, gentleness, resiliency, strength, character, and kindness.

Whatever your family makeup, there is always hope that you can build a kingdom home. Stay on the nest, and you'll find that the principles in this book can transform your family.

Horton the elephant isn't the only elephant with a moral to teach. In fact, we can learn a lot from a group of orphaned adolescent bull elephants in South Africa's Pilanesberg Park that began to act unruly. These elephants had reached an age where they experienced periods of high hormonal levels, resulting in their more aggressive behavior. Left unchecked by their parents, these adolescent bulls became extremely dangerous—able to go on a rampage at any time. The park rangers chose to address the situation by adding mentors to the elephants' natural environment.

When adolescent bulls break away from the herd in the wild, older bulls become their mentors. As a result, the adolescent bulls submit to the presence and the power of the older bulls among them. In fact, they learn how to direct their hormonal upswings in responsible ways that are productive to the herd rather than destructive.

When the park rangers introduced adult bulls into the living space of the adolescents, the result was exactly what they had anticipated. Where there had been chaos, there was now calm. The "father" elephants completed the environment so that the young elephants received the guidance they needed to live well.[3]

While elephants can't be compared to humans on all levels, the principles evident in their interactions reflect what psychologists observe in teenagers today. So many teenagers are living a life of chaos simply because they are lacking parental involvement and dedication. Parenting is so essential to the development of a boy becoming a man and a girl becoming a woman that many, if not most, of the issues that plague us as a nation today would be eradicated if we

Rather than looking to the White House to fix all of our ills, we ought to be looking to our own houses to do just that.

would just master this one thing. Rather than looking to the White House to fix all of our ills, we ought to be looking to our own houses to do just that. As goes the family, so goes the nation.

When the family breaks down, everything that's supposed to be built on that sacred foundation crumbles with it. And so God's kingdom on earth (made up of the body of Christ) is now reaping the devastation of family disintegration. When parents fail to provide their children with the tools necessary to resist the culture's onrush, the rising tide of secularism washes away a generation of children like sand castles on the shores of life.

As we saw with the illustration of Horton, the bull elephants, and as I have personally witnessed in many successful blended homes, family commitment is a trait that transcends DNA and can produce great results. A strong sense of commitment is the foundation for a strong, fully functional home. Aspects of commitment include dependence on each other, loyalty, honesty, and trust—as well as developing goals and dreams together as a family.

> *A strong sense of commitment is the foundation for a strong, fully functional home*

Commitment focuses on a child's proper development. In fact, a child's development is so critical that, in biblical times, whenever a young boy was earmarked to become a king, many people took much care in training that child about how to be a king. Yet somewhere along the line, we have come to believe that the princes and princesses in God's kingdom don't need any significant training at all. Just as we saw in the illustration of the elephants, parental modeling and involvement impact the young. We see this impact show up in the life of a man many of you have never heard of: Asher.

Asher's Blended Home

Let's face it: The Chronicles aren't the most exciting read. But hidden among the myriad difficult-to-pronounce names lies one of the greatest treasures of kingdom parenting we have. His name was Asher, which in Hebrew means "happy."[4] In 1 Chronicles 7 (as well as in Genesis 46:17), we read the genealogy of his descendants. It starts with his five children—four boys and a girl. As the only girl in the group, no doubt his daughter, Serah, held a special place in Asher's heart. We know this for a number of reasons.

It is said in Jewish rabbinical literature that Serah is actually Asher's stepdaughter, thus making Asher a father of a blended home. She was the daughter of a woman named Hadurah, who had become a widow early on. History records that Hadurah married Asher when Serah was just three years old, and he raised her as his own child.

So loved and welcomed into the family was Serah that she is the only granddaughter mentioned in the entire lineage of Jacob, her grandfather.

Piety and virtue, though, were not something Asher could have claimed for himself when he was a young man, although he later went on to live a life accented with great wisdom. In his youth, Asher did something that was terribly wrong—by anyone's standards. He joined in on a selfish and hard-hearted scheme to have his half-brother, Joseph, thrown into a pit and later sold as a slave to a traveling caravan headed to Egypt.

Perhaps due to his own early misdeeds, the ensuing guilt as he watched his beloved father grieve, as well as the subsequent near-starvation of his people at the start of the seven-year drought, Asher became a changed man. Maybe it came through witnessing Joseph model a spirit of charity, mercy, and grace to his family. We don't really know what brought about his transformation, but we do know the legacy he ended up leaving behind—a legacy of great wisdom, faith, character, and service to his nation. It's a legacy that has impacted generations of his descendants.

Asher's legacy ought to give each of us hope, especially those who may not have started out on the best possible footing as parents. Asher made mistakes early on—big ones that harmed his original family. He certainly didn't have it all together. In addition, he was raised in one of the most historically dysfunctional homes ever to be recorded biblically. Sprinkle on top of that the added burdens of a blended family of his own—four sons and a stepdaughter—while married to a woman who had been married once before, and most might not have considered that Asher would have produced much of anything lasting at all.

But he did. In fact, his is a great legacy and a model for kingdom parenting today.

That legacy is recorded for us in 1 Chronicles 7:40 where we read, "All these were the sons of Asher, heads of the fathers' houses, choice and mighty men of valor, heads of the princes. And the number of them enrolled by genealogy for service in war was 26,000 men."

They Call Me "Mommy"

by Chrystal Evans Hurst

They call me Mommy. It's a five-letter word that my children use all day, every day, hundreds and thousands of times a day. And it means . . .

I need you . . .

I'm hurting . . .

Help me . . .

Can we talk? . . .

Love me . . . and

What's for dinner?

They use that word so loosely. They use that word a lot. They use it whenever they need to find me.

Why? Because they know that I hold the keys.

They know I hold the keys to whatever will make it onto their dinner plates that evening.

They know that if anybody can get the splinter out, I can.

They know that if anyone will love them, I will.

But that common name means so much more. It means that I am responsible, along with my husband, for training them in righteousness. It means that I have to shape their hearts and their character in a way that will prepare them for the plans God has for their lives. It means that they will learn from me how they are to parent their own children someday.

And it's scary.

It's a little unsettling to think that you could mess up your kids, isn't it?

I know I'm not perfect, but somehow that fact is grossly magnified under the lens of my role in the lives of my family.

Asher's story comforts me. He didn't get it right at first either.

And then, when he grew up and became a man, he didn't have the picture-perfect family. But that didn't stop his children from becoming leaders characterized by bravery, excellence, and influence.

My parents did a great job raising us. Really. They did. They will tell you that they don't harbor many regrets. That's wonderful to hear.

But I want to encourage those who may be reading this book on raising kingdom kids and thinking, *Well, this couldn't apply to me. I've messed up too badly to be a positive influence in the lives of my children.*

Enter Asher.

He messed up too. After bad decisions, he committed himself to make good ones going forward.

Enter the blended family.

A perfectly nuclear family was not a prerequisite for God to work through Asher to produce godly people.

Enter impact.

As I've heard my father say many times, "God can hit a bull's-eye with a crooked stick." And while Asher—and maybe you and I—may not have had a straight start, God can work miracles.

So as you read this book and arm yourself with knowledge to help you in your parenting journey . . .

Know that when your children call out for you, Mommy and Daddy are not titles to be held loosely.

You are not common.

You hold a crucial place and have significant value in the life of your children, now and in the future they will experience.

And if you choose, starting now, to have a kingdom home, you can have an impact beyond your wildest dreams.

No wonder Asher was a happy man. He did not look at his five children as getting on his last nerve. Rather, he was a satisfied man who was intentional in caring for his offspring and those under his care. As a result, he and his descendants truly lived out his father's blessing: "Of Asher [Moses] said, 'More blessed than sons is Asher; may he be favored by his brothers, and may he dip his foot in oil. Your locks will be iron and bronze, and according to your days, so will your leisurely walk be'" (Deuteronomy 33:24–25).

Raising Leaders

The first parenting principle we can learn from the life of Asher is that his sons were the "heads of the father's houses." Asher raised his sons, and also his daughter, to be leaders. They weren't just hanging around the house, eating food and taking up space. According to 1 Chronicles 7:40, these men grew up to fulfill a leadership role. (In the Bible, "headship" refers to a leadership position within a home.) Asher took his role as the head of his home seriously and subsequently raised up leaders over their homes as well.

As a leader, Asher and his sons set the tone and direction for their homes and ensuing generations. One of the worst things that can happen to a family is to have parents who do not adequately fulfill their leadership roles. They want to be called parents without the commitment of parenting. Yet "headship" in the Bible isn't a title; it's a responsibility. In order to claim the title, a leader must also own the responsibility that goes along with it.

I can't say that I want to be a preacher and not want to preach. I can't say that I want to be a pastor and not want to shepherd my congregation. That would be taking a title and misusing it. Likewise, parents need to fulfill the responsibilities that come within their role, and that includes preparing their children to do the same.

Second, Asher raised his children to excel in all things. We discern this from the descriptive terminology used to introduce them. The Bible says they were "choice" men. It was rare in historical Jewish culture to record much of anything about women, but taking into account other verses referencing Serah, we can discern that she grew to be a choice lady as well.

Asher's descendants went on to become "choice" men; these individuals grew up to become top of the line in all that they did. Asher and his wife raised choice children, those of great ethical character who accepted their responsibilities. They held high standards that wouldn't allow them to settle for mediocrity. As parents, they most likely communicated high expectations to their children. Clearly expressed expectations coupled with consistent follow-through produce responsible kids.

These children were not just trying to make it and get by, still living with Mom and Dad long after they were physically able to work and provide for themselves. Neither were these young adults postponing the responsibilities of life as long as possible by pursuing degree after degree. Asher didn't raise his children to be like that. Rather, he raised them in a spirit of excellence and integrity. Even though he didn't have a perfect track record, he sought to better his own character while steering his children to a higher plane than he had experienced.

Kingdom parents, if you are satisfied with your kids being mediocre, then mediocre might be all that you are going to get. If you don't raise the bar, how can your kids experience anything better? You run the risk of

Clearly expressed expectations coupled with consistent follow-through produce responsible kids.

them becoming mediocre adults who marry mediocre spouses because that's all your kids know and understand. But if you raise the bar, what might happen? Your kids could become like Asher's children. You could raise them to be the cream of the crop—to aim for excellence in all things.

These days, in a room that is crowded with no more seats available, it amazes me that men will allow women to stand for an inordinate amount of time. My father would have corrected me sternly if I ever let a woman stand for an extended period of time while I was seated. Today we've got a generation of children being raised without the simplest notion of etiquette, common courtesy, respect, honor, excellence, and integrity. Why? Because we have a generation of parents who are so distracted by the sights, sounds, and smells of life's adventures that they simply settle for mediocrity in both themselves and their offspring. It's easier that way. However, trifling children typically grow up to become trifling adults—and, in the long run, that isn't easy at all.

Obviously not everyone is going to excel in everything. Raising kingdom kids who are "choice" simply means they will maximize their personal potential and God-given gifts. Maybe they won't be in the top of their particular class in every subject, but whatever it is that God has created them to fulfill, they will do so with a degree of excellence, and they will do all else to the best of their abilities.

The third lesson we can learn is that Asher raised warriors. According to 1 Chronicles 7:40, he raised "mighty men of valor." This describes individuals who are brave, courageous, and willing to risk themselves for the betterment of the whole. Valor means boldness. A person of valor is willing to take a stand when a stand needs to be taken. Asher raised children who grew into adults of conviction.

Too many of our children crumble under the pressure of their peers rather than rise above the fray. They are indecisive, taking a stand for little or nothing at all. To raise kingdom kids, we must instill in them a heart of valor—a spirit that will stay strong despite the challenges and enemies that they might face on any given day. Scripture tells us that Satan roams around like "a roaring lion looking for someone to devour" (1 Peter 5:8). A kingdom kid must be adequately equipped with knowledge and wisdom in order to be prepared for the spiritual battle that surrounds him or her. Asher raised children who were ready.

Finally, Asher raised children who would serve others. They became mentors. We read that they were "heads of princes." Essentially, Asher mentored leaders who were then positioned to influence the kingdom as mentors themselves. A prince is a king waiting to happen. By raising princes, Asher's children influenced society. Parents, keep in mind that strong families are always connected to the community in some way. A healthy home is not an isolated home—it's a home where family members are encouraged to get involved in local activities, as well as service opportunities in the community and beyond.

Asher's children not only took care of themselves (choice men), their own homes (heads of the fathers' houses), their own community (mighty men of valor); they also took care of their country (heads of princes). Asher raised kingdom kids who understood that the stability and advancement of the kingdom began with them, weaving through their families into their congregations and communities and ultimately impacting their nation.

Unfortunately, today many parents have lost sight of the long-term impact their children will one day make. As a result, some parents spend more time training their dogs than they do their kids. They rarely play with them, study the Bible with them, take them to church, discuss what was taught, correct them when they are wrong, give them a vision and a dream, develop their character, instill godly virtues, and so on. They don't do any of these things—or they do them halfheartedly—and then they wonder why their children turn out the way that they do. Rather than reaping the generational cycles of victory Asher and his wife experienced, they wind up with generational cycles of collapse passed on from their kids to their grandkids and so on. Instead of positive patterns being transferred, they transfer a DNA of defeat.

Some parents spend more time training their dogs than they do their kids.

First Chronicles 7:40 concludes with this summary of successful parenting: "And the number of them enrolled by genealogy for service in war was 26,000 men." Keep in mind that Asher had only four boys and a girl. Yet by the time those five children raised their own families, there were 26,000 choice men of valor (not including the women of valor who were undoubtedly produced as well).

I'll never forget the birth of my first son. Our first two children were girls, so when Lois gave birth to our third child, I waited anxiously in the sitting area outside of the labor room with my mind fixated on one thing: Will this be a boy? I desperately wanted to have the legacy of a son. I was so excited when I first saw him that, without even thinking, I blurted out, "His name is Anthony Tyrone Evans Jr." I gave him my name because I was so thrilled at having the legacy of a son.

As I grew older, God began to develop in me the ability to see His creation more as He does. He opened my heart to think like a king. Legacy is much more than simply passing on the family name. Legacy involves passing on a kingdom worldview and perspective, whether that involves sons or daughters.

Perhaps because we think our daughters will grow up and take on someone else's name, we don't always look at them through the legacy-lens. But when we live life as parents from a kingdom perspective, we grow in our understanding that we aren't just passing on our name through our children—we are passing on God's name, His character, and His kingdom agenda. We are reminding them that they no longer have only our blood flowing through their veins; they have God's—they have royal blood.

Many of our children may struggle with issues of ethnicity as well. One of the greatest lessons my father instilled in me as a child growing up in the midst of a country torn by racial disparity and injustice was that I was not primarily to identify myself by my ethnicity, but rather by my citizenry. As a citizen of heaven and a child of the King, my father always taught me to remember that I had royal blood flowing through my veins. If people called me names or treated me unjustly, he would remind me that it wasn't a reflection of who I was—it just meant they failed to realize that I was a prince in God's kingdom.

As a citizen of heaven and a child of the King, my father always taught me to remember that I had royal blood flowing through my veins.

Parents, there is a world of princes and princesses in our nation today who have no one to tell them who they really are, as my father told me or Asher told his four sons, stepdaughter, and subsequent grandchildren. No one studies the Bible with them, takes them to church, corrects them when they are wrong, teaches them about life, shows them how to treat others, or tells them what it means to be responsible and make wise decisions. This has resulted in a form of spiritual castration on the part of our young men and spiritual barrenness on the part of our young women. Their royalty has been stripped from them by a culture that fails to even recognize them as princes or princesses.

Today our nation needs men and women who will fulfill the high call of kingdom parenting. Our world needs parents who will act as a police escort, guiding their children safely into the future as they oversee the covenantal transference of the faith. Parents who will walk with their children along the checkerboard of life until they finally reach the destination where each child can stand tall and say, "Crown me."

And then repeat the same cycle in their own home.

It's an Elephant

One day a father decided to take his daughter to the zoo. She asked if she could bring some friends along, and her dad agreed, so she invited ten friends to join them. At the zoo, the kids ran over to where they were giving elephant rides. Excitedly, the daughter jumped up and down and asked her dad if they could all go on an elephant ride. The father looked at the price, multiplied it by eleven, and shook his head no. "It's too much," he said.

"Too much?" his daughter replied. "But Daddy, it's an elephant."

"Yes," he said, "but that's a lot of money."

"I know, Daddy," she replied, "but that's because it's an elephant."

The father was looking at the price. The daughter was looking at the size. It seemed like a lot to him because he just saw the cost, but it didn't seem like a lot to her compared to the size of the elephant. Parents, raising kingdom kids comes with a high price tag of time, energy, investment, and many other things, but when you take your eyes off the cost and focus instead on the size of the legacy you are producing, you will realize that it's worth every single thing that you invest.

3

~⁊~

THE HEIR AND
HEIRESS APPARENT

Today we live in a world of outsourcing. Everything from manufacturing to customer service and computer programming to website development frequently is sent overseas by large corporations needing to limit payroll, human resource costs, and office space. As outsourcing options have increased, even smaller companies now view this as a viable option for shrinking costs while expanding the bottom line.

Yet consider with me what might happen if the prince and princess of Cambridge opted for outsourcing the upbringing and training of their little one, Prince George. What if they relied solely on nannies situated outside the palace walls for his primary teaching and care? Not only would the media have a heyday, but Prince George wouldn't receive the proper training he requires to one day fulfill his potential role as heir apparent of Great Britain.

While children won't always do what they are told, they will do what they see. For a prince in line for a kingship to know how to fulfill his role both in the palace and out, Prince George needs the mentoring and modeling of his father, William. He also needs the devotion and nurturing of his mother, Kate.

Raising kingdom kids requires more than simply outsourcing them by sending them off to Sunday school on the weekends and school during the week. It takes more than access to the television or peer groups. It involves more than what your children will learn through surfing the Internet or texting their friends. In order for you to properly raise your child as the heir or heiress apparent that he or she is, it will take time, attention, investment, and training. Healthy families must be intentional in passing on the traits necessary to thrive in relationships, work, morality, manners, and leadership, as well as in personal fulfillment and purpose.

While children won't always do what they are told, they will do what they see.

It is said that in the early years of the British monarchy, the heir apparent would receive an entirely different type of training than the rest of his siblings. From an early age on, this child was surrounded with success in order to instill a leadership mindset of triumph. For instance, games would be rigged so that the child would always win, thus building confidence for when wars would be later fought. The monarchy employed a variety of intentional instruction aimed at preparing the young heir for his ultimate ascension to the throne.

Our King has a kingdom, and your children have a significant place in it—one that requires specialized instruction and preparation if they are to experience a victorious kingdom life. When your children trust in Jesus Christ for their salvation, they enter into a position of royalty and priesthood, becoming heirs or heiresses with Christ. In the book of Romans we read, "The Spirit Himself testifies with our spirit that we are children of God, and if children, heirs also, heirs of God and fellow heirs with Christ" (8:16–17).

First Peter 2:9 says, "You are a chosen race, a royal priesthood, a holy nation, a people for God's own possession."

And in Revelation we read, "You have made them to be a kingdom and priests to our God; and they will reign upon the earth" (5:10).

When you look into that sweet, cherubic face of your young child, you are not just viewing a little angel—you are viewing royalty. And as royalty, your child needs to receive the training befitting such monarchy in the kingdom of God. Keep in mind that as children's legs get longer, their wings get shorter. Thus they will need the foundational mindset of healthy kingdom living in order to navigate through life with a sin nature that has the potential to derail them, and in a world that aims to defeat them.

Surviving and Thriving

One of the most essential instructions on how to raise kingdom kids is found in the book of Deuteronomy. The Israelites are about to cross over into the Promised Land. And while the Promised Land holds a host of promises and potential, it also holds a host of sheer messes. Canaanites, Hittites, Jebusites, and more roam the land, both ready and able to defend it from conquest. Difficulties surround the people of Israel, and culture shock awaits them. Thus Moses instructs them that, if they want to not only survive but also thrive in this land of promise, the family must become the primary place where faith is transferred. To make it generationally out there, they will need to make it generationally in the home.

The starting point for transferring faith, of course, is the salvation of your children. The greatest thing parents can do for their children is to lead them to the Lord. As soon as your child has the cognitive ability to understand both sin and the gospel, you have the opportunity to bring that child to a saving knowledge of Jesus Christ. Be careful, though, not to rush this process; far too many children have no recollection of their salvation experience because they were so young when it happened. As you seek to communicate the gospel to them, children need to truly understand for themselves both sin and their need for forgiveness. In addition, after they are saved, make sure you do not pressure them to get baptized, but rather allow them the opportunity to fully comprehend what baptism expresses publicly. That way they can initiate this declaration of their faith—as well as remember it when they get older.

To make it generationally out there, they will need to make it generationally in the home.

The single greatest reason why we are losing our young people today is that the home is no longer the place where faith is transferred. Parents, the primary purpose of the home is the evangelization and discipleship of your children. You cannot outsource this vital component in the rearing of your children. Their discipleship requires time and commitment, even though your time and commitment might be divided among too many things already. I struggled greatly in this area during the first decade of our family. I had a hard time choosing where my time and commitments needed to be, largely because I have this "man thing" about my personality—if I can do something, I don't want another man doing it for me. Even to this day, I don't let the bellman take my luggage when I'm traveling. When he reaches for it, I think, *I don't need you picking up something for me! Put that back down—I've got it!*

Raising your child is about much more than raising your child. It is about raising the future.

Because of this, I tried to carry all of the other responsibilities around the home—mowing the lawn, changing the oil in the car, fixing things—when I was already stretched thin by starting a church, leading my family, going to seminary, and ministering to people. One day I finally had to step back and admit that it was just too much. It was more than I could handle. At that point, I decided to outsource the things that didn't require me personally to do them, such as the lawn care, fixing things around the house, and maintenance on the car. And while that was difficult for me to swallow, it was a choice I had to make in order to free up my time to focus on the things I needed to do—like teach my children God's Word on an ongoing basis. That's no small calling, and it requires time and commitment.

Let's read what Moses had to say:

> Hear, O Israel! The LORD is our God, the LORD is one! You shall love the LORD your God with all your heart and with all your soul and with all your might. These words, which I am commanding you today, shall be on your heart. You shall teach them diligently to your sons and shall talk of them when you sit in your house and when you walk by the way and when you lie down and when you rise up. (Deuteronomy 6:4–7)

Moses said that parents are to teach their children diligently and continually—when they sit in the house, when they are out walking, when they go to bed, and when they get up. That pretty much sums up every possible time. Yet for the generation of parents today, the home is no longer the central place for spiritual development. Raising your child is about much more than raising your child. It is about raising the future. Moses opened his instructions by declaring that this is a multigenerational task that carries with it a future-oriented promise. Look at the first two verses of Deuteronomy 6:

> Now this is the commandment, the statutes and the judgments which
> the LORD your God has commanded me to teach you, that you might
> do them in the land where you are going over to possess it, so that you
> and your son and your grandson might fear the LORD your God, to
> keep all His statutes and His commandments which I command you, all
> the days of your life, and that your days may be prolonged.

The job of kingdom parenting is imparting a biblical worldview to your children, who will in turn impart the same biblical worldview to your grandchildren in order for it to be lived out into the future so that generations to come will not only survive, but also thrive.

A Kingdom Point of View

A worldview is the lens through which a person views life. It informs decisions, values, and responsibilities because it is the grid by which a person both thinks and functions. Parents, if you are providing a home, clothes, food, and education to your child but not providing them with the foundation of a biblical worldview, you have not fulfilled your role as provider. If a baseball player hits a home run yet fails to touch first base when rounding the bases, he will not score when he crosses home plate. Likewise, your children need you to cover all the bases for living a productive kingdom life or, when they reach the place of creating their own homes, they will lack the skills necessary to transfer that faith to their kids.

Mothers and fathers are meant to be the dominant spiritual influences in the lives of their children. Likewise, a strong marriage has a direct impact on raising strong kids. One of the greatest things a father can do for his children is to biblically and visually love their mother. If your marriage is not strong spiritually, then a primary focus in your parenting needs to be the strengthening of your relationship with your spouse. Couples with weak marriages tend to rely more on others to "parent" their children.

The church's job is to supplement the training of your children as well as to disciple you as parents. What is preached on Sunday should not be the only spiritual food your children receive throughout the week. You don't feed your children dinner just one day a week. Legally that would be considered neglect. Similarly, it is spiritual neglect to fail to honor your children by providing the tools they need to develop spiritually. So let me ask you a question before we dig much deeper: How often do you sit down with your children with the intention of imparting a biblical worldview?

Eating God's Words

by Jonathan Evans

I remember vividly dinnertime in the Evans household: sitting down, getting ready to eat my mom's awesome cooking, and feeling excited about all of the fun and laughter we would have at the table. However, dinnertime at the Evans table, which happened every evening without fail, was about much more than eating good food and having fun. I remember dinnertime being the setting where my father and mother would teach me God's Word. My father would lead us in devotions and have each of us read a Scripture and talk about its meaning. Every evening I remember being reminded that God's Word is to be the centerpiece of our lives through which all decisions are to be made. I was taught that God's Word is the only thing certain in an uncertain world. At the dinner table I learned how to live by the truth in a world full of lies, how to serve the true God in a world full of false gods. Now that I'm older, I realize that the dinner table in the Evans household was the place where my siblings and I discovered the kingdom of God. I am now over thirty years old, with a wife and three kids of my own, and I find myself subconsciously repeating with my children what my parents started with me. Every evening without fail we eat dinner together, and my three little children are slowly but surely learning about the kingdom of God.

I know your schedule is probably busy, and you are most likely tired when you get home. But that doesn't mean you have been relieved of your responsibility. When my children were still in the home, it was one of the busiest seasons of my ministry. With Promise Keepers exploding on the scene, our church growing exponentially and quickly, and our national ministry taking off, I was under a lot of legitimate pressure for meetings, speaking events, management, and the like. Yet to the best of my knowledge, we missed few—if any—family meals when I was in town. And when I was out of town, Lois did an excellent job of continuing the discipleship routine in our home. In addition, I limited my traveling to that which was agreeable to everyone in the family.

Consistency in relating to your children, whether it's at the dinner table or elsewhere, is essential for discipling them. As Moses said, we are to talk with them morning, noon, and night concerning the things of God. There were times when I accidentally double-booked a speaking engagement and a family event. I can remember flying back (covering the costs myself) from a speaking engagement so I could attend one of our children's school events. I overheard my daughter Priscilla telling a friend one day that, as she grew up, she never really knew that her dad was a prominent national preacher simply because he always seemed to be around. Comments like this warm my heart today because, even though at the time I may have sat there tired and perhaps even frustrated at the extra effort and expense (my family will attest that I don't like to spend money) needed to attend both functions, I knew that the value and honor I sought to communicate to my children through my actions would be worth it.

As much as possible I made it a priority to be around during normal, everyday activities because that set a pattern of both availability and stability in our home. Driving the kids to school was always my duty, as was homework time at the end of each day. I volunteered for this task because I wanted to show my kids honor in that way. Leading the kids in devotions, Bible study, and manners occurred routinely around our table. The boys were taught how to seat a lady at a table. The girls were taught how to respectfully be seated by a gentleman. And whenever my kids called me, whether I was in a meeting or not, I took their call. Parents, accessibility communicates commitment and value more clearly than almost anything else you can do. Make it your goal to increase your accessibility to your children if this isn't already a strong point in your home.

Now that my kids have grown into not-perfect-but-still-God-fearing-and-kingdom-serving adults, I am grateful for every moment I invested in them. They continually seek—although they sometimes struggle—to put God and His precepts first in their lives. I couldn't be more proud of the kingdom men and women they have become. All four serve in ministry, and all four amaze me with their spiritual insight, depth, maturity, and dedication to their families. If you don't know them already, you'll get to know them a little through their own contributions in the pages of this book.

Parents, I understand *busy*. Been there, and still am there. I get it, and I hear you. But the busier you are, the more important it is to carve out time for your children. If you are going to raise kingdom kids, they must be a priority.

I also understand *tired*. I know what it's like to get home from a crowded, noisy day and just want to sit in front of the television. In our home, we made it a rule that television time was significantly limited during the week. Thirty minutes per day is what the children got, meaning that's what we as their parents got as well while they were awake. I admit there were days when I broke that rule—when I would turn on the television and just sit there while I sent the kids off to do something else.

However, I tried not to make breaking that rule a habit. You see, setting standards in your home doesn't mean being legalistic and never making mistakes. It does mean that you aim for excellence and allow for grace when you experience one of those tiresome days. As long as you aim high, you'll hit that goal more often than not. Kingdom parenting isn't perfect parenting. Kingdom parenting is purposeful parenting.

Go ahead and set times for family meetings, guidance, and direction. Moses' instruction was composed of a comprehensive approach to parenting: "When you sit in your house," and "when you walk by the way," and "when you lie down," and "when you rise up." This describes a home like a pinball machine where no matter where your children go, they can't get away from learning to have a kingdom mindset and a biblical worldview.

Moses went so far as to say, "You shall bind them as a sign on your hand and they shall be as frontals on your forehead. You shall write them on the doorposts of your house and on your gates" (Deuteronomy 6:8–9). God and His precepts are to be *everywhere*. Whether it's a plaque hanging on the wall, a Scripture memory project for the day, a note written to your child and placed in his or her lunch box, a song playing on the speakers, or simply words out of your mouth, God's viewpoint should dominate the environment of your home. That way God becomes the point of reference for your child at school, with friends, on the sports team, and into adulthood as they establish their own home.

> *Kingdom parenting isn't perfect parenting. Kingdom parenting is purposeful parenting.*

Kingdom Mom and kingdom Dad, do not delegate the spiritual development of your children to someone else. Moses said it is *your* job to train them diligently. You are to create a bungee-cord effect so that if your children grow up and run away from God, they will bounce back to Him, so saturated with Him that they can't escape His influence and presence.

And while the primary responsibility of training your children lies with you, part of that responsibility involves being intentional about seeking out things that will supplement, or add to, that training. Parents literally will move to a different home in order to provide the best possible school for their children. In that same vein, seek out the best possible church within which to raise your children in order to reinforce the values you are teaching at home.

I see a disturbing pattern emerging in parenting these days: For many parents, it is far more important for their kids to make the team than to make it in God's kingdom. They'll get their kids to baseball, football, basketball, or soccer practice on time, but not to church. But raising heirs and heiresses of the kingdom takes purposefully positioning them in an environment where they will learn, understand, and apply a kingdom mindset.

Two Fundamentals of a Kingdom Mindset

Before the Israelites reached the Promised Land, they were delivered out of Egypt and developed in the wilderness. The Promised Land—Canaan—was their destiny. It was not heaven, though. Their destiny included God's provision, but it also came riddled with obstacles, temptations, and challenges. Due to the sinful world that we live in, your child's destiny also will contain obstacles, temptations, and financial, relational, emotional, spiritual, educational, and career challenges.

In order for your children to live out their destiny, it's necessary for them to be delivered from sin, developed through sanctification, and dependent on God to play the divine role in the unfolding of His kingdom plan. To achieve this, it's important for you to cultivate in your children two fundamentals of a kingdom mindset: remembering God and fearing Him.

Remembering God

The next part of the Deuteronomy passage says:

> Then it shall come about when the LORD your God brings you into the land which He swore to your fathers, Abraham, Isaac and Jacob, to give you great and splendid cities which you did not build, and houses full of all good things which you did not fill, and hewn cisterns which you did not dig, vineyards and olive trees which you did not plant, and you eat and are satisfied, then watch yourself, that you do not forget the LORD who brought you from the land of Egypt, out of the house of slavery. You shall fear only the LORD your God; and you shall worship Him and swear by His name. (Deuteronomy 6:10–13)

As Moses reminds the Israelites in this passage, sometimes when we experience God's blessings and provision, we can forget Him. Now that the television is bigger, the family time is smaller. Now that the beds are more comfortable, the chairs at the table seem harder. Unfortunately God's provision can sometimes eclipse God's rightful place in our hearts.

That's why after the Israelites had eaten, Moses instructed them to say grace once again. The meal prayer wasn't to be offered simply before they ate; it also was to be given after they ate as a reminder of God's faithfulness and their recognition of it. "When you have eaten and are satisfied, you shall bless the LORD your God for the good land which He has given you" (Deuteronomy 8:10). After the Israelites were satisfied by the food God had caused to grow in their land, they were to bless Him for that land. They were to continually remember God lest in their comfort they forget Him altogether.

We are living at a time in our culture where many families experience the blessing of God's hand. I remember growing up at a time when a new pair of jeans was a rarity, yet kids today get much more than jeans on a regular basis. While it is good to experience God's provision, it can also be dangerous. Material satisfaction can quickly lead to spiritual starvation. That's why Moses commanded the Israelites to teach their children God's precepts daily so that they would not forget Him in the midst of their success.

It's easy to remember God in a trial when there seems to be no one else to turn to. But the true test of faith comes at those times when all seems well. Real faith never forgets the real Source. But when you disconnect the goodness of God from the God who is good, you have walked away from your destiny. Destiny

When you disconnect the goodness of God from the God who is good, you have walked away from your destiny.

is always God-ward—tied to advancing His kingdom and bringing Him glory.

What does it mean to forget God? It doesn't necessarily mean that you are skipping church. It means that His guidelines no longer govern your decisions. It means that, in your mind, His power no longer trumps your own. Forgetting God leads to pride, and pride gives birth to rebellion. Moses shares this concept here:

> Beware that you do not forget the LORD your God . . . Otherwise, you
> may say in your heart, "My power and the strength of my hand made
> me this wealth." . . . It shall come about that if you ever forget the
> LORD your God and go after other gods and serve them and worship

them, I testify against you today that you will surely perish. Like the nations that the Lord makes to perish before you, so you shall perish; because you would not listen to the voice of the LORD your God. (Deuteronomy 8:11, 17, 19–20).

Establishing a kingdom mindset within your children that puts God first as the centerpiece of all of life prepares them to not only reach their destiny, but also to remain in it. If you have ever seen a turtle on a fence, you know that somebody put it there—because turtles can't climb fences. Likewise, whatever success you achieve as parents—and as adults—and whatever success your children achieve as they grow will be the result of God's divine favor and His provision. He is the source of all that is good (James 1:17). Guard that mindset within your home by continually remembering God in all that you do.

Fearing God

In addition to teaching your kids to remember God, raising them with a kingdom mindset means teaching them the fear of the Lord.

The word *fear* in the Bible combines the concept of "awe" along with the concept of "terror." When you put the two together, it boils down to taking something very seriously. For example, let's look at electricity. Electricity is a good thing—it keeps our food cold and our houses warm.

I got a wake-up call about just how good electricity is not too long ago when we had a winter ice storm in Dallas, with the temperature dropping to near zero. As a result, hundreds of thousands of homes lost power—including ours. For days, Lois and I huddled next to our only source of heat in the home, a gaslit fireplace, as we were reminded just how important electricity is.

Yet that same electricity that can help keep you warm can also fry you. I would not advise taking a screwdriver and sticking it in an outlet. The same electricity that can illuminate your home can also make your hair stand on end. It's dangerous. Electricity must be handled properly, or it will cause harm.

Creating a kingdom mindset in your home includes cultivating a healthy fear of God. Yes, God wants your children to reach their destiny. Yes, God has a plan for them. He desires to guide and direct us, but He also demands reverence and respect. God is a jealous God, and when the fear that rightfully belongs to Him is misplaced, He doesn't take it lightly. Moses told the Israelites that if they revered idols rather than God, then "the anger of the LORD your God will be kindled against you, and He will wipe you off the face of the earth" (Deuteronomy 6:15).

Now, here Moses was talking to a national society, but the principle still remains: broken fellowship with God brings about the removal of His favor and His blessing. He wants to be recognized as the ultimate definer and authority over life in your home and in your children's lives. He won't share His honor with idols—with anything that eclipses God's rightful place in your life. His Word makes this explicitly clear: "You shall not follow other gods, any of the gods of the peoples who surround you" (Deuteronomy 6:14). In fact, He won't even share His glory if that idol happens to be you.

The king of Babylon, Nebuchadnezzar, made a terrible mistake after his kingdom got established. He said, "Look at this great Babylon that I have built! Look at what I have done!"

God quickly reminded him who the true source of all good things is. We read:

> While the word was in the king's mouth, a voice came from heaven, say-
> ing, "King Nebuchadnezzar, to you it is declared: sovereignty has been
> removed from you, and you will be driven away from mankind, and
> your dwelling place will be with the beasts of the field. You will be given
> grass to eat like cattle, and seven periods of time will pass over you until
> you recognize that the Most High is ruler over the realm of mankind
> and bestows it on whomever He wishes." (Daniel 4:31–32)

In other words, "Nebuchadnezzar, I am God, and you are not." Scripture records that the king subsequently went insane, and it would be seven years before God brought him back to his senses.

The reason why so many of our children are not living out their destinies as adults is that they have been raised with a mindset that is too tied to the culture. It is also too "me centered." But you can't worship the culture's god, or make yourself a god, and still have the one, true God. He won't share His glory with anyone else.

Raising kingdom kids is more than singing sweet lullabies about Jesus to them. It involves introducing them on an ongoing basis to the King of Kings and the Lord of Lords. It requires teaching them that God is highly exalted and reigns supreme. That His Word is the law of the land. That His name is the name above all names, at which every knee will bow.

Our God is the essence and purity of royalty, and the author and finisher of our destiny. If your hope is for your children to reign well in their promised land as the heirs and heiresses that they are, then you must give them the kingdom keys to do so; you must make sure that they both remember and fear their King.

4

LIFE OUTSIDE THE PALACE WALLS

Not too long ago some parents at the church I pastor asked if I would come and personally speak to their high school seniors. They wanted me to meet with their kids before they wrapped up their final year of high school and headed to college.

These parents had done all that they could to provide their children with a strong Christian foundation. They had carefully chosen where their kids would attend high school and had made great sacrifices on behalf of their children's development. Yet as they prepared to launch their young adult children out into the world—many of whom would be attending secular universities on scholarship—these parents grew concerned about whether their kids' foundations would be solid enough to withstand the crucible their faith was about to encounter.

I was more than happy to spend some personal time with these young adults in hopes of reinforcing the principles their parents had taught them—principles related to living as healthy individuals now that they were going out on their own. Principles such as respecting other people's boundaries as well as their own, developing critical thinking skills, and creating a balanced emotional, spiritual, physical, and mental life.

I wanted to encourage these young people to keep the faith in a faithless society. I wanted to share with them how they could wisely and effectively go against the grain when the grain is going against God. How they could act with both courage and honesty at the times when they needed to the most.

As we met together, the youth had some very important questions for me, and I enjoyed our discussion. I could tell they were mature and wanted to do well. But I also knew that they were probably not aware of the severity of secularism they would soon be facing when they transitioned out of the home and into the broader society. Because of this, I sought to reinforce biblical principles of living for the kingdom specifically within a secular context. I took the bulk of those principles from the book of Daniel.

In fact, most of what I shared with them came from illustrations given to us by four teenage boys in the Old Testament. What better way to teach young adults how to maintain their faith and purity in a foreign environment than with role models from their own age group? As you might have noticed with your own kids, teens sometimes tune out adults when we seek to instruct or mentor them. However, it is the rare teen that won't pay attention to what another teen is saying or modeling.

> *Children need to learn how to wisely and effectively go against the grain when the grain is going against God.*

As a matter of fact, one of the most successful school outreach initiatives we've ever implemented, High School Heroes, seeks to capitalize on this truth. First we identify high school students in the public school setting who are exhibiting the virtues and character qualities of kingdom living. Once chosen, we mentor and arrange for these students to speak to junior high and elementary groups in the same school system in order to encourage the younger students along a positive path. These younger students are captivated when the older students talk about the importance of making right choices, studying, moral purity, and other principles of kingdom living.

If the Old Testament city of Babylon had a High School Heroes outreach in place, there's no doubt the four young men we are about to look at as our examples in this chapter would have been chosen. These teens exhibited the qualities that demanded respect and set them up for future success.

Four Boys in Babylon

Before we look directly at the four boys in Babylon, I want to spend some time exploring the process that a secularized society often puts in place—sometimes knowingly and other times simply by nature of the society—in order to strip Christian values and a kingdom worldview from those who have it.

When these four young men lived, Babylon was known as a pagan society. It was also a powerful society. Babylon had recently seized Jerusalem out of the people of Israel's waning grasp. In so doing, they confiscated not only a number of the people of God but also the vessels of God, and they transferred them to a new, even more ungodly realm.

We read in the opening passage of Daniel:

> In the third year of the reign of Jehoiakim king of Judah, Nebuchad-
> nezzar king of Babylon came to Jerusalem and besieged it. The LORD
> gave Jehoiakim king of Judah into his hand, along with some of the
> vessels of the house of God; and he brought them to the land of Shinar,
> to the house of his god, and he brought the vessels into the treasury of
> his god. (Daniel 1:1–2)

You'll notice that Babylon didn't take siege of Jerusalem all on its own. They had help from above. It says that "the Lord gave" the city of Jerusalem over to Babylon. This came as a result of the Israelite's rebellion against God. As His people continued to turn further and further away from Him, He turned them over to secularism. In fact, He eventually gave them entirely into the grip of a nation who didn't know Him at all.

Before the four boys ever reached Babylon, their parents must have been very intentional about instilling kingdom virtues in them while in Jerusalem. Jerusalem was already spiritually off-target. The scenario in Jerusalem before the siege doesn't seem too different from where we are now in our nation.

As the people of Israel continued to put God on the periphery of their lives and marginalize Him through their rebellion, God withdrew His hand of bless-ing, favor, and protection. He allowed their hearts to become harder and their minds duller. This wasn't the Jerusalem that had once been founded firmly on

God's Word. Families no longer echoed Joshua's battle cry, "As for me and my house, we will serve the Lord." People did what they wanted to do, what they saw fit in their own eyes.

Similarly, the nation in which you and I are living, the one in which we are seeking to maintain kingdom families and raise kingdom kids, is not the same nation we were born into. At warp speed, we are witnessing the devolution of our country. In every arena you can name, we are watching the spiritual unraveling of a culture imploding upon itself.

While there has always been evil, sin, and negativity in our land, we were at least in a position collectively where we recognized evil, sin, and negativity for the most part. But all of those definitions have now been placed on the sidelines, while new definitions have taken their place.

Our culture used to be defined by a Judeo-Christian framework. In those days—not so long ago—even non-Christians understood, valued, and respected the biblical worldview. However, that is no longer our reality. The implications of this shift are staggering, but the even greater tragedy is that even the worldview and opinions of Christians seem to be shifting with the secular society just as swiftly. It is as if the church now thinks that God checks with popular opinion polls before He decides what is legitimate and what is not.

Jerusalem's atmosphere may have differed little from Christian culture in America today. But Babylon could easily be compared to the secular culture in our nation as well. It was precisely in this secularism and humanism that the four boys found themselves.

> Then the king ordered Ashpenaz, the chief of his officials, to bring in some of the sons of Israel, including some of the royal family and of the nobles, youths in whom was no defect, who were good-looking, showing intelligence in every branch of wisdom, endowed with understanding and discerning knowledge, and who had ability for serving in the king's court; and he ordered him to teach them the literature and language of the Chaldeans. (Daniel 1:3–4)

In other words, the leaders of Babylon said, "Let's get the next generation." It would be by procuring the minds and wills of the young teenagers—effectively

"Babylonianizing" them—that these leaders knew they would uncover the greatest assets for the future of their civilization. Therefore, they sought to strip the spiritual heritage out of the Israelite young men while simultaneously capitalizing on their strengths as they reoriented them to a new way of thinking and living.

One of the ways they opted to do this was relocating the chosen young men to Babylon. This is similar to what many of our kids face as they go from a Christian home and environment into a college setting. When you consider the vast number of hours children spend in secularized school institutions and compare that with the amount of time parents pray with them, lead them in God's Word, and take them to church, it is frighteningly out of balance. A relocation to a dominant secular atmosphere is one of the first ways a kingdom worldview is challenged.

Another way the Babylonians sought to strip the spiritual heritage from these Israelite young men was by isolating them. After relocating them, they made certain that the exposure the young men had was to Babylonian culture and nothing else. In no way did they want the God-centered, theistic orientation of these young men reinforced in anything they

A relocation to a dominant secular atmosphere is one of the first ways a kingdom worldview is challenged.

were reading or learning. Instead, they isolated them to the literature and the language of the Chaldeans.

In fact, in verse 5 we discover that the Babylonians knew this wouldn't happen overnight, so they opted for a three-year program—giving enough time for the Israelite heritage to be replaced by the Babylonian belief system. Essentially, the goal was for these young men to attend a Babylonian school located in a Babylonian city where they were taught by Babylonian teachers while being forced to read only Babylonian literature and speak the Babylonian language so that after three years they would think, act, talk, and walk like a Babylonian. The dominant culture would have a dominating effect on them.

As they were being indoctrinated into the Babylonian way of life, the king also wanted them to learn the Babylonian way of eating. In verse 5 we read, "The king appointed for them a daily ration from the king's choice food and from the wine which he drank . . . ." In this way, the Israelites got to experience the fanfare of Babylon. It was more than food and drink—it was the king's *choicest* food and drink. It was "living large." As the Israelite youth enjoyed the choicest food and drinks, their resistance to every other bit of propaganda being pushed at them from the Babylonian empire no doubt lessened. This is similar to the free drinks that are offered in gambling casinos or other businesses, where the owners want to reduce the rational thought of the potential consumers so they will be more inclined to gamble their funds or make that purchase.[1]

As the young Israelites began to hang out with the king's crowd and enjoy the finest food and drinks, it would become easier for them to adopt everything else that came along with the culture—including their names.

Lessons Learned in LA
by Anthony Evans Jr.

My phone rang, and on the other end was someone from NBC asking if I would come to Hollywood and be a part of a new show called *The Voice*. That's how it all started for me. Until that time, a couple of years ago, I had never been immersed in secular culture. I never knew the meaning of "living outside of the palace walls." When I received an invitation to be on *The Voice* and then decided to move to Los Angeles, I was confused. I had never performed outside of our church, and I wondered if it was wrong to live and work in such a secular environment. I will never forget calling my dad as I tried to figure this all out and hearing him say to me in the first three minutes of our conversation, "As long as you don't compromise your faith, I want you to go and have a great time." Those were the words that freed me up to experience what I consider to have been a life-altering experience.

I now know what it means to literally have to make a choice to be countercultural daily, because most of my friends in LA aren't Christians. They're confused by what "we" do in church and turned off by how judgmental they consider "us" to be.

It would be very easy to adapt to a new way of thinking in a town like this. But, there are a few things my parents did that bring me back to my core belief system whenever it's challenged. If you're wondering what they did, I can tell you for sure that it has nothing to do with pastoring a ten-thousand-member church, being on more than five hundred radio stations, or having countless books published and numerous invitations to speak. All of these things are inconsequential to me as the son of "well-known Christian parents." What my parents did is nothing other than live an example that I now have engraved into my consciousness. It was watching my parents make decisions to follow the Lord in spite of circumstances. It was the time we spent around the table as they taught me the meaning of making daily decisions to acknowledge the presence of God in my life. At times, just like any "training," it definitely felt rhetorical, but now "living outside the palace" has given me an opportunity to actually experience this training as a reflex. I find myself recalling Scripture and making decisions as a reflex due to the training that I received—just like any athlete repeats a motion until it becomes muscle memory, until it's recalled without having to "think" about it. This is what my parents did. They actually lived and trained us up in the way we should go (see Proverbs 22:6). And this training, although hard at times, has given me an unwavering example of what it actually means and looks like to trust in the Lord with my whole heart.

What's In a Name?

In the tragic play *Romeo and Juliet*, Shakespeare wrote these famous words: "What's in a name? That which we call a rose by any other name would smell as sweet."[2] While the English playwright didn't place a lot of merit on a name, God has a very different idea about its importance.

Our name is the first thing we're given when we arrive in this world. If we're fortunate, it's one that's been carefully and lovingly chosen for us by our parents. Throughout history, names have had specific meanings, and those meanings give them power. While today's culture may not focus as much attention on the meaning behind a name, the Bible makes no secret of its importance. Perhaps no passage more beautifully illustrates the significance of a name as Isaiah 43:1, which tells us, "Do not fear, for I have redeemed you; I have called you by name; you are Mine!"

A name in biblical times signified much more than nomenclature. Parents chose names impregnated with meaning, often both in the present tense and hope for the future. The parents of the four boys in Babylon followed this tradition. They gave the boys Hebrew names filled with significance, presumably because the parents wanted to leave a spiritual legacy. We can deduce this by examining the endings of those four names. In Daniel 1:6 we read, "Now among them from the sons of Judah were Daniel, Hananiah, Mishael, and Azariah." Two of their names end in the Hebrew word *El*. The other two end with *Iah*. *El* is the singular form of the Hebrew word for God, *Elohim*, while *Iah*, found at the end of our word *hallelujah* comes from another name for God, Jehovah.

We can reasonably speculate that when these parents brought their children into the world, they purposefully named them in a way that would baptize them daily with a remembrance of God. Every time these boys would hear their name, they would be reminded of the God in whose image they were made and to whom they were to offer their lives in service. Even though Jerusalem was inhabited at that time by individuals who were rebelling against God, the names of these four young Israelites indicate that their parents had a different lifestyle in mind for their children. There's strong evidence that Daniel, Hananiah, Mishael, and Azariah were raised as kingdom kids.

The Babylonians knew the importance of a name as well, so one of the very first things they did was to rename the four young men. Instead of Daniel, Hananiah, Mishael, and Azariah, they were now called Belteshazzar, Shadrach, Meshach, and Abednego. The Babylonians sought to change the young men's identities by giving them new names.

"But Daniel . . ."

While the young men didn't seem to have much of a say in what was going on around them or concerning the changing of their names, Daniel drew the line on one thing—the food. In verse 8, we read a very critical phrase: "But Daniel . . . " Daniel's parents most likely hadn't raised him to go along with something without thinking it through. Perhaps he knew he couldn't keep his name because it tied him too deeply with his spiritual heritage. Perhaps he knew he had to live in Babylon and study the Babylonian culture. Yet, strong in his faith, perhaps he also knew that none of those things would affect him spiritually the way Babylonians hoped.

But perhaps Daniel also knew that he would not be able to control his body's responses to eating the king's choice food or drinking the king's wine. In fact, in the Israelite spiritual heritage, he knew that to do so would literally defile his body. Likewise, Daniel knew that whatever he put into his body would affect his body, and—in the case of the king's wine—would also affect his mind, so that is where Daniel drew the line.

It's fair to assume that it was his parents who had trained him so well. We see this young man, most likely around the age of fifteen, emerging into a kingdom man. The entire verse reads, "But Daniel made up his mind that he would not defile himself with the king's choice food or with the wine which he drank; so he sought permission from the commander of the officials that he might not defile himself."

Daniel had his limits. And he would do everything he could not to cross them.

Daniel lived in a secular environment. He couldn't change it, just as your kids can't change the secular conditions they are exposed to on a daily basis. As parents, we normally don't have any control over those conditions, either. We can't control the environments our children will walk into or what they will be pressured to do. Yet, as a parent, what you do have control over as you are raising kingdom kids is this: You can create a "But Daniel . . ." Daniel hadn't become a kingdom man on his own. Someone had taught him the importance of his faith and the essential nature of setting spiritual boundaries in spite of whatever is happening in the culture at large. The most likely scenario is that, while Daniel was living at home, his parents taught him the value of autonomy so he could capitalize on its strength once removed from it. They gave him a kingdom mindset that transcended location, connection, country, and environment. In fact, Daniel took advantage of what was in the culture without submitting to that culture. He had made up his mind. The role of kingdom parenting is to instill such a foundation in your children that they will make decisions consistent with their faith even though they live in a secular society.

Maybe Daniel googled "food in a foreign land," and up popped Exodus 34:14–15, recalling his parents' instruction in the Scriptures: "For you shall not worship any other god, for the LORD, whose name is Jealous, is a jealous God—otherwise you might make a covenant with the inhabitants of the land and they would play the harlot with their gods and sacrifice to their gods, and someone might invite you to eat of his sacrifice."

The role of kingdom parenting is to instill such a foundation in your children that they will make decisions consistent with their faith even though they live in a secular society.

From that passage and others, Daniel knew that food was never just about eating. It was opening the door to fellowship with another culture's god. And Daniel wouldn't choose to commune with any other god but the true and living God, nor would he break God's commands. That is where he said no.

Notice that Daniel didn't run away from the Babylonians and hide in some mountain retreat while growing his hair long and singing praise songs. He was *in* the culture; he just wasn't *of* the culture. He took the king's job; he just didn't take the king's food. Daniel received the king's salary; he just didn't adopt the king's society. In other words, he didn't lose his identity just because he was in a secular land.

Daniel worked hard for Babylon, benefitted Babylon, was productive for Babylon, but he also set his own boundaries in Babylon. He remembered the two letters on the end of his name, *El*, and to whom he belonged. Thus, Daniel lived fully in the culture without surrendering to the values of the culture.

"Now God . . ."

The interesting thing to keep in mind is what happened after the "But Daniel . . ." Verse 9 tells us that when Daniel made up his mind to set his spiritual boundaries, God intervened. We read, "Now God granted Daniel favor and compassion in the sight of the commander of the officials."

In verse 8 we see, "But Daniel . . ." In verse 9, we get, "Now God . . ." Often we fail to train our children to understand that this doesn't happen in reverse. We aren't meant to live the kingdom life by "Now God . . ." and then "But Daniel . . ." We all pray for favor, compassion, and blessings in our own lives, and we teach our children to look to God for these things too. But if we do not give them the proper formula for receiving God's great favor, we haven't instilled in them the foundation of kingdom life.

God's blessing and favor, more often than not, come through commitment to Him. Yes, He gives the rain to both the righteous and the unrighteous, but what we are looking at here isn't rain—it's favor. God's favor is the greatest thing anyone can have. Daniel took his stand, and *then* Daniel got God's favor—which was then extended to the commander of the officials over him.

Daniel's request to refrain from the king's food and drink intrigued the official. As a result, Daniel and his three Hebrew friends were able to perform a ten-day test to show the com-

> *God's blessing and favor, more often than not, come through commitment to Him.*

mander how they did after ten days on their diet versus how the other Hebrew boys fared after ten days on the king's food and drink. When the ten days were up, it was clear to everyone that the four boys in Babylon were stronger, healthier, and had more energy than the other Hebrew boys. As a result, they were allowed to eat the food and drink of their heritage and spiritual upbringing.

In raising your kingdom kids, always remember that verse 8 comes before verse 9 in Daniel chapter 1. Daniel first had to make up his mind and then act before God responded. What's more, God didn't make up Daniel's mind. Daniel's parents didn't make up Daniel's mind. The young Daniel had to make the right decision himself, and when he did, he was blessed with great favor.

Parents, train up your children in God's Word and His principles so that the Holy Spirit has something to work with when they are no longer under your direct influence—and do it diligently. One of the key traits of a healthy family is a shared spiritual foundation. As you grow together through studying God's Word, devotions, attending church, praying together, and teaching and modeling morality and character, you will be transferring a living faith to your children that they will then own when they are out on their own. In addition, try to surround your children with other families with like values. Notice that Daniel had three Hebrew boys around him who shared his character qualities. Kingdom parents connect their kids with other kingdom parents who are raising kingdom kids—all four of these young men had a name of God at the end of their own names.

> *In raising your kingdom kids, always remember that verse 8 comes before verse 9 in Daniel chapter 1.*

Yes, I know that sometimes you feel like you are wasting your time when you pray for your kids, have family devotions, or make them go to church. They sit there sulking or looking like they are about to fall asleep. Maybe they argue or complain, and you wonder if it's worth continuing. But remember that they are kids; they may not always look like they want to know what you are teaching them, but they need it. One day they will be older and find themselves in a Daniel situation where you can't bail them out, and no one else will answer for them. It will be up to them at that time to either be a "But Daniel . . ." or not.

There were times when our four kids would be acting up around the table while I was trying to lead devotions, and it would irritate me. They would be talking out of turn, or one would be pouting. It just seemed like a lot of commotion rather than devotion! I admit there were even times when I called it quits and told everyone to go to their rooms because they weren't paying attention or they were being disrespectful.

But more times than not, I stuck it out, and then, at a later point, I would be surprised how one child or another would bring up something I thought for sure no one had heard during the devotions at the table simply due to the noise. They were listening—even when it didn't look like they were listening. Those were the moments God used to remind me to hang in there when I would want to walk away from the table early and call it a night. I would remember that it was my responsibility to train these children to the best of my ability—imperfectly but consistently. I was called to show up and do my part, leaving the hard work of getting the truth into their hearts to God.

Our culture's system has been set up to own our children—to pluck them from us and strip them of the values they need to live well. Babylon is not just a far-off land with no bearing on how we live today. In many ways we live in our own Babylon, and it's a sophisticated one at that—one which seeks to redefine value systems, morality, order, and more.

But we *can* give our children what they need to retain their identity despite the society around them. It will take effort, prayer, and sacrifice. Trust me—it will also take patience. In the end, however, they will remember the last few letters of their name. Despite where they live, they will know the true kingdom to which they belong.

I'll admit it—I was fearful when Anthony moved to Hollywood. My concern was rooted in the idea that such a broad level of exposure to the secular world would invade his Christian worldview and erode his values. I had similar concerns when our daughter Priscilla started participating in (and winning) beauty pageants at college, and when our son Jonathan was signed by the NFL and thrust into an environment that included being surrounded by people who partied and drank a lot.

At these junctures, I always wondered, *Did we raise them with enough of a kingdom mindset to resist the world's temptations?* And while I'm sure none of our kids were squeaky clean and never made a wrong choice, by and large they made it through those times strong.

Parents, one of the hardest parts of parenting is letting your child go out into a world that you no longer can control or heavily influence. But each child will eventually have to make his or her own decisions. That's why it is so critical that you provide your children with a deep foundation while they are still with you, making sure you have equipped them with what they need in order to live as a Daniel in their own Babylon.

Have you ever witnessed the building of a downtown high-rise? When a construction company sets out to build a skyscraper, they begin the process by digging deep into the ground. In fact, the higher the building is to go up, the deeper they need to dig in order to lay the foundation. A tall building set on top of a shallow foundation will ultimately topple and fall.

As parents, you have lofty dreams and aspirations for your children, and your role is to provide them with what they need in order to reach them. Your responsibility is to give them the depth of character, faith, hope, love, and esteem they need in order to soar to the full height of their personal destiny. Focus on the foundation—it will be the bedrock of their life's success.

5

TRANSFERRING THE ROYAL BLESSING

The suburban railway rolled through the city, passing in front of residential dwellings on the quiet streets of Oslo, Norway. The energy crisis of the early 1970s had increased the traffic on this previously low-traveled metro so that it nearly burst with passengers. Everyone had to squeeze in as tightly as possible so everyone could fit.

It didn't help that one stop on the metro's line included a popular location for recreational ski jumping. It also didn't help that ski jumping in Norway attracted more people than nearly any other activity. That being the case, the suburban railway not only held passengers but also held the accompanying conglomeration of skis, equipment, and additional layers of clothing. The rail-car was packed.

An onlooker watching the metro pass by that cold, wintry morning would not have noticed anything extraordinary. In fact, most of the passengers did not notice anything either. After all, it is not every day that a king rides the metro. It's just not something that most people expect to see.

But there he was, seated next to the window in a heavy jacket and hat, the young female passenger sitting next to him trying to cover a shy grin of knowing. She recognized him from both his face and his voice as he greeted her when she sat down. Dare she tell anyone else? Was this truly her king, the leader of Norway, rumbling along with them on the cold and slow-moving railcar? Maybe he wanted to go unnoticed, she might have thought, choosing not to say anything to the others. Yet going unnoticed as a king in your own country can be a bit tricky.

Eventually, one person said something, and then another, and ultimately everyone found out as the murmur spread like lit coals throughout the railcars. A passenger with a camera stood to take his photo while the conductor asked to take his ticket, no doubt in shock at whose ticket he had just asked to see. After all, this was their king, King Olav V of Norway, having been crowned more than fifteen years before.

The king had not boarded the railcar with an entourage that day. He had not even taken along any bodyguards. When asked later why he chose not to do so, thus putting himself potentially at risk, he answered frankly, "I didn't need to—I have four million bodyguards already," referring to the population of Norway at that time.

Thus the king had chosen to travel the metro alone, even though he had no need of traveling on it at all. While driving on certain weekends had been banned in Norway during the energy crunch, it certainly hadn't been banned for the king. He had retained his rights to drive and could have easily, and legally, driven himself to the ski jump nearby.

Yet in an act of respect and honor toward his people who had been forced to take the railcar due to the weekend driving ban, he chose to do the same. A one-time Olympic gold-medal winner in sailing, King Olav V loved his sports. Wanting to get to the ski jump, he had taken the only transportation available to those over whom he reigned.[1]

That is just one of the many reasons why this unique king who served his country for over three decades was known as *folkekongen*, "the people's king." Throughout his lifetime, he modeled both humility and grace, subsequently receiving great favor from God and man.

Something else worth mentioning occurred during King Olav V's ascension to the throne. I mention it because it reveals the heart and insight of this respected royal man. By that time (1957), a coronation ceremony signifying the rite of passage into kingship was no longer performed in many Nordic countries. For a variety of reasons, this ritual had been discouraged. Yet having watched his father serve faithfully as king through many ups and downs—including the resistance of Norway to Hitler's Nazi regime—Olav knew that he could not carry out his position alone. If he were to perform it successfully, it would require nothing short of divine favor and intervention.

Knowing this, he asked the ruling government to implement a royal consecration upon his reign. The primary focus of this consecration, following a sermon, would include the bishop laying his hands upon the king's head and the proclamation of a blessing. The recitation was simple yet profound:

> Eternal, Almighty God, Heavenly Father, we thank thee whose grace in need has always gone over our land in woeful and good times to this day. Hear, today, our king's and our prayer. We pray thee, send thy grace to King Olav the Fifth, assist him by the Spirit and give him wisdom and peace from thee that his reign be a benefit and a blessing on Norway's land and people. Deceitful and burdensome days will come; may truth and goodness from thee be his power and gladness. Eternal, powerful God, bless our king, be thou always his Lord and his King and grant his House all good days in time and eternity. Amen.[2]

King Olav V went on to reign well and reign long. Having passed away as he neared the age of ninety, history records his rule as one truly blessed. He governed his land wisely, administered his people compassionately, and left an example for any with eyes to see of what it means to live up to the name of royalty. Not too long ago, Olav's nation honored their king by declaring him the "Norwegian of the Century."[3]

When There Is No Blessing

King Olav V knew intuitively that if he were going to reign successfully, he needed to receive a blessing from above, so he asked for it. In biblical times, every Israelite parent knew this truth as well. In fact, every child in the Jewish culture looked forward to receiving the blessing. This blessing wasn't reserved simply for kings or monarchs because each child was an image bearer of the one, true King. Neither was it limited to shaking someone's hand and saying, "God bless you," as we often do today in mainstream Christianity. The blessing wasn't merely a trite statement in the movement of time. Rather, it was an

ongoing and profound transference of faith, favor, and destiny from one generation to the next. The blessing provided continuity to a future not isolated from
the past, and a present not irrelevant to tomorrow.

*The blessing provided
continuity to a future
not isolated from the
past, and a present not
irrelevant to tomorrow.*

In historical Jewish culture, the
blessing bestowed favor and acceptance
upon each child (both sons and daughters), based not on their accomplish-
ments but on who they were as children
of God. And while there were many in-
formal blessings in the life of the child
as he or she grew, these ultimately cul-
minated with a formal blessing when
the child reached the age of fourteen or
fifteen. This formal ceremony was attended not only by the parents but also
their peers, with many of the adults present speaking words of wisdom and
blessing upon the child. Today, many Orthodox Jewish families still give their
children a formal blessing. In the context of biblical society, though, to miss out
on the blessing would devastate anyone involved. And this is having a similar
effect in our culture as well.

The greatest story in the Bible concerning the absence of the blessing is
found in the book of Genesis when Jacob, the twin brother of Esau, stole his
brother's blessing. Pretending to be Esau in the presence of his aging father,
Jacob tricked him into giving him what rightfully belonged to Esau. As a result, Esau cried out in agony. We read, "He cried out with an exceedingly great
and bitter cry, and said to his father, 'Bless me, even me also, O my father!'"
(Genesis 27:34). Esau knew that without the blessing, he faced a difficult path
ahead. His entire life and future were tied to this blessing. Yet due to the bro-
kenness between him and his father, all he could do was scream. Fathers have
a critical role in the transference of the faith, and that role involves imparting
a blessing.

When individuals do not receive the blessing, they often feel as though they
have lost their significance. They have lost what makes them distinct. Just as
a flower needs the right kind of environment in which to grow, we have been

made with a desire for blessing in order to move fruitfully into the future. I've preached in enough prisons and talked to enough prisoners to know that most of them—if not all—are men or women who have never received the blessing. They've never heard a parent speak over them the words of favor and future that come from being a child of the King.

One of my greatest failures as a father occurred early on in this area of transferring the blessing to both my sons equally. Because our youngest son, Jonathan, struggled greatly in school, the time I spent with him was disproportionate to the time I spent with Anthony and my daughters. In addition to that, as Jonathan grew, he also played football, so my natural affinity with football drew us into conversations more easily and just added to the time we spent together.

In light of everything else on my plate during those days, I realize now that I didn't spend as much time with Anthony as I should have, and in many ways he may have felt like he wasn't receiving the blessing that was due him as my firstborn son. It wasn't until Anthony was in college and began singing that this truly dawned on me. Since I couldn't change the past, I made every effort to engage with him in his singing career, and I continue to do so to this day. It is exciting to see how many times God has brought the two of us together in recent years at events across the country where I'm there to speak and Anthony has been brought in to sing. Often we don't even know this until we get there, but it's always a pleasant surprise.

Fathers have a critical role in the transference of the faith, and that role involves imparting a blessing.

As a father, I could have looked at my failure in prioritizing the transfer of the blessing to Anthony early on and just given up and walked away. I could have assumed it was too late to undo the message I had communicated to him. But parents, even in areas where you know you did not live up to God's standard, start where you are. I made a conscious choice to work at reversing my actions with Anthony and give him the blessing even though he was now older, and I have seen the Lord honor that effort over the years, even through bringing us together regularly at events. And now that Anthony is an adult, rarely do two or three days go by that we don't talk, either in person or by phone. Not only do I enjoy him and his company, but I also want him to know that he has the transference of the blessing.

Parents, realize that there are things in your past—and in your parenting—that were mistakes or even failures. None of us are perfect. But you can start where you are and move forward. Even if your children are grown and are now adults, your role as their parent still exists. Develop and nurture that relationship as much as you can. And remember that grandparenting is often God's way of giving parents a second chance. In the Bible, Jacob (the father of Joseph) blew it as a dad in many ways. Yet the end of his life is recorded with him placing his hands on his two grandsons (Joseph's children) in order to bless them. Never look at parenting as something that is finished. It is always an ongoing process, no matter what stage your family is in.

And while the blessing may seem meaningless to many of us today, it was not meaningless to Esau when he lost it, and neither is it truly elusive to our own children at the time that they need it the most. The blessing may no longer contain inheritance rights such as land and cattle, but its spiritual significance still remains. It refers to the God-ordained role of transferring the faith and its implications in history through the family line to the child. It concerns God's covenantal covering. Like an umbrella that shelters someone from the rain, the blessing covers a person through the storms of life. The blessing doesn't stop the storm, but it shelters you under it.

The blessing doesn't stop the storm, but it shelters you under it.

Parents, our culture is raining down evil, promiscuity, immorality, materialism, selfishness, and a deluge of other disasters upon our young people today. If you are not careful to position yourself underneath God's covenantal covering, and likewise position your children through how you choose to raise them, then they are going to get drenched.

As you might imagine, Satan's goal is to cut off the blessing. His job is to clip the line and keep what God is giving you from ever reaching your kids.

Satan desires to usher in discontinuity where God wants continuity, and one of the ways that Satan does this is through removing the blessing.

The Blessing of Destiny

In Genesis 12, we witness one of the best explanations of the blessing when the Lord speaks to Abraham, Esau's grandfather:

> Go forth from your country,
> And from your relatives
> And from your father's house,
> To the land which I will show you;
> And I will make you a great nation,
> And I will bless you,
> And make your name great;
> And so you shall be a blessing;
> And I will bless those who bless you,
> And the one who curses you I will curse.
> And in you all the families of the earth will be blessed. (Genesis 12:1–3)

As we see in this passage, the blessing is completely tied to purpose. Through Abraham, the peoples of the earth would also be blessed as God made him into a great nation. Your child's blessing comes tied to his or her purpose as well. God has a divinely ordained destiny for your child that includes his or her passions, personality, skills, dreams, and experiences. All of these merge together to enable your child to live out all he or she is created to be. Your child's destiny may be defined as the customized life calling God has ordained for him or her in order to bring Him the greatest glory and achieve the maximum expansion of His kingdom. Keep in mind, your child's blessing and purpose are never only about him or her. They are about God and His kingdom agenda.

God is a God of both purpose and plans. "The counsel of the LORD stands forever, the plans of His heart from generation to generation" (Psalm 33:11). He has a plan that is specific to your child. Jeremiah 29:11 says, "'For I know the plans that I have for you,' declares the LORD, 'plans for welfare and not for calamity to give you a future and a hope.' "

Your children are here for a reason. It's a tragedy if your children never discover what that purpose is. One of the most important things you can do as a parent is help your children discover their spiritual gifts, passions, and vision so you can guide them into their calling. Keep in mind that a gift is different than a talent. I define a *gift* as "a divinely bestowed ability which is used to strengthen others in order to best serve God and His kingdom." A *talent*, on the other hand, is "a human ability in general, not infused with the Holy Spirit's unique touch and power."

Many believers don't live out their destiny simply because they are not aware of their spiritual gifts. They may be stuck trying to utilize a talent instead of seeking God for the gift He has given to them, or discovering how God wants to transform that talent into a gift. Still others don't fulfill their destiny because they never discover their gifts at all. In raising kingdom kids, be aware of the difference between gifts and talents as you try to guide your children toward their personal purpose.

> *In raising kingdom kids, be aware of the difference between gifts and talents as you try to guide your children toward their personal purpose.*

Will it take time and effort? Yes, but it will be worth it. Before our son Anthony developed a strong interest in singing, he was fascinated with animals and wanted to be a veterinarian. Even when he reached college age, he planned to study to be a vet. As Anthony was growing up, it was our job as his parents to help him along this path of exploration so he could discover if this was truly God's call on his life.

I'll never forget the time that Anthony announced to us that he wanted to buy a donkey. Now, we don't have a huge backyard—and we live in the city. But, regardless, we took the effort to go to different animal farms with Anthony to explore the idea of bringing home a donkey. I even went so far as knocking on our neighbors' doors to ask if they would mind if we had a donkey in our yard.

Needless to say, we didn't end up getting the donkey, but my point is that sometimes we may need to go to great lengths to give our children the option of discovering their gifts. We didn't get the donkey, but we did get a number of different animals over the years—and we also provided Anthony with the experience of riding horses and being with animals at family camps or elsewhere—so he could learn whether or not this was truly his calling.

Too many families today live with conflict and stress simply because they are comprised of individuals who don't know their destiny or are simply not living it out. Anytime you put frustrated or disappointed people in the same home, and add to that the normal trials and tribulations of life, there is going to be stress. One of the greatest ways of passing on the blessing is by providing wisdom, opportunity, and guidance toward your child's destiny.

God has a plan for your child's life—and it is a good plan filled with purpose and hope (see Jeremiah 29:11). As parents, you may sometimes feel you have a better plan for your children. Maybe you have different dreams for them—perhaps to be successful as a doctor, lawyer, or accountant—so you steer them in those directions rather than truly humbling yourself before the Lord to discover His plan for them. Yet trying to improve on God's plan for your child is like trying to improve on a Picasso with a Sharpie: You'll only mess up a masterpiece. God wants you to view your children through His eyes. He wants you to view their future through His plans because He is all-wise, and He knows the best way for them to live fulfilled and abundant lives.

The Gift of Song

by Chrystal Evans Hurst

My mother sings. We grew up listening to her practice in the bathroom for her solo on a Sunday morning. Her father, our late grandfather, sang loudly and with vigor anytime he sat in that second row at our church. We used to chuckle at how loudly he would sing. He took hymns seriously. My dad sings. He wouldn't sign up to enter a vocal competition, but he can definitely carry a tune. In fact, he will break out in the chorus of "My Girl" by the Temptations at the drop of a hat. My dad's father sings. He also plays the piano and has been a fantastic musician his whole life.

You could say that we have been mentored in music over the years.

It's no surprise then that my brother Anthony Jr. sings—and sings well. He has a few albums to prove it. Both my sister, Priscilla, and I sing. We even have formed a quartet on special occasions, with Anthony and Jonathan joining us.

One could argue that we have inherited this gift of song as a part of our DNA. While that may be true in part, it's not the whole story. I know lots of people who can sing but have siblings or children who absolutely cannot. So vocal aptitude is not solely a product of a particular gene pool. This trait must also be related to environmental osmosis. Plain English? In my family, we were around song. We picked it up.

What is true for song is also true of our spiritual heritage. While the four of us Evans kids are grateful for our upbringing, we are acutely aware that what we have received is largely a result of spiritual traits, aptitudes, or abilities that we were exposed to. We had the privilege of hearing our parents pray. We have been blessed to see them serve Christ and His body when it was not necessarily easy to do so. We have witnessed them taking their faith seriously.

And not only were we able to observe and absorb the beauty of their commitment to Christ, they invited us to join them. Just as we might gather around the piano and sing in unison, we would similarly gather around the kitchen table and pray together in unity and be prayed for by our parents—our spiritual mentors.

Herein lies the blessing.

What my grandparents gave to my parents was the gift of a spiritual inheritance. My parents in turn gave that same gift to us.

From generation to generation, the blessing was transferred. We were mentored in ministry and cultivated in Christianity. And for that we are grateful.

Abraham's blessing was not only tied to purpose—it was also tied to his posterity. When Esau missed out on the blessing from his father, Isaac, he missed out on what God had initiated in Abraham. There was a glorious future for Abraham and his descendants—as long as the blessing was passed down. As believers we are all children of Abraham, having been adopted into God's royal home. Therefore, hope for a glorious future is available to your children as well.

Because kingdom parents have the ability to pass down Abraham's legacy of blessing, Satan tries very hard to keep parents from understanding the significance of their role. If he can keep a father or mother from being a responsible parent who raises his or her children according to the principles of the blessing, then Satan has a good chance of limiting the subsequent fulfillment of their destinies. In my counseling to families, I've seen this happen time and again. If Satan can keep marriages in a state of conflict rather than in a state of united commitment, the prince of this world can hinder the blessing. A strong marriage is invaluable, and it goes a long way toward producing a healthy home where the transfer of the blessing can occur.

And not only can Satan limit the next generation's destinies by causing disruption within marriages and in the home, he can limit succeeding generations as well.

Because kingdom parents have the ability to pass down Abraham's legacy of blessing, Satan tries very hard to keep parents from understanding the significance of their role.

Over the course of my life, I've had the privilege of preaching to stadiums filled with more than 65,000 individuals, and I've even spoken to a gathering of a million in our nation's Capitol. Yet there is one time I got to preach that ranks at the top for me. I was in my late forties at the time, and a church in Baltimore had asked me to come and speak at their event on a Friday night. I always liked to include the kids whenever I could, so I decided to take Anthony with me on this occasion, especially since I knew we would get to see his grandparents who lived nearby.

I'll never forget my parents picking us up from the airport and taking us to do what we always did when we were in Baltimore—eat some crabs. Later we picked through those crabs in my parents' kitchen in the home where I had grown up. After that, we headed to the church for the evening's program. Midway through my sermon, I looked out and noticed something very significant. There was my father, sitting in the front row with a big grin on his face, saying amen to my message time and time again. In between his amens, he would turn to Anthony and encourage him to do the same. Now I knew I had my father's blessing all along, but at that moment I felt it in an especially strong way. I felt his blessing linking to me and then transferring through me to my son. It is one of the most treasured memories I have.

Parents, if you are going to raise kingdom kids who live lives worthy of the royalty for which Christ has redeemed them, they need the blessing.

Unfortunately today, most children don't get the benefits of the blessing. We have a generation of boys on our streets not knowing what to do because they know nothing of the blessing. We have a generation of young girls looking for love by selling themselves cheaply, not knowing their true value as inheritors of the blessing. We have a generation of children growing into adults without aim, lacking focus, and neglecting responsibilities because they don't have the motivation of a future and a blessing. Parents, if you are going to raise kingdom kids who live lives worthy of the royalty for which Christ has redeemed them, they need the blessing.

Truth and Touch

The substance of the blessing is made up of multiple things. One of them involves meaningful touch. We see this illustrated in Isaac's deliverance of the blessing when we read, "Then his father Isaac said to him, 'Please come close and kiss me, my son.' So he came close and kissed him" (Genesis 27:26–27). In other places throughout Scripture we read that in transferring the blessing, or anointing, the one giving the blessing laid hands on the one receiving it or kissed him or her on the forehead.

In the New Testament, parents brought their children to Jesus so He could touch them. The disciples tried to dissuade the parents so the children would go away, but this is what happened: "When Jesus saw this, He was indignant and said to them, 'Permit the children to come to Me; do not hinder them; for the kingdom of God belongs to such as these.' . . . And He took them in His arms and began blessing them, laying His hands on them" (Mark 10:14–16).

Whenever you see the transfer of the blessing in the Bible, it involves the use of touch. Touch symbolizes identification, removes distance, and communicates intimacy.

Vince Lombardi is considered to be one of the most successful coaches of all time with multiple league championships and wins in both of the first two Super Bowls. His record is impressive, but his legacy is profound. Lombardi had a special gift for motivating mediocre players to somehow achieve championship play. In fact, Lombardi twice transformed losing teams into winning teams in just one year. He made his players believe they were winners, could play better than they had ever played before, and achieve more than they ever imagined.

This belief motivated them to practice harder than they thought they could and dedicate themselves more fully than they ever had before. Lombardi is known for saying, "Man responds to leadership in a most remarkable way, and once you have won his heart, he will follow you anywhere."[4]

Children are the same.

It's interesting to note that Lombardi coached during an era of great racial division. In fact, when he started, most teams in the NFL didn't even have black players at all, and the teams that did treated them poorly. But not Lombardi. Similar to the touch of the blessing, Lombardi was known for a certain pat that he would give to his players on the back of their neck while speaking to them or as they were coming in from a game or practice. In addition to the fact that racial tensions were at an all-time high, keep in mind that touch can connote both negative and positive intentions.

One particular black player, Dave Robinson, spoke of this pat on his neck in a recent documentary: "My father taught me never to allow a white man to pat me on the head," he said, "but Lombardi was different." A smile broke over his face while remembering his former coach. "I loved it when Lombardi patted my neck." This player later said that Lombardi's funeral was the only time he ever cried at a white man's funeral. "He had become a father-figure to me," the former Green Bay Packer said, "and I loved him."[5]

Touch coupled with words of belief and truth became a blessing that transformed Robinson's heart—a heart that had been hardened by a legacy of racial hatred and pain. He acknowledged that not only did it help him become a great football player, it also made him a great man. Consider how much more impact you might have as a parent if you give your children the positive, loving touch of the blessing. Combine that touch with words spoken that express truths of belief, honor, and favor concerning your child's future and destiny, and you will set your child up to fully live out the plan God has for him or her. We'll look at the blessing of the spoken word—encouragement—in an upcoming chapter so we won't go into it deeply here, but both touch and truth are necessary components of passing on the blessing.

Blessed to Bless

Today we have a generation of kids who are looking for a blessing; they are looking for someone to place his or her hands on their head, believe in them, and let them know that a glorious future awaits them. Remember that the blessing is always future-oriented. We witness this in Isaac's verbal blessing to Jacob: "Now may God give you of the dew of heaven, and of the fatness of the earth, and an abundance of grain and new wine; may peoples serve you and nations bow down to you" (Genesis 27:28–29). The blessing gave Jacob something to look forward to.

I'll never forget the way my father blessed me on a regular basis. Due to financial difficulties in his own home growing up, he had to drop out of high school in order to help earn money to buy food for the family. As a result, he ended up doing manual labor his entire life. For nearly four decades he worked as a longshoreman, loading and unloading ships. It was backbreaking work. I frequently remember my dad coming home exhausted at the end of the day. Sometimes, based on how the ships would come in, he would have to work for twenty-four hours straight.

But even though my dad was tired, he always found time to pray with us, have devotions with us, and take us to church. Yet even more than that, he communicated to us that what he was doing was so we could have a better future. He'd say, "Tony, I'm working hard like this so that you won't have to work quite so hard when you grow up." He wanted me to go to college and earn a living using my brain, and not just my back like he had to. He wanted me to have his blessing of a brighter future, but to give me that required more than words—it required his commitment.

I never saw my dad complain about working, and I never saw him not go to work simply because he didn't want to. My dad's commitment modeled for me his investment in me, and his example therefore encouraged me to be diligent in investing in my future as well, and in my children's futures. As a result, I've tried to honor him with my decisions every way I can.

The tragedy today is that we have a generation of children without a future. They don't have anything to look forward to. They don't know how to dream about tomorrow because they have no one to first dream about it for them and with them. And so they make poor decisions, risking both their lives and their futures, to live for what they can get in the next minute—all the while throwing away the discipline and dedication it takes to live out their destinies.

Giving your children the blessing means giving them a long-range view for a greater tomorrow. It means speaking hope, favor, and dedication over them and letting them know that you will always be there for them on their journey to reach their destinies. A great way to begin this process is by dedicating your child to God as a baby. We offer this as a ceremony at our church, and it is done more so for the parents as a reminder of their calling as parents than for the child's benefit. If you've not had the option of doing this and your child is no longer a baby, consider having a "blessing ceremony" when he or she reaches a specific age. In fact, even if you did dedicate your child as a baby, having an additional ceremony once he or she reaches an age of understanding

Giving your children the blessing means giving them a long-range view for a greater tomorrow.

should prove beneficial as well. It doesn't need to be formal, although it can be. Invite others to join in and pray for your child. Perhaps you can present your son or daughter with a Bible to signify the passing of the blessing.

Bear in mind that passing on the blessing to your children isn't simply saying some magic words and then, *poof*, it's there. You don't just sit down and passively wait for it while doing nothing to secure it. Giving the blessing to your children involves passionately setting them up for it on your part. In Genesis 18, we read about such a commitment concerning Abraham's blessing: "For I have chosen him, so that he may command his children and his household after him to keep the way of the LORD by doing righteousness and justice, so that the LORD may bring upon Abraham what He has spoken about him" (Genesis 18:19).

Abraham's transference of the blessing to his children and descendants required his responsibility. As parents raising kingdom kids, we have an equal responsibility. Abraham's destiny included bringing his children to the fulfillment of their destinies as well. He was to command his household to keep the way of the Lord by doing righteousness and justice. Like Abraham, we are not simply here to exist—we have been selected to be part of the royal family; we have been chosen to bring up the next heirs and heiresses apparent to their rightful positions as rulers in God's kingdom.

That is one of the reasons why I have chosen to dedicate an entire section in this book to instilling kingdom virtues. In order for you to teach your children the ways of the Lord, it is critical to first know them and practice them yourself. And while these virtues may be ones that you have already mastered, it is important to review the foundational principles involved with each one so that you can better know how to transmit them to your children.

It's also why I've put together a workbook you can use with your children as a means of transferring and reviewing these virtues. Character development and the passing of the blessing require effort on your part as a parent, and there is no better way of doing that than setting aside specific times to talk with your children about God's Word and its impact on life. Of course the list of virtues covered is not exhaustive, but it provides a good foundation on which to build.

As parents, you set the pace and the standards for everyone in your home. You establish the goals; you take the lead in discipleship. That is one of your primary roles, and it is critical for bringing about the transference and realization of the blessing. And, fathers, let me just remind you—in biblical times, it wasn't the mothers who were charged with the primary responsibility of raising the kids. It was the fathers' job. The mother was there to help. But it was the father who saw to their apprenticeship, their spiritual training, their teaching and training. Somewhere along the line, we as men have misunderstood the high calling of fatherhood. We are not put in the family to help, but to lead—and to lead well.

> *We are not put in the family to help, but to lead—and to lead well.*

Remember the example of King Olav V of Norway, a king who ruled well. The blessing upon his reign manifested throughout his years and even into his legacy. May your children experience the same level of God's favor as you position them to receive God's greatest blessing upon their lives, along with the manifestation of their dreams and destinies.

PART II

CULTIVATING A KINGDOM ATMOSPHERE

6

~❧~

LOVE IS AS LOVE DOES

Kingdom parenting involves intentionally overseeing the generational transfer of the faith in such a way that children learn to consistently live all of life under God's divine rule. The greatest kingdom rule, given to us by God, is that of love. We have been called to love Him with all of our heart, mind, soul, and strength as well as to love others as ourselves (see Luke 10:27).

Loving God ought to be your child's highest priority in life. And it should be your highest priority as well, both as a parent and a child of the King yourself. Loving God should translate into passionately seeking His glory and submitting to His will as your chief motivation in life. We are to love God

- with all of our heart—the core of our desires and affections;
- with all of our mind—conforming our thinking to His Word;
- with all of our soul—placing the uniqueness of our personalities under His control; and
- with all of our strength—using our body and energy to perform His will.

Our love for God, then, is meant to overflow into compassionately seeking the well-being of others and treating them as you would have them treat you.

Love is God's idea, and it's the most important element in cultivating a kingdom atmosphere in your home. If we are going to raise kingdom kids, we have to lay this part of the foundation carefully and securely. Anything built on a weak foundation will come crashing down sooner or later, and today we can observe many beautiful-looking homes that are falling apart. They were built on the world's misguided definition of love, which is often rooted merely in emotion or convenience. Yet God's kingdom definition of love—if we choose to apply it—will transform not only the atmosphere but also the dynamics of our home.

Love always involves an element of connectedness, an important trait for establishing a healthy family. It can best be defined as the degree of closeness and warmth between children and their parents. It includes spending quality time together, having fun, sharing leisure times, and being involved in school events and homework.

> *God's kingdom definition of love—if we choose to apply it—will transform not only the atmosphere but also the dynamics of our home.*

So how do we build connectedness in our families and raise our children according to God's definition of kingdom-based love? God has provided some practical directions in a familiar passage of Scripture. First Corinthians 13 is commonly called the "Love Chapter." Although its message is usually discussed in terms of personal growth, its portrait of love applies equally to the family.

Love Lesson #1

"If I speak with the tongues of men and of angels, but do not have love, I have become a noisy gong or a clanging cymbal" (1 Corinthians 13:1). In chapter 13, the apostle Paul says a lot about what it means to truly love. When we apply these principles to our home, we will see the resultant fruit. The opening verse hits me—as a husband, father, and a preacher—right in the heart.

As a kingdom man and a kingdom father, I've had more than enough opportunities to do plenty of talking to my children, whether it's around the dinner table having devotions, gathered around the fireplace discussing the day's events, or simply sharing with each one a principle that God had taught me that day. And—at least when my children were little—they hung on every word I said. Daddy knew best, or so they thought. To be honest, I enjoyed their rapt attention and their confidence in me. It made me feel strong and knowledgeable—and loved.

As a preacher for over four decades, I've also had more than my fair share of opportunities to speak in front of people. One time I tried to add up the number of people over the years that I've addressed, and I lost track somewhere around ten million. Speaking is my passion, particularly when it relates to God's Word. I especially like those times when the congregation is really tracking with me and I can't go more than two or three sentences without hearing a chorus of amens. Hopefully during those times the Holy Spirit is driving home a principle for the majority of my listeners. Whatever the case, I'm always delighted to impact people through words.

However, no matter how effective I may think my speech is, 1 Corinthians 13:1 says that words ring hollow unless they are backed up by genuine love. While congregations, clients, Sunday school classes, coworkers and children may hear the voice of an angel, God hears an out-of-tune soul that sounds more like an old gong or an irritating and crashing cymbal that won't stop making noise. He covers His anthropomorphic ears and cries, "Hush!"

The ability to sound good means nothing if it doesn't stem from a truly loving heart. As the title of this chapter says, "love is as love does." Talk is talk, and when it is not backed up by actions that reflect a heart of love—a heart committed to someone else's well-being and good—it's just words.

Whether it's a text message to your children saying, "I love you" or a heart-to-heart talk with someone before he or she leaves home, when it is not backed up with action, it's just cheap, clanging gongs. Your actions must demonstrate to them that the things they are struggling with get addressed, the areas where they need comfort get comforted, the esteem that they legitimately need is awarded, and the time they crave with you gets offered, or it's just cheap clanging gongs.

Sooner or later they will see through the words only to hear your actions instead, leaving them with a heart that was once soft toward you now bitter and cold.

Love Lesson #2

The next verse we're going to examine is 1 Corinthians 13:2: "If I have the gift of prophecy, and know all mysteries and all knowledge; and if I have all faith, so as to remove mountains, but do not have love, I am nothing." This passage tells us that it's possible to look, act, and even sound very spiritual and still amount to nothing. It's possible to be blessed with many gifts of the Spirit and still be bankrupt. It's possible to be a great teacher and yet leave no lasting impact for good. You may know all the verses, understand the principles of the faith, and comprehend the proper lessons and discipline to impart to your children. But if you are more focused on *you* than on your home, that's what will come through. As a father, if your motivation for teaching your family about God's Word is so you can look good publicly, then it's not authentic. Paul says clearly that when your gifts are built on a foundation other than love, they are *nothing*.

Ladies, this goes for you as well. If you treat your husband with disrespect, belittle him in front of your children and others, or fail to open your home in gestures of hospitality and friendship, it doesn't matter how many church committees you're on or how many luncheons you attend. It doesn't even matter whether others in the church look to you as a paragon of faith. If the foundation for your spiritual appearance is something other than love, in God's eyes it is "nothing at all."

Emotions Don't Have Intellect

by Anthony Evans Jr.

One of the most poignant things my dad has ever told me is this: "Anthony, emotions don't have intellect." Those words have continued to resonate throughout the ups and downs of my life. One of the main areas I've felt the impact of these words has been in the area of love. For most of modern culture, love is all about emotions and feelings. It is rarely defined by making a decision and moving in a particular direction in spite of the way one feels. I have had the opportunity to watch my parents express love in spite of circumstances that made many things "unlovable." I've seen this clearly when it comes to the church, our family, and the ministry.

The greatest example I can think of is myself. There were moments in my childhood and early adulthood when my actions made me the hardest person to love. In the Evans household, I'm the emotional kid who wears his feelings on his sleeve and—good or bad—lets you know what's resonating in his heart. There was a time where my internal emotional struggles surfaced in a way that could have been seen almost as hatred toward my parents and their ministry. I didn't want to have anything to do with the church, and although I didn't have a desire to hurt my parents, I could not separate them from the hurt I blamed on "that big building across the street." Early in my life I subconsciously considered the church an enemy, an institution that competed for my father's attention and often won. It took me until I was well into my late twenties to talk with my father and communicate things he never knew.

My father's response to my "complaints" could have been irritation and self-defense, but I will never forget what he did after hearing me tell him how I felt in the depths of my heart. I had gone back to my room, and then I heard his familiar footsteps coming down the hall. The door gently opened, and in one breath my father said, "I apologize for the way I hurt you." No excuses, no disclaimers, no reference to the way I responded. He just empathized with me and loved me. My father defined for me that day the true meaning of love. He looked beyond his intentions into my experience and loved me in spite of the incongruence with what he intended.

My encouragement to you as a Christian parent is to lead by example when it comes to loving. My own desire is to be the kind of man that can do what my dad exemplified, not just what he said.

Love Lesson #3

"Love is patient, love is kind" (1 Corinthians 13:4). The essence of a good teacher is patience—and as parents, we are teachers. Our children are the students. Sadly, we usually have a harder time being patient with our own kids than we do with other people's kids. When our children attempt a task for the first time and make a mistake, our tendency is to run over, correct it, and finish it ourselves. After all, it's easier that way. At least the task will get done. Yet the best thing to do at such moments is to let them make the mistake, explain how to do it right the next time, and provide them with the opportunity to try again. Sometimes the most loving thing we can do is to let go, even if we cringe while doing it.

I remember a time I faced a situation requiring patience in our home. My younger son, Jonathan, struggled in school due to ADD, which severely hindered his ability to read early on. As the self-appointed "homework assistant" in the Evans home, I would often spend hours with Jonathan in the evening, sitting at the kitchen table trying to help him read or helping him complete another homework assignment that involved reading. Reading is so foundational to everything else, and it was difficult for him to complete any of his schoolwork because he struggled in this key area.

Dealing with this issue came at the height of my traveling and preaching opportunities, as well as at a time of unprecedented growth at our church. Promise Keepers had exploded on the American scene and required a significant portion of my attention. I needed to spend intentional time managing our church growth, in addition to my normal counseling sessions and preparation for preaching. I don't think Jonathan's need for help could have come at a worse time as far as my availability both physically and mentally were concerned.

Yet Jonathan was my son, and as such, he was my first priority. His needs trumped all others, and so—whether I was tired or not, whether I was worn out or not, whether I had had a long day or not—every night I would sit with Jonathan and help him with his homework, often staying up until midnight.

Now, if anyone might have been tempted to just read it for him, answer it for him, and fill in the blanks for him—it would have been me back then. But I knew that wouldn't have prepared him to perform well as he continued in school and later into adulthood. As an hour would pass, and then two each night, I had to call on my patience to guide Jonathan as he deciphered what to do each step of the way. More than that, I couldn't let Jonathan see my lack of patience, because nothing can crush a child more than the feeling that his parent is trying to off-load him quickly so as to move on to something else.

As we continued to spend time together regularly at the table at the end of each day, I actually began to look forward to this time with Jonathan. He's always had a unique and special spirit, and I got to see even more evidence of that when I saw how he faced challenges. In time, Jonathan learned to read on his own. In fact, he went on to attend Baylor University on a full football scholarship, and he completed his degree in only three-and-a-half years. Jonathan, now a husband and father himself, spent a few seasons in the NFL, and he's now studying for his master's degree at Dallas Theological Seminary. At the time of this writing, with several classes under his belt, he is an honors student. He also serves as the team chaplain for the Dallas Cowboys.

Those hours with Jonathan at the table paved the way for what God would later provide as he lives out his destiny. I did what I could and left the rest with God. As a parent, loving requires an investment of time. Leading with patience and love involves doing all that you can for as long as you can, while leaving the results with God. Had I tried to force the results I wanted early on, I may have ended up frustrating Jonathan and causing a rift in our relationship as well. Maybe Jonathan would have gotten the notion that he could never do well in school and wouldn't have had the resolve to pursue his education. In any case, I wouldn't have had his best interests in mind, and that would not have been love. Raising kingdom kids always keeps the best interests of the child at heart, no matter how busy your schedule, how tired you feel, or how hopeless the situation may appear—and it always requires patience. Did I ever feel like giving up during a homework session and just saying, "Let's call it a night"? Yes. And sometimes I did—especially when I could see that Jonathan was tired too. At times he would sit there crying because it was just too hard for him to focus, and it would literally break my heart to watch him struggle. But I had made a commitment to help him, and no matter how much patience that would require, I was going to do my part. I would tell him, "Jonathan, it's going to be all right. We're going to get through this. I'm here with you, and I'm not going to leave."

> *Raising kingdom kids always keeps the best interests of the child at heart, no matter how busy your schedule, how tired you feel, or how hopeless the situation may appear—and it always requires patience.*

At the time, there was a great push to put children diagnosed with ADD on medication. While his doctor had recommended this for Jonathan, Lois and I prayed through this decision and ultimately decided that we would seek to empower Jonathan to learn how to succeed in life without medication. That decision meant I would have to invest additional hours to teach him how to complete assignments and also make sure he *did* complete them. But in the end, these lessons Jonathan learned have stayed with him and still help him to this day.

Love Lesson #4

"Love is kind and is not jealous; love does not brag and is not arrogant, does not act unbecomingly; it does not seek its own, is not provoked, does not take into account a wrong suffered" (1 Corinthians 13:4–5). We can see from this verse that jealousy, pride, and conceit are three deadly enemies of family unity and health. Family members who love one another encourage one another's talents and gifts. They do not seek to "one up" each other. Parents, watch this one particularly in yourselves. When you compare one child with another, you may think your motivation is helping that child improve, but this kind of comparison is hurtful. Many parents encourage the talents of one child at the expense of another. Even worse, some parents devalue the gifts of one child with the line, "Why can't you be more like your brother or sister?"

Remember, even if your children's gifts or talents are not the ones you would have chosen for them, they are the gifts and talents God has chosen. Don't let your pride or selfishness get in the way of encouragement. If you and your spouse both graduated from college, for instance, and want your kids to do the same, be careful to guard against any negative reaction you may give a child who chooses to go to a vocational school and pursue a trade. Instead of wishing that child were more like you, offer encouragement and support for his or her choice.

They say that confession is good for the soul, so here goes: If you've read any of my books or have heard me preach, you probably already know how much I loved football when I was growing up. As a young boy in the bustling Baltimore–Washington Metroplex, I dreamed of one day playing professional football. I would eat my mom's "famous" double-decker sandwiches or that extra piece of fried chicken to try and be big enough to eventually play. Unfortunately, an injury just before my eighteenth birthday brought that dream to an end.

So what did I do instead? Well, I tried to live out my vision through my older son, Anthony. From the day of his birth, he was surrounded by footballs. He had a football waiting in his crib when he came home from the hospital. Playtime with Daddy meant tossing a football or watching a game together.

Can you guess how all my efforts to indoctrinate my now widely acclaimed professional singer son turned out? Yes, he hates football—or at least he used to. And the more I would bring it up when he was younger, the more he hated it.

Because of my own inability to achieve my dream, I wanted Anthony to play for me. I wanted to live vicariously through him. I gave little thought to his enjoyment, and in so doing, I was loving *myself*; I wasn't loving him. I was raising him in the way I wanted him to go, not in the way he should go, which is what Proverbs advises. It says, "Train up a child in the way he should go, even when he is old he will not depart from it" (22:6). In the original language of the Scripture, the phrase "in the way he should go" refers to a child's bent, or uniqueness.

Unfortunately, this is one of the most misinterpreted biblical passages. It is not a promise that if you train up a child in Christian principles, he or she will stay faithful to those principles when he or she is older. What it is referring to is that if you have enough wisdom and insight to train your child according to the unique fingerprints of his or her personality—God-given skills, gifts, and interests—when that child is older, he or she will remain on that path. It is an admonition to parents to study their children well, and then guide them in the direction that best fits their interests and natural abilities.

Had I studied Anthony well, I would have noticed the football lying in the corner of the room under a pile of clothes as an indication of what it truly was: He just wasn't interested in football. I wish I could go back and change what I focused on where he was concerned during those early years, but I can't. And I'm grateful today that he has a thriving music ministry, crossing into both Christian and secular audiences and sharing God's love through the power of his voice. But learn from me—never try to live out your unmet dream through your children. Rather, study your children to recognize their abilities and talents, and then point them in the right direction at a young age. If you do, Scripture tells us that they likely will not depart from it.

> *True love is seeking God's will and destiny for the other person, not seeking your will and destiny through the other person.*

True love is seeking God's will and destiny for the other person, not seeking your will and destiny through the other person. Love is compassionately and righteously pursuing the well-being of another.

Love is not a loud parent boasting of providing for their children while ignoring deeper needs that should be met. It is not saying, "Of course we love you. Look at this house. Look at your clothes. Look at what we've given you." Love is quiet. It's a thoughtful deed done for a child with the expectation of nothing in return. It's going the extra mile with your children, even when you feel too tired to do it. Love is never rude, nor is it selfish.

Why is it that we're often gentle and courteous with business associates, friends, and even complete strangers, yet for some reason we don't feel the need to extend any of this to our own families? Common courtesy is a lost art, even in many Christian homes. It doesn't take too much effort to offer a kind word or once in a while clean up a mess around the house that you didn't make. The largest love is often revealed in the smallest acts.

Men, remember when you were dating your wife and you couldn't wait to open the car door for her? Now she's lucky to get into the car before you drive off. Ladies, remember when you would go to great pains to fix your husband's favorite meal? Now he's lucky to get something to warm up in the microwave. Love never forgets the little things.

Paul tells us in 1 Corinthians 13:6, "[Love] does not rejoice in unrighteousness, but rejoices with the truth." One of the most painful experiences of life is to watch one of your children stumble and fall while you're absolutely powerless to do anything about it. It's harder yet to sit by helplessly and watch that child suffer the consequences. Yet, if we think it through, we know that stumbling, falling, and getting back up again are common parts of spiritual (or any other kind of) growth.

I remember how nervous we felt when our first child, Chrystal, was learning to walk. We were caught up in the tension of wanting to be close enough to catch her if she stumbled yet far enough away that she had to take the risk of walking in order to get to us.

The largest love is often revealed in the smallest acts.

The nature of life's bumps and bruises changes over time, but what remains constant is giving your children room to grow, comforting them when they fall, and helping them get back on their feet again. What is critical is that you are there for them. What kind of parents would we have been if we saw Chrystal trying to walk and left the room? The same is true as our children grow older. They need us to be with them when they choose wisely as well as when they make poor decisions. No, it won't always be fun—the scripture says that love does not take pleasure in others' sins—but we can use those opportunities to demonstrate unconditional love and teach our kids how to make a better choice next time.

We don't need any more cotton-candy parents, full of nothing but sugar and sweetness. You are not meant to buy your children whatever they want, applaud everything they do, and say yes to whatever they demand. Permissive parenting doesn't produce kingdom kids; it creates cotton-candy kids—kids without the strength or substance to make it through when life gets challenging. To develop strength and substance in your children, you'll need to model it for them and with them during the trials and mistakes that you both will encounter along life's path. Remember, one day the toys are going to break and the clothes will get too small, but a spiritual heritage will cross generations. That is the thing you give to your kids that will last forever.

Love Lesson #5

"[Love] bears all things, believes all things, hopes all things, endures all things" (1 Corinthians 13:7). How many times do you bring up the past while correcting your children in the present, long after they have apologized and truly tried to live according to the rules you've set? What a child learns from that is that Mom and Dad don't really forgive; they keeping a running count of all misdeeds. What's the point of doing what you're told if Mom and Dad keep bringing up things from the past?

It's true with your spouse as well. I can't even count the number of times during counseling sessions when I've heard a husband or wife refuse to acknowledge the present problem in their relationship, instead going back years in the past to dredge up a hurtful moment that has long been atoned for. When I tell a couple we can't proceed without some forgiveness being extended, I hear the clincher. One spouse chimes in and says, "Well, I can forgive, but I can't forget."

Far too often, we hold the pain of the past over our loved one's head like a club, or we remind them of the burden we still carry because of something they did years ago whenever we want to get the upper hand.

How grateful we should be that if we're repentant and earnestly desire to turn our lives around, God will "remember [our] sins no more." If He operated on the principles we often use with one another, we'd all be bound for hell on a fast track.

I know that true love and forgiveness work in families. While I've seen many families hold each other in bondage because of the sins of the past, I've also seen others overcome incredible odds to forgive, forget, and restore broken relationships. I've seen rebellious kids who have run off into a life of alcohol and drug abuse turn their lives around, and I've watched with great joy as parents and children worked together on the hard path of reconciliation.

What 1 Corinthians 13 boils down to is unconditional love—love that is not based on your child's performance or on how you feel about your family on any given day. Ultimately, unconditional love is one of the greatest ways of showing someone honor. As husbands and wives, we must never lose sight of the vow of unconditional love we made to each other during our wedding ceremony, and we should be aware of how that should extend to our children. The depth to which we adhere to those vows will determine the spiritual strength of our home.

Children are vulnerable and sensitive. They are affected by our actions even when we think they may not notice. Love requires effort. Though good feelings, positive emotions, and serenity may be known through love, they are not (as our culture tells us) the goal. The aim of love is to promote another's well-being, and that especially applies to those within our own home. It means more than merely teaching your kids kingdom principles and virtues—it means modeling them.

Giving yourself for the betterment of another is difficult work, no doubt. Our pride is strong, and we often would rather not make the hard choice of going out of our way for our families, especially if we feel that we're giving a lot already. It's much more comfortable to sit in church and say amen to a sermon on love than to spend hours tutoring a child in spelling or math. It's a lot easier to keep busy with church activities or work long hours all week than it is to go to your spouse or your kids when you've neglected or dismissed them, admit you're wrong, and seek to make things right.

Love is as love does. Your children will follow what you model. They will know they are loved by what you do.

The truth about kingdom love is simple and biblical: Love is as love does. Your children will follow what you model. They will know they are loved by what you do.

7

〜

THREE PILLARS OF PARENTING

Families determine the future, making parenting one of the most critical tasks on earth. Unfortunately, today Satan has done a great job of dismantling the family. Satan despises the family because he knows that God's plan is for the earth to be blessed through the family.

Not only that, Satan has also been after the family since the beginning of time. If you recall from the book of Genesis, he never bothered Adam until after Adam got married. Satan wasn't just after a man; he was after the future. Satan wants your children because he wants to control tomorrow by advancing a culture of rebellion.

However, God has instructed us in His Word concerning three pillars of parenting which—if followed—can stabilize and protect your home, as well as future generations, from the attacks of the enemy. Raising kingdom kids involves carrying out each of these three important pillars on a regular basis: encouragement, discipline, and instruction. Doing so helps to establish a strong family with consistent expectations and follow-through.

Encouragement

We learn about our first pillar through the words of Paul when he penned what will serve as our primary verse for this chapter: "Fathers, do not provoke your children to anger, but bring them up in the discipline and instruction of the Lord" (Ephesians 6:4). Paul reiterated the same concept in his letter to the church at Colossae when he wrote, "Fathers, do not exasperate your children, so that they will not lose heart" (Colossians 3:21).

Yet before we dive into this arena of encouragement, I want to point out that in both verses Paul used the Greek word that has been translated into "fathers." It applies to the male parent, but it can also encompass both parents in its application. The same Greek word is used in Hebrews 11:23 when talking about Moses' mother and father, and it is often translated as "parents."[1] In choosing that term, Paul wasn't limiting this pillar of parenting to just the man. These verses could have just as easily been translated as "Parents, do not exasperate your children " or "Parents, do not provoke your children to anger."

I also want to point out what they could *not* be translated to read. They could not have been translated as, "Government, do not exasperate your children," or "Village, do not exasperate your children," or "School system, do not provoke your children to anger." This is because the onus of raising kingdom kids is on the parents. It is on you and me, not the government, or even our schools.

A child needs parents to raise him or her well, not a village. Unless the village has kingdom values, that village will mess up a person. After all, gangs are villages. Entertainment is a village as well. In fact, entertainment is probably the most prevalent village raising kids in our nation today. The average child spends thirty-two or more hours a week in front of the television, tablet, gaming devices, or other forms of electronic media.[2] We don't need more villages raising kids; we need more parents raising kingdom kids.

It is the parents' responsibility to raise their children well, and one of the first ways to do this is by not exasperating them. This means that parents are not to provoke their children. They're not to create irritation, anger, and frustration in the lives of their children. We can easily turn this verse around and say that, rather than discouraging them, parents are to encourage their children.

Scripture tells us, "Death and life are in the power of the tongue" (Proverbs 18:21). A parent who discourages his or her children instead of encouraging them speaks failure and curses into their future. Instead, as parents we are called to give encouragement. There's a difference between encouragement and praise, though. Praise is tied to what a person accomplished. Your child did something you want to acknowledge. Praise is good. But children need encouragement even more. Encouragement is not tied to *what they did*; it's tied to *who they are*. Encouragement relates to their identity in Christ and their inheritance as image bearers of God Himself as children of the King.

Have you ever seen a drooping plant quickly perk up when someone pours some water on it? That's what encouragement does. Encouragement will take a droopy kid and perk him or her up again. As the Bible tells us, "Pleasant words are a honeycomb, sweet to the soul and healing to the bones" (Proverbs 16:24). Encouraging your children gives them an expectation of God's goodness and favor on both their todays and their tomorrows. It sets within their hearts an anticipation of a glorious future. Encouragement tells them they are fearfully and wonderfully made and have been gifted by God. It helps them believe that God has a plan for them filled with both a future and a hope.

One reason so many teenagers get caught up with negative groups of their peers today is because that's where their encouragement is found. They get more affirmation from their peers than their parents, and so they respond to that which makes them feel significant.

> *Encouraging your children gives them an expectation of God's goodness and favor on both their todays and their tomorrows.*

Parents, let your words reach deep into your children's hearts with encouraging truths that communicate to them that you know their personalities, dreams, hopes, struggles and that it will all turn out okay because of who they are and to whom they belong. Give them the hope that they need to face each day.

On top of that, don't "provoke" your children to anger, as Paul said. Provoking them can happen by disrespecting them in your words or actions, comparing them to others, or even showing favoritism to one child over the others. We all remember what Joseph's brothers did when his father showed favoritism by giving him the multicolored coat. Be fair with your treatment, time, and attention, because your children are all equally valuable to our heavenly Father.

Being critical, finding fault, and setting up your children with negative thoughts about the future can also develop in them a spirit of frustration. These things have a profound impact on children, more so than we might even know or realize, so always be mindful of whether you are speaking life to them or discouraging them with your words and actions.

There are times when it may not feel very easy to encourage your child, but those are the times you need to dig deep and find the patience and commitment required. Lois and I faced a time like that with our oldest child, Chrystal. Chrystal was around twelve years old when she developed what I would call an identity crisis. I had never seen anyone struggle with his or her identity on such a profound level, let alone at such a young age, and I was literally at a loss for what to say to her. At times she would be crying and asking us to help her, but neither of us knew what to do. Lois and I would look at each other as if to say, "You handle this."

This went on for so long that it became frustrating, and at times I just wanted to give up and walk away. But even though I couldn't understand where it came from or where it was going, I had to dig deep to find the patience to walk with Chrystal through it. Part of parenting is in connecting your child with a healthy esteem. Some children are more difficult than others in this area. Some kids seem born with a strong esteem, while others are more fragile. As a parent you must be committed to walk with each child as he or she discovers his or her personal identity and esteem. Thankfully, Chrystal came through this challenge and discovered her strengths and purpose. But getting through it required much patience from us as her parents—and a lot of encouragement.

Above all else, encourage your children and build them up.

Discipline

Pillar number two is discipline. Paul wrote, "Fathers, do not provoke your children to anger, but bring them up in the discipline and instruction of the Lord" (Ephesians 6:4). Discipline involves a number of things. It is not only a corrective influence in a child's life, it also involves instilling personal discipline within his or her life.

Discipline is a key factor in any victorious Christian life, whether it is discipline in money management, time spent, or personal morality. Job wrote during his distress that he had disciplined his eyes so as to not lust on a woman: "I have made a covenant with my eyes" (Job 31:1). And Paul spoke of the discipline he had maintained so that he would finish his race strong: "I discipline my body and make it my slave, so that, after I have preached to others, I myself will not be disqualified" (1 Corinthians 9:27).

Parental discipline, when done well, trains your children to apply personal discipline as they grow older, as well as prevents them from making poor decisions later in life.

The parents of the great missionary to China during the 1800s, Hudson Taylor, strove to teach him personal discipline by putting a piece of dessert on the table in front of his evening meal and giving him the option of not eating it because he trusted them for a greater reward at a later time. In this way, he had the option to eat it, but he also received the greater reward of his parents' affirmation and an unexpected treat later on when he chose not to do so.

> *Parental discipline, when done well, trains your children to apply personal discipline as they grow older, as well as prevents them from making poor decisions later in life.*

"See if you can do without " was [one of Hudson Taylor's father's maxims]. This of course applied, among other things, to the simple pleasures of the table. Porridge with bread and butter for breakfast, meat once a day, and bread and butter or toast for tea was the usual routine. But sugar and preserves were allowed in moderation, and extra-nice cakes or puddings occasionally found a place. As a rule the children shared whatever was provided, their parents delighting to give them pleasure no less than other fathers and mothers the wide world over. At the same time they fully realised the lifelong influence of little habits. At any cost to themselves and within wise limits to the children, they felt they must secure to them the power of self-control.

"By-and-by," the father would explain, "you will have to say 'No' to yourself when we are not there to help you; and very difficult you will find it when you want a thing tremendously. So let us try to practise now, for the sooner you begin the stronger will be the habit."

It was a principle difficult of application, no doubt, when a favourite dish was in question. But though it was at least as hard for him as for them, he would encourage them to go the whole length on occasions, saying cheerfully, "Who will see if they can do without today?"

The children were not blamed if they could not respond as he desired, but were commended if they did, the mother generally arranging some little surprise at night—a few almonds and raisins, or an orange, with an extra-loving kiss.[3]

That reward of their affirmation would stay with Taylor over a period of several days as a reminder of his choice. He said that this affirmation, even more so than the greater reward later on, was a critical learning opportunity for him as a child. Not only that, it later transferred to his adult life when he had choices to make on a much larger scale. Because he was able to delay the rewards of immediate gratification for an even deeper, more meaningful, and lasting reward from his heavenly Father, he had a positive impact on the nation of China.

There are also corrective measures a parent must apply in order to raise kingdom kids. Essentially, your children are born with hell in them—a sin nature—and it is your job to correct and train them so the Holy Spirit is the dominant influencer in their life instead of their flesh.

Corrective discipline is designed to break a strong, rebellious will that a child might have—yet without breaking the precious spirit God has placed within that child.

Discipline comes in a variety of different forms, and depending on your children's personalities, what works for one may not work for another. For some children, the greatest discipline might include being sent to their room alone. For another child, however, that could be a reward. This is why it is so critical to understand and know your children so you are able to raise them according to their individual personalities and needs.

My father knew what worked with me. And because he did, he didn't have to discipline me much. When he did, it was done in such a way that I would never forget it. My dad called my discipline "sessions," and they took place in the basement. What's worse is that he would send me down for a "session" and then make me wait. I knew what was about to happen, and he wanted me to have plenty of time to think about whatever I had done to get myself into this mess in the first place.

Before my dad started a session, he would say something like, "Now, are we ever going to do such-and-such again?" I would always say, "No, Dad." He usually asked me again to confirm it, and I would say no again—often loud enough that the neighbors could hear. And I meant it.

> *Corrective discipline is designed to break a strong, rebellious will that a child might have— yet without breaking the precious spirit God has placed within that child.*

Now, keep in mind, disciplining your child is not the same as child abuse. That is completely wrong and has nothing to do with love. While discipline ought to produce some level of pain—whether by removing games, reducing socializing or spending, putting your child to work on an extra laborious chore, or some other rational form—it should be *constructive* pain, designed to teach your child not to engage in the wrong behavior again. The goal in discipline is always correction. You're trying to create obedience while maintaining your child's personal dignity and esteem.

Discipline is not yelling at your child—that's venting. It must be coupled with love or your child will not see it for the good you hope to gain through it. You will end up only provoking your child to anger by being angry yourself. Discipline must flow out of a heart of compassion for your child's well-being and future, just as we read in Hebrews concerning God: "For those whom the Lord loves He disciplines" (Hebrews 12:6).

Another critical element in performing discipline that will establish kingdom principles in your child is setting clear boundaries ahead of time. Disciplining your children for something they didn't realize was wrong—and maybe was something that just irritated you—will bring about only confusion and animosity in them, not spiritual growth. God always sets clear boundaries with us, and we should do the same with our own children.

When you teach your children that boundaries are actually an open door to freedom, they will be more receptive to them. You can establish freedom by instructing your children that they are free to do what they want within the boundaries you have provided. As they continue to honor those boundaries, they earn more freedom. Let's say they faithfully adhere to a 10:00 p.m. curfew. In time you could reward them with more freedom by moving that curfew to 10:30 p.m. This will teach them that rewards come from obeying boundaries.

Parents, remember that it's okay to reward obedience. God modeled this for us all the time throughout Scripture. Often His promises to the Israelites were dependent upon whether they obeyed His commands.

Teach your children to obey with honor. This means the child is not walking around with a scowl on his or her face, "obeying" you but at the same time making the atmosphere smolder. If that happens, you need to let your child know that it is not obedience until he or she also fixes his or her facial expression and attitude.

Along with the area of boundaries, parents must establish clearly defined expectations about what children are to contribute to the function of the home. Whether that means chores they perform, meals they prepare, or helping out with siblings, a healthy family atmosphere is one where there is clear communication about expectations. In addition, be consistent in enforcing those expectations.

Instruction

The third pillar of parenting is instruction. As parents, we are to raise our children "in the instruction of the Lord." We are to duplicate in them the same instruction we receive from Him.

When I preach at our church in Dallas, the message gets recorded onto a master CD. This master CD is later inserted into a duplicating machine to produce CDs for our church members and distributed through our national ministry, The Urban Alternative.

Only one master CD exists for each message, but thousands of duplicates are created. I learned something interesting about this process long ago when we first began it—the blank CDs (audio-cassettes when we first started) are inserted into a machine called the "slave unit." The slave unit has one mission: to duplicate the message of the master. It doesn't add to it, take away from it, or distort it.

What a great illustration this is for us as believers in Jesus Christ! As His followers, we are to replicate His image on earth. We are His slaves and He is our Master (see Ephesians 6:6). The goal of discipleship is to reproduce the Master as completely and accurately as possible. That is also the goal of instructing your children in the Lord. In doing so, you are intentionally discipling them to embody and live out the message of the Master, Jesus Christ. You are teaching them the values of righteousness before God and justice among men—how to live lives punctuated by equity and fairness, kindness, compassion, and love.

My Mouth, the Culprit
by Priscilla Shirer

I'll admit it—I got into a lot more trouble than my siblings. Honestly, during my teenage years, I probably got into more trouble than all of them put together. Of the four of us, I was the one who kept my parents up late at night worrying about my fierce rebellious streak, wondering how in the world it had gotten there and what to do about it.

I brought home notes from teachers explaining why I'd been sent to the principal's office . . . again. My parents would take me to the one bedroom that was down a different hallway from the rest, where we'd talk . . . among other things.

If there was a theme to my troublemaking, it was usually because of something I'd said or the way I'd said it. *"My mouth,"* as my mother called the culprit. And that mouth appeared all set to cause me a lifetime of trouble if I didn't do something to soften it and restrain it and put it to good use.

So my parents, um . . . they *helped* me with that problem.

Every time I spoke out of turn or spoke too much or too rudely or too grown-up for my age, they faithfully disciplined me appropriately. But the discipline part was never the end of the situation. There would also be a conversation afterward, when my parents would talk with me about *why* my mouth was getting me into trouble and how I could change all of that if I'd just take it seriously. Or maybe if I'd just take it in a different direction . . .

My parents were the first to plant the idea in my head that my aptitude for talking could actually be a benefit to me, and even to others. They encouraged me, for example, to read to our family some of the poetry and monologues I had written, occasionally even allowing me to present them at church during service or at a special program. Rather than stifling me, they put a microphone in my hand and encouraged me to edify others.

My mother's sister, who directed the children's ministry at our church for nearly three decades, put me in front of a Sunday school class of six-year-olds and let me teach them a Bible lesson when I was only ten. That was my first time teaching the Bible, and it lit a fire in my soul that has never gone out.

Then, as college drew closer, my dad directed me to think about taking up communications as a major. (I didn't even know such a degree existed.) He even set me up with an internship at a Christian radio station in the city where I'd be studying. And after graduation, he was the one who advised me to consider speaking and teaching as a career and ministry.

It turns out that this mouth of mine didn't need to be *stifled* as much as it just needed to be *redirected* by loving, caring parents who could see beneath the surface of my youthful foolishness and imprudence. I'm so glad they did—I'm so appreciative that they valued encouragement and instruction every bit as much as correction and discipline. It's made all the difference for me.

When Paul talks to parents about our third pillar of parenting, he clearly says that we are to "bring them up . . . in the instruction of the Lord." Bringing our children up "in the instruction of the Lord" is meant to be a joint venture between you and God. Simply instructing your children without including the truths and principles of God's Word may provide them with information, but it won't give them wisdom to make right choices in their lives.

Bringing your children up in the instruction of the Lord requires a substantial time commitment. You can't teach your children if you are not there, or if you are too preoccupied when you are there that you never spend any time with them. Our nation is facing an epidemic of the devolution of the family, and it is largely due to the negligence of parents who are simply not available to instruct their children.

The last few verses of the book of Malachi record a similar scenario. "Behold, I am going to send you Elijah the prophet before the coming of the great and terrible day of the LORD. He will restore the hearts of the fathers to their children and the hearts of the children to their fathers, so that I will not come and smite the land with a curse" (Malachi 4:5–6). The land would be saved when the fathers' hearts were once again turned toward home, indicating that when they are not turned toward home, the land suffers. You know a nation is cursed when you can't even find the fathers. You know a home is cursed when the same holds true.

I understand that schedules are busy, workloads are full, church programs are important, children are involved in sports—the list goes on and on. But we cannot ignore the supreme importance of instructing our children in the Lord until it's too late and they are on their own. Don't fall into the enemy's trap, thinking there will be time enough tomorrow, when you are not so tired, or you have finished that important project, or the holidays are over. The Bible tells us to ask God to "teach us to number our days, that we may present" to Him a "heart of wisdom" (Psalm 90:12).

As parents, we have to seize the day, make it count, live it to the fullest, not allowing any opportunity to pass to invest in the lives of our children. Trust me, I know—they grow up a lot faster than you could ever imagine. One minute you're wrestling with them on the floor, the next minute you're giving them away at a wedding.

And when time is really tight, the good news is that you can always teach your children while you go about your everyday life. My father was a master at this. He could turn any situation into an opportunity to share a spiritual principle. Because he made himself available to us, whether it was going with him on an errand or being accessible at home, we were learning all the time.

I have to admit, though, that wasn't my strength as a father. Looking back, I wish now that I would have taken advantage of more teachable moments. I placed a lot of emphasis on family devotions around the table, but not as much on discipling my children in the everyday activities of life. Yet in hindsight, those moments are as important, if not more so, than the more structured times of teaching. Maybe I inherited this mindset of formalizing the instruction because my kids were young while I was in college, seminary, and then getting my doctorate—I don't know. Or maybe the pressure of my schedule caused me to feel more comfortable with a formal structure than a relational one. For whatever reason, I didn't take advantage of unstructured, casual times as much as I could have. But since I can't change the past, I try to look for teachable moments with my kids even now that they are adults, and I do the same with my grandkids.

We all have the same twenty-four hours in the day. Seizing the day, then, doesn't merely have to do with the amount of time as much as with prioritizing that time. It means keeping first things first. The fact is that we always make time for the things that are most important to us, whether we realize it or not. The activity that takes you away from your children may be a good thing in and of itself, but that is not the question. Your children are your primary responsibility, and they deserve your time.

Samuel was a prophet in the Old Testament busy performing the work of God. But he lost his children because he spent so much time on the road (see 1 Samuel 7:16; 8:1–5). Eli, the high priest, ended up forfeiting his ministry and his very life because he ignored his responsibility to discipline and instruct his sons (see 1 Samuel 2:12–17, 22–25; 3:10–18).

What about your priorities and your schedule? Do you find yourself saying "tomorrow" a lot? Too often, when those tomorrows come, the kids don't feel like hanging around with you anymore. Parents, forget about tomorrow. Seize today.

Instructing your children in the Lord means spending time with them so they can see how you live out the gospel. It means letting them see you praying and studying the Bible. It means involving them in any ministry you are engaged in. As I mentioned earlier, my dad would often take me along when he went downtown to preach on a street corner or visit the prisons. My kids can tell you that they came with me to different speaking engagements, often manning the book table in the back when they were still small. Things may have felt chaotic or busy at the time, but those times made for some good memories. Now that they are grown, all four of our kids are fulfilling their calling by doing God's work. Now I see them involving their own kids in similar ways.

By being with your children on a regular basis during normal, everyday life activities, you are able to capitalize on the teachable moments that present opportunities for you to mentor your child in the faith. Something as simple as

Instructing your children in the Lord means spending time with them so they can see how you live out the gospel.

looking at the night sky together can easily lead to a discussion about the creation and how God knows every star and every hair on our heads. Playing games together can open up topics on the importance of integrity, communication, and focus. Watching a television show or movie together provides a natural conversation starter for an analysis of the character's motives, choices, and actions.

At times these teachable moments might be simple, while at other times they may be more graphic. I remember one time sitting on my parents' front porch with my kids when several policemen chased a drug dealer onto my parents' lawn, tackled him, and handcuffed him right there, just a few feet in front of us. It didn't take much for me to capitalize on that moment and let my kids know that breaking the law is a serious matter.

Discover the lesson I've learned through the years: You don't have to sit your children down and have them sit up straight for you to teach them. They can learn with you while you are cooking, driving, studying, or otherwise going about your day. The goal isn't just shaping the way they think and believe; it's shaping the way they live. Instructing them in the Lord isn't being as concerned about how much they *know*, but with how much they can *apply*. When people try to learn a foreign language in a classroom, it often takes years upon years of study and practice before they reach a competent level. Yet when people learn a foreign language by immersing themselves in that culture and language, they can pick it up within half a year, if not sooner. Instructing your children in the Lord ought to be done by the immersion method; it ought to be a lifestyle.

It's also important to intentionally create an atmosphere where your children feel free to ask you questions. This provides the greatest opportunity for learning because they will ask you about things that concern them the most.

Raising kingdom kids is not a task for the weary or lazy. It is a full-time responsibility. But it also brings with it an eternity of rewards. It is an investment with great returns.

As our world seeks to threaten and mislead our children in so many ways, it might be tempting for us to surround them with a cocoon and never let them out of our sight. But at those times when you feel overwhelmed at the size of your task, here's a verse I took comfort in—and still do—with regard to raising my children: "Trust in the LORD with all your heart and do not lean on your own understanding. In all your ways acknowledge him and he will direct your path" (Proverbs 3:5–6).

> *Raising kingdom kids is not a task for the weary or lazy.*

Ultimately we must trust God with this endeavor of raising kingdom kids. As we seek Him and acknowledge Him in all of our ways, He will guide us every step of the way. In training our children, our job is to give them what they need to make wise choices both while they are under our roof and once they leave our home. If we've equipped them well, done all we can while trusting God with the rest, we have done our job.

8

HONOR *AND* RESPECT

I'll never forget one of the biggest disappointments of my childhood. I brought it on myself, and that only added to the pain. My parents were adamant that my brothers and sister and I be model students. Any disciplinary problems in our classes were to be caused by "other people's kids." That was important to my parents for a number of reasons. The first was that a teacher was someone to be highly respected and obeyed. Another was that the Evans family honor was at stake; what one child did reflected on us all. Yet another was that my parents were concerned about the kind of adults we would become. And lastly, but just as important, was that, as followers of Jesus Christ, we were to honor those God had placed in authority over us.

My mom and dad also made it clear that if we misbehaved in school, there would be consequences at home. My dad especially cut no slack when it came to breaking the rules at school—or anywhere else, for that matter. As much as I loved and respected him and knew that he loved me, I also knew he would never fail to administer discipline when I had it coming. There were certain things that I did not do simply because I did not want to have to give an account to my father afterwards.

Well, as you've probably guessed by now, there came a day when I forgot all of those things and acted up in school. I misbehaved so badly the teacher called my father to let him know what I had done. The penalty for my behavior was stern discipline from my dad . . . in the basement. In addition, I also lost some of my privileges.

It just so happened that on that particular day, my school baseball team was playing an important game, and I was the starting catcher. But after finishing up in the basement, my dad said those dreaded words, "No game for you today."

You have to understand that when I was a child I loved sports more than anything. Plus I was having a great season that year on the team. To hear that I couldn't play devastated me. As if that weren't enough, though, my dad made me go and apologize to the coach for not playing and tell him why I couldn't play, which embarrassed me all the more.

That episode from my childhood is only half the story, though. While the incident caused me a lot of pain, it also accomplished my father's greater purpose, which was far more important in the long run. It taught me the importance of respect for my parents' rules, but it also impressed upon me the importance of showing my teachers respect and respecting authority in general. I learned there is a price tag to disrespect, and it was a price tag I didn't want to pay.

My father also "ruined" many a Saturday night during my youth by saying as I went out the front door, "When you are out there tonight, remember that your last name is Evans." Obviously, he didn't need to remind me of my name. But he wanted to remind me that my name represented something bigger than just me. It stood for honesty, integrity, morality, and dignity in the community. In short, it represented a commitment to Christian living, and my dad didn't want me to do anything to jeopardize that testimony. That reminder always stayed in my mind as I made youthful choices. I sought to respect my dad by honoring his name, which he had given to me, and I felt it inside when I didn't live up to that name.

> *There is a price tag to disrespect.*

Not every child in my community was taught those lessons, and I see the results every year when I go back to visit Baltimore. Many of my boyhood friends died early from taking illegal drugs or participating in other ill-fated activities, and many others are still living purposeless lives with little or no direction. But the respect and honor my parents instilled in me helped me to progress beyond the limitations of the neighborhood.

What Is Honor?

The Greek word for *honor* means "to value highly, to hold in highest regard."[1] This, by the way, holds true at any age. There may be some areas of controversy and disagreement when it comes to obeying parents, but children never reach an age when they don't owe their parents honor. Honor is an important trait to have in a healthy home because it involves unconditional love, affirming the value and uniqueness of each person in the family, celebrating and acknowledging the family's strengths, respecting the privacy of each family member, and serving one another.

The reason we have so much dishonor in the streets and in our schools is that children have never learned honor in the home. If kids don't learn to honor Dad and Mom, how will they learn to honor police officers, judges, or anyone else's person or property?

It used to be that when adults were walking down the street and met a group of kids coming the other way, the kids moved over. Now we see kids coming, and we get out of the way. They are not afraid of us; we are afraid of them. Why? Because we don't know what these kids might do if we make them mad. Because parents don't instill honor in the home and allow their children to get away with dishonoring them, we all pay the price in our society. It is no secret that Satan wants to destroy the home; if he can do that, he can destroy the culture.

If kids don't learn to honor Dad and Mom, how will they learn to honor police officers, judges, or anyone else's person or property?

All human relationships are based initially on what a child learns at home. If a child learns that it is okay for a man to push a woman or disrespect her verbally, he may grow up to beat his wife or abuse her verbally. If a son learns that it is okay to be lazy, sarcastic, and unemployed, he may grow up to be an unproductive man. When parents model a lack of responsibility, their children are on track to grow up to be irresponsible and unaccountable adults. If the parents are absent in the home—or they are physically present but emotionally absent—their children will rely on what they learn from television, music, movies, video games, and their friends to form their character and worldview.

Because Satan wants to destroy the home, he will use whatever he can to accomplish his goal. You need to understand, parents: Satan *hates* your family. He knows the family determines the future. If he destroys your family today, he can mess up many people's tomorrows. Satan is after the future, and he's all about destruction.

He is not just after you or your marriage—he's after your kids. He wants them damaged because he knows that if he can damage them, he can damage their future families. Let's say you have three children, and Satan manages to infiltrate and ruin all three of them. He's now potentially ruined four families—yours and theirs when they are older. Eventually, the society as a whole is in jeopardy as families continue to crumble.

That's why God made it unequivocally clear from the beginning of recorded history that honor and respect are critical elements in every home. How important is it to God that children honor their parents? We find the answer in Exodus 21. Verse 15 says, "He who strikes his father or his mother shall surely be put to death." According to verse 17, "He who curses his father or his mother shall surely be put to death."

> *God understands it's not simply about having a good day or a peaceful home—the whole picture is about advancing His kingdom on earth versus Satan advancing chaos.*

Lifting your hand against your parents or cursing them, both terrible forms of dishonor, meant death in ancient Israel. That's how serious God is about children honoring their parents—because God understands the whole picture. He understands it's not simply about having a good day or a peaceful home—it's about advancing His kingdom on earth versus Satan advancing his chaos.

Seeing Clearly

by Jonathan Evans

"Children, obey your parents in the LORD, for this is right. 'Honor your father and mother' (this is the first commandment with a promise), 'that it may go well with you and that you may live long in the land'" (Ephesians 6:1–3, ESV). I have already had my kids memorize this passage of Scripture, not simply because it's convenient to do so as a parent, but rather because through my own life experiences, I've learned how true this passage really is. Having a promising future and living life all of your days more abundantly are welded to honor and respect. Keeping that fact in mind has helped me to see things more clearly.

As a kid I definitely had blurry vision about the future. The problem was, as is with all kids, that, to me, my blurry vision was 20/20. Therefore, there were many circumstances I faced growing up when I didn't see things the way my parents saw them. At the time I thought my vision in regards to decision making about the future was better than theirs. However, as I grew up, life experiences taught me differently. I learned the true meaning of the famous phrase, "Hindsight is 20/20." There are so many situations in my life that I would handle differently now. I admit it—I would see things the way my parents saw them. I came to realize that because of my parents' experiences which preceded mine, they already had hindsight; they already saw with 20/20 vision. I learned the truth of Ephesians 6:1–3, which says that honoring and respecting one's parents creates the foresight for a promising future. Simply put, a parent's job is passing on their clear vision to their children. Therefore, the children's job is honoring and respecting their parents' biblical foresight instead of their own blurry eyes.

Teaching Respect and Honor

In Scripture, honor and respect are first spoken of with regard to parents. Exodus 20:12 says, "Honor your father and your mother, that your days may be long in the land that the LORD your God is giving you" (ESV).

God has an order established in all that He does, and He works through that order. In the home, the mother and the father have the responsibility of raising the children and the children have the responsibility of honoring and respecting their parents. When you disregard God's order, you invite damage to come into your life. When you go around His way—or dishonor His way—you enter into His consequences.

> *When you disregard God's order, you invite damage to come into your life.*

For both children and adults, how we respond to God's established flow influences how God will respond to us. When Adam and Eve responded to the devil in the garden and violated God's order, it affected how God responded to them. Some of us as adults have not responded to the way God has arranged things to flow; we failed to make the connection, and now we wonder why we have troublesome issues in our lives. We see our children disrespecting us, and this is a reflection of our own disrespect for our parents.

Let's look at a biblical case study of how God feels about dishonor and how He deals with it. It's an unusual story, found in 2 Kings 2:23–24. The prophet Elisha was being dishonored and cursed by a group of young men:

> Then [Elisha] went up from there to Bethel; and as he was going up by the way, young lads came out from the city and mocked him and said to him, "Go up, you baldhead; go up, you baldhead!" When he looked behind him and saw them, he cursed them in the name of the LORD. Then two female bears came out of the woods and tore up forty-two lads of their number.

The word used here indicates that these were not little kids being irresponsible. These were older boys who were, in effect, cursing God's prophet. And their disrespect brought death. The reason so many children are dying in the streets is because they have never learned honor, and it's costing them their lives. They look only to each other as examples because there is a lack of parents who hold their kids accountable to this kingdom principle.

Let's say you have two sons, one fifteen years old and the other ten. You tell your fifteen-year-old son that he can go to the movies but he must be home by 11:00 p.m., but instead he comes home at 4:00 a.m. You get upset with him and tell him not to do it again, but he continues to break his curfew anyway, and he continues to get away with it without consequences. By failing to address the rebellion in your older son, you are potentially encouraging rebellion in your ten-year-old son. Rebellion that is ignored only leads to more rebellion—and not just in one child. As the younger brother watches his sibling rebel without accountability, he will learn to do the same. That's why instilling honor and respect as virtues within the home is so important. If you fail to do this, a wave of disrespect grows as you move on down through the ages of your children.

For example, when Chrystal was in high school, she didn't want to go on our family vacation because she didn't want to miss out on some social activities going on that month. This was also a time in her life when she was openly struggling with a contentious attitude. I knew that how we handled Chrystal's request (demand might be a better word) would subsequently affect each of our other three kids when they would get older, so we decided to make Chrystal go on the family vacation. Now, I'm not saying she went with the right attitude. But sometimes parents have to realize that, even if they can't quite get the *heart* to show honor or respect, the *actions* still must.

God takes honor very seriously. Look at another passage that spells it out in detail. What did Israelite parents do when they had a rebellious child who refused to obey them? The Mosaic law was very specific:

> If any man has a stubborn and rebellious son who will not obey his
> father or his mother, and when they chastise him, he will not even
> listen to them, then his father and mother shall seize him, and bring
> him out to the elders of his city at the gateway of his hometown.
> They shall say to the elders of his city, "This son of ours is stubborn
> and rebellious, he will not obey us, he is a glutton and a drunkard."
> Then all the men of his city shall stone him to death; so you shall
> remove the evil from your midst, and all Israel will hear of it and fear.
> (Deuteronomy 21:18–21)

This passage is not talking about misbehavior. All children are going to misbehave. This is talking about serious, deliberate, long-term rebellion. Children, especially teenagers, need to know that they cannot live any way they want and expect to cruise right along with no consequences.

These days it is customary to blame your problems and the way you behave in general on your parents. It reminds me of two brothers who went through a counseling session together. They had been brought up in a home where the father was an alcoholic. One of the brothers had also become an alcoholic, but the other didn't drink at all. When asked to explain their behavior, they said in unison, "Well, what else could you expect with a father like mine?"

Both men told the truth: One followed their father's example, even though he probably didn't want to, and the other—the stronger of the two—managed to stick to his resolve not to end up like their dad. The story also illustrates the truth that parents sometimes get blamed for far too much and receive praise for far too little.

The fact is, however, that parents need to teach their children to respect and honor them, and they also have to model that respect.

When my dad disciplined me for acting up in school, as much as I disliked it, I grew in my respect for him. He had given me plenty of warning that misbehaving in class would not be tolerated. He had always followed through on his warnings in the past. And by being consistent that day by spanking and grounding me, he showed me once again that he was a man of his word, that his rules counted, and that he was not a person to be trifled with. In short, he was a man to be respected.

Parents, remember that honor flows out of a heart of respect; establishing that respect mindset in your children is critical. It doesn't always come through physically disciplining them. This is important, because all children are different. Out of our four kids, one got spanked far more than the others, and one hardly got spanked at all. I had to discover the best way to communicate to each child.

For example, one day Jonathan came home from being out with his friends, and he had gotten his ear pierced. Now, Jonathan knew that I did not want him to get an earring, but he did it anyway. He wasn't typically a child who dishonored Lois or me, so this decision startled me. Not only did it surprise me, it also deeply disappointed me—so much so that when I walked in the house and saw him sitting there with an earring in his ear, I had nothing to say. I was speechless due to the depth of disrespect I felt he showed. I just looked at him, turned around, and walked out of the room.

Jonathan could sense my disappointment, despite my not saying or doing anything. He took out the earring and never wore it again. Parents, disciplining your child goes far deeper than an action in one moment. It's an ongoing process that instills in them a respect for you so that when they deviate from the right path, their hearts will be tender and they'll want to get back on it.

> *Honor flows out of a heart of respect; establishing that respect mindset in your children is critical.*

As the Bible says, "We had earthly fathers to discipline us, and we respected them [for it]" (Hebrews 12:9). Proper discipline naturally creates respect, as God intended. My father's first name is Arthur, but I would never call him that. To me, he'll always be Dad. And when I used to take my kids to visit him during the summer, I always came under his authority. My age makes no difference. That's the kind of respect that I have for him.

Parents, remember that proper discipline takes time and effort on your part. We need to make sure we have all the facts straight before we act. We have to make time and put forth the effort to discipline when there are a million other things we would rather do, like put our feet up and relax at the end of a long, hard day. It's also vital that we combine our discipline with love. I would often follow up grounding, spanking, or lecturing one of my children with a hug, telling that child that I loved him or her. I wanted him or her to both hear and see the heart from which the correction came.

Teaching respect and honor requires something else, too: a long-term perspective. At the moment when discipline is needed, it's not pleasant for anyone. But you must see beyond the moment. "No discipline seems pleasant at the time, but painful," we read in Hebrews 12:11. "Later on, however, it produces a harvest of righteousness and peace for those who have been trained by it" (NIV).

God has an eternal perspective in disciplining us, Hebrews 12 reminds us, with the goal of making us more and more like Christ. In the same way, be careful not to simply think of your sons and daughters as the boys and girls that they are now, but rather as the men and women they will one day become. Consider the quality of relationships they will one day have because of the honor and respect you instilled in them at a young age. They need to know how to honor and respect themselves, their parents, and those around them in all that they do—in their words, actions, and even in their thoughts.

At the moment when discipline is needed, it's not pleasant for anyone. But you must see beyond the moment.

Parents, when we're inconsistent with our discipline, when we favor one child over another, or when our children observe us treating others with dishonor and disrespect, we make it difficult for our children to respect us. Although the command for children to honor their parents is all-inclusive of children, I believe that one way to help your children to honor you is by honoring them. If you want your children to give you honor and respect, honor and respect them, too, by setting a good example and being consistent in your words and actions.

Honor Comes with a Prize

The book of Ephesians tells us that when children honor their parents, they will receive a blessing: "Honor your father and mother (which is the first commandment with a promise), so that it may be well with you, and that you may live long on the earth" (Ephesians 6:2–3).

This verse says that children who honor their parents will be blessed with a greater quality and quantity of life. They will avoid the consequences of rebellion and disobedience that can bring about the loss of God's blessing and can even lead to a premature death.

These children will also experience God's blessing. This principle of honoring parents was given in the Old Testament, and it carries right through the New Testament. It still applies today, and it remains a central feature for anyone who is serious about experiencing God's blessings.

Does Ephesians 6:3 promise that every child who honors his or her parents will live to be ninety and experience only good things? No, the biblical idea of long life is that you will get all the life God ordained you to have. He won't have to cut you off before your time because you refuse to stop dishonoring your parents. You won't die at forty if you're supposed to live to be seventy. You'll live all your ordained days.

How to Show Honor

How do children honor their parents? Let me suggest several ways.

First, children need to honor their parents emotionally. This includes spending time with them and showing them some concern and love. Some mothers and fathers are wasting away in retirement homes and care centers for lack of attention and honor from their grown children.

Someone may say, "But you don't know my mother. She was a terrible mother." Or, "My father was bad news." But this person is still your parent. He or she must have done something right, because you're still here. This doesn't imply that you have to honor what your parents did wrong. But you can still recognize and honor your parents for their position.

You can also honor your parents verbally. When I visit my parents' home in Baltimore, I don't say to my father, "Hey, Art. How's it going?" It's "Yes, sir" and "No, sir."

Paul told Timothy, "Do not sharply rebuke an older man, but rather appeal to him as a father" (1 Timothy 5:1). In other words, even if he's wrong, you must still speak to him with respect. A mother and father are not, "Hey, you" to their children. Parents are to be spoken to—and spoken about—with honor.

God also calls children to honor their parents financially. In 1 Timothy 5:8 Paul wrote, "If anyone does not provide for his own, and especially for those of his household, he has denied the faith, and is worse than an unbeliever." In verse 16 we read: "If any woman who is a believer has dependent widows, she must assist them and the church must not be burdened."

As children, we have a financial responsibility for our parents when they can no longer take care of themselves. This means more than buying them a Mother's or Father's Day card. It means seeing to their well-being when they need our assistance. Maybe they can't live with us because of the kind of medical care they need, but honor still demands that we look after their welfare.

Notice that in 1 Timothy 5:4, Paul described what we do for our parents—in this case, our mothers—as making a "return" for what they have done for us. Your mother carried you for nine months. She went through painful labor to bring you into the world. She fed you, clothed you, and housed you.

In the case of many poor families in our generation, your mother may have boarded a bus every day to go to the other side of town and scrub other people's floors so you could eat, have clothes, and go to school. Your dad may have worked like my dad did, until he was so tired he could hardly drive home. That kind of sacrifice deserves to be honored.

When an elder in our church was a child, he was abandoned by his father. Not long ago, the father fell ill, and the elder went to the hospital regularly to visit him, even though none of the elder's siblings would have anything to do with their father.

This elder showed his father honor, not because he was a great dad, but because his position as father deserved respect. And who knows? This man's honor may win his father to Christ.

Honor is also shown through obedience. You don't have to have teenagers to recognize that we are living in a day of changing values and role reversals. The culture has turned up the heat on our families. As this thing boils, what has come to the top is a rebellious spirit that tells children to ignore, disregard, and disobey their parents—and all authority, for that matter. We could say that what we are seeing today is the "adultification" of our nation's children. Paul taught the importance of showing honor through obedience beginning with verse 1 of Ephesians 6: "Children, obey your parents in the Lord, for this is right."

As parents, part of your role is creating an atmosphere where obedience comes naturally and easily. This is done partly by setting standards and boundaries for what you allow in your children's lives, and bringing the appropriate correction when your children cross them. For example, when our children were young, we limited their television time to thirty minutes during weekdays. Essentially, that meant they could watch one show, and typically that show was *The Cosby Show*. This not only kept out negative and ungodly media influences, but it also encouraged quality time together since we spent the bulk of our evenings either talking, playing games, or reading together. Because that allowed for deeper relationships to develop between us, when we asked the children to obey certain rules or do their chores, they didn't feel as if that was the only thing we were asking them to do. They reciprocated more easily out of a heart of trust and mutual esteem.

As a Christian parent, your job is to filter the culture in such a way that its evil influences don't dominate your kids' lives. You must strive to filter out the sinful tendencies within them in such a way that you bend their will without breaking their spirit.

Why is this necessary? Because no matter how cute your children are, they are sinfully cute. Foolishness and rebellion are built into the heart of a child (see Proverbs 22:15). That's why children must learn obedience.

When Paul said that children are to obey their parents "in the Lord," he is reminding us that obedience to

> *As a Christian parent, your job is to filter the culture in such a way that its evil influences don't dominate your kids' lives.*

parents is akin to obedience to God, because that is how God has set up the hierarchy of the home. Said another way, when a child rebels against his or her parents, he or she rebels against God. Several times throughout the Bible, God emphasizes this need for obedience. Here are just a few:

> Hear, my son, your father's instruction, and do not forsake your mother's teaching. (Proverbs 1:8)

> My son, do not forget my teaching, but let your heart keep my commandments. (Proverbs 3:1)

Hear, O sons, the instruction of a father, and give attention that you may gain understanding, for I give you sound teaching; do not abandon my instruction. When I was a son to my father, tender and the only son in the sight of my mother, then he taught me and said to me, "Let your heart hold fast my words; keep my commandments and live." (Proverbs 4:1–4)

My son, keep my words, and treasure my commandments within you. Keep my commandments and live, and my teaching as the apple of your eye. Bind them on your fingers; Write them on the tablet of your heart. (Proverbs 7:1–3)

The book of Proverbs also says that a disobedient child brings grief to his parents (10:1; 17:21; 19:13) and shame to the entire home (19:26).

Obedience—couched in a spirit of both honor and respect—is an essential component of a kingdom atmosphere and a healthy home. Make it easy for your kids to honor and obey you. Live honorably. Treat them with respect, and let them see you honoring your spouse and showing respect for their grandparents. Don't just give them rules; they desire a relationship with you. Rules without relationship leads to dishonor and rebellion. Hug your children, pray for and with them, encourage them and thank them for the things they do to contribute to the well-being of your home. Be a part of their world. Let them know you love them. When all of that is in place, they will more easily listen to your rules because they will believe that those rules are for their best interest. They will learn to trust you, and trust is the bedrock of all true honor and respect.

9

LOL, SMHS, AND CC (CULTIVATING COMMUNICATION)

People today benefit from the most advanced information systems ever devised. Those who died just fifty years ago would be astounded if they came back to life and saw the incredible ways we can communicate today. Through television and satellites, we can watch what's happening on the other side of the world as it occurs. Social media have changed everything we used to know and understand about communication. Over 1.2 billion people use Facebook. Over 250 billion photos have been uploaded to Facebook alone, not to mention Instagram. And since they say a picture is worth a thousand words, that's an awful lot of communication right there.

Families can sit in the same room these days with everyone on either a mobile device or a tablet and go hours without communicating with each other. Tweets are substituted for talk. Posts have taken the place of conversations. Words have been reduced to mere letters—acronyms such as LOL (laugh out loud) and SMHS (shake my head silly), for example. Complete sentences have lost their once-valued standing in our culture. Slowly but surely we are losing our finesse in coherent speech patterns, grammar, and the art of listening. After all, social media don't necessarily require two-way interaction.

We call this communication, but it would be better defined as mere transmission. Communication takes place not only when a message is sent but also when it is received, understood, and acted upon. Given that definition, there is very little real communication going on today. Yet communication is a vital and critical component of a healthy family.

In addition to the lack of true communication happening in most homes, an awful lot of negative messaging is getting through to kids, and this is driving a young generation into an unprecedented depth of hopelessness and irreverence toward life.

The effectiveness of that negative communication, coupled with the scarcity of quality communication within families, is a large part of our problem in raising kingdom kids. A kingdom home should have open and frequent sharing of feelings or mutual concerns, listening, understanding, empathy, affirmation, and accessibility to discussion and information. In this chapter, let's explore how we can create an atmosphere conducive to healthy communication patterns and skills by implementing a few key strategies and principles.

The Kingdom Principle of Healthy Communication

In my years as a pastor, I've read a number of books and heard countless lectures on family communication. With few exceptions, they've all been excellent. But based on my own experience, both in my own family and in counseling, I believe the primary principle has to be this: There is no quality time without quantity time.

There is no quality time without quantity time.

I cringe every time I hear parents say that because their schedules are really full, they make a great effort to spend "quality time" with their children. Think what this idea would look like if transferred to another area of life. What if star quarterback Peyton Manning decided that, since he was already pretty good, he needed to practice only twenty-five minutes a day? What do you think would happen to his team, or to the atmosphere and attitudes of those around him? Of course this isn't the case, as Manning has a reputation for being one of the most dedicated players in the NFL, often

putting in more hours than those around him, whether it's practicing or studying game film or plays.[1]

Another Super Bowl-winning quarterback, Russell Wilson, who exploded
on the NFL scene with some of the best fundamental football ever played, is
usually the first to show up in the morning—sometimes by 5:30 a.m.—and the
last to leave, often logging fourteen-hour days. Wilson's motto is "The separation is in the preparation."[2] Quantity time has definitely translated into quality
play in both Wilson and Manning's case.

Unfortunately, while we would not tolerate an attitude of "quality time"
being better than "quantity time" in any other profession or endeavor—certainly not in professional football—we have no trouble shortchanging our parenting and calling it "quality time."

Parents, that is simply not acceptable. In order to foster an atmosphere of
healthy communication in your home, there first have to be plenty of opportunities for communication. Family communication takes work and skill, and
you can't develop those skills if you're not present.

In our family, when the kids were still at home—and even now as they
live nearby and often visit, bringing their kids with them—we found that one
of the best places for family communication was around the kitchen table.
It's a time when we are all together, we are all relaxed, and we are enjoying a
shared meal. It's a great time to catch up on the events of the day and discover
what is pressing on the hearts of all involved. But the kitchen table isn't just
for mealtime.

What about your home? Are your kids around the table? Do they look
forward to coming home because their parents will be at dinner tonight? Or
are you rarely there? Do they know they'll have your attention when they are
talking to you, or are you busy texting or on the phone with someone from
work?

Communication isn't always effortless and easy, of course. One of your
children might be easier to talk to than another, or there could be an age level
that lends itself to deeper communication more so than others. But regardless
of the investment it takes to create an atmosphere for healthy communication,
it is worth it.

Part of the effort required to communicate is due to the fact that there are different personalities within a family. Because people are unique, they will respond to the same message in different ways. If I correct a strong-willed and confident child in a stern voice, for example, that child could possibly take it well, either obeying because of the sternness or feeling free to ignore me.

A sensitive child, on the other hand, might be crushed emotionally by the same tone of voice. The sternness could be interpreted as an overwhelming personal attack. Clearly, parents need to know their children's personalities so they understand how to communicate effectively with each one without causing hurt. And how do we learn to read our children's personalities? How do we discover the best ways to communicate with them? It takes time—quantity time; there's just no other way. And there is no other way for children to truly feel valued and appreciated than by their parents spending time with them.

> *There is no other way for children to truly feel valued and appreciated than by their parents spending time with them.*

You can tell someone's priorities by how they spend their time. Children are smart enough to discern that as well.

Consistent investment in the lives of those you care about is necessary to achieve effective family communication. Put simply: Making an investment in your family may cut back some of the profits at work. It may mean letting someone else in the office land the big client or get the promotion. It could mean less time in front of the television watching your favorite shows, or fewer shopping excursions to the mall. But in sacrificing these things, you will be fulfilling your role as a kingdom parent raising kingdom kids.

Kingdom Keys for Communication

We've talked about why you need communication in the family and what it will take. Now let's talk about the principles of effective communication—I call them the kingdom keys for communication. These include how you send messages and how you receive them.

In all communication, there are three parts. The *encoder* is the person who wants to say something. The *message* is what's actually said. It's supposed to convey the encoder's intended information and emotion, but it has a life of its own and is easily misinterpreted. The *decoder* receives and deciphers the message, making sense of it.

If the decoder doesn't understand what was received, no matter how clear the encoder thought the message was, the encoder might have to repeat himself. If the message is still not understood, the encoder might become frustrated at the decoder.

If you are married, you are probably well aware that most marital problems stem from poor communication. When a couple tells me in counseling about how they fight all the time, they're actually saying that they don't communicate well. When a wife says, "He doesn't understand me," she's really saying that who she is and what she says are not getting through to her husband. Good communication is critical to lasting and fruitful relationships. Giving these powerful principles to your children—through modeling and teaching them—is an important step in raising kingdom kids.

Kingdom Key #1—Be Honest

Ephesians 4 contains excellent counsel regarding communication. The first principle found there states: "Therefore, laying aside falsehood, speak truth each one of you with his neighbor, for we are members of one another" (verse 25).

The first kingdom key is honesty. One reason families break apart is the lack of honesty and consequent lack of trust. People are afraid to tell each other what they really think and feel. They are afraid to be vulnerable. Parents especially have this need to always appear right in front of their children and won't always admit when they've made a mistake.

One of the greatest things you can do as a parent is let your children know when you've made a mistake. This way they can see how you respond to it, and thus you model for them how they are to respond when they make mistakes. Honesty is a critical component of all communication—without honesty there is a lack of trust, and trust is fundamental in all relationships.

Turn Off the Television

by Chrystal Evans Hurst

Thirty minutes a night. That's all the television we got on school nights. We watched every episode of *The Cosby Show* and probably rewatched them all at least once. Thursday nights at seven o'clock was our main night to watch television. What did we do the rest of the time on weeknights? We finished our homework, helped with dinner, and completed our chores.

And we talked.

Dinnertime was talk time. My mom had a home-cooked meal ready every night and we lingered over it in conversation.

We played.

I can't tell you how many memories I have of being doubled over an empty plate laughing hard at some corny joke or playing "who stole the cookie from the cookie jar" for the umpteenth time.

We engaged with one another.

Homegrown talent shows were the order of the evening. Long games of Monopoly took forever, and my dad was a barracuda. Uno was the game that all ages could play and have an equal chance of winning.

From tot to teenager, each person had many opportunities throughout the evening to share his or her life. I knew about what happened in my brother's kindergarten class. He got to hear my reasons for wanting to run for sophomore class secretary.

My parents gave us thirty minutes a night to engage with a portal that delivered the message of someone else's home. The rest of the week, we engaged with the message of our own abode.

My parents weren't afraid to be the "not-cool" parents who tortured their children with limitations on television, secular radio, and hours of talking on the phone.

My parents weren't afraid to ensure that we connected.

I am constantly fighting the battle of making room in my house for connection. It is no easy task with the Internet, laptops, cell phones, video games, and yes . . . television. I don't pretend to have it all figured out. The elusive goal of balancing the joys of present-day media and the pains of kids that are overly wired is not one I can say I've met yet.

But I was given a standard.

A standard that made space for the people sharing four walls to look each other in the eye and *know* each other. A standard that made time with family a higher priority than hours of phone calls to teenage friends. A standard that gave us time to talk, play, and engage with one another. A standard that made sure we connected.

Kingdom Key #2—Be Angry, Yet Do Not Sin

"Be angry, and yet do not sin; do not let the sun go down on your anger" (Ephesians 4:26). Take a moment to understand the flow of that statement. It puts to rest something that many of us heard as we were growing up in the church—that it's sinful to get upset or angry. Many of us heard only the "do not sin" part. We missed "Be angry, and yet . . . ."

Because of that misinterpretation, many of us held back, even when our anger was justified. And when people don't allow, acknowledge, or address their anger, they build up deep resentments that come to the surface months—sometimes years—later. They can explode over seemingly small things—a missed phone call here, being late there, a child not completing his or her homework. Whatever the case, it ends up drawing out a heart full of repressed anger and empties a huge storehouse of bitterness, leaving the recipient defensive and offended by an overreaction to something they thought was small.

Yet the Bible tells us that even Jesus became angry. He took a whip and drove the money changers out of the temple. He became very angry with people turning His Father's house into a place of profit. Anger, in and of itself, is not the sin. It's what we do with anger that either leads to sin or to an improvement of the situation.

In Ephesians 4:26, Paul told us what we must do with our anger: "Do not let the sun go down on your anger." At times in life, there are justifiable reasons for anger, as it was in Jesus' case. But anger can become sin when it's not dealt with properly and—according to Paul—promptly. If you get angry at your spouse or your children and don't at least begin to resolve the conflict right away (implied by the reference to the sun going down), your anger can easily become sin. If you harbor unresolved anger in your heart for anyone, you set yourself up for bitterness, resentment, and unforgiveness. And you model for your children the opposite of what God has called us to do.

> *If you harbor unresolved anger in your heart for anyone, you set yourself up for bitterness, resentment, and unforgiveness.*

Sadly, the seeds for unresolved anger are often planted in the church. Instead of coming to church to be real—which is the only way the body of Christ can ever help us—we sometimes put up a façade, even if we're not doing well inside. We act as if nothing's wrong in the very place where those wrongs could be addressed and healed. We've trained ourselves that church is the place where we are meant to look our best, even when God knows better.

When Paul told us not to let the sun go down on our anger, he didn't intend to impose some burdensome rule on us. He wrote those words so that we could open the lines of communication and restore emotional health to our lives. Take that verse literally when it's within your power to do so. Settle issues with your children and with your spouse before the end of each day or, at a minimum, at least attempt to do so.

If a member of your family is angry with you, ask his or her why and then listen. If you're the one who is angry, tell the person why; don't make your spouse or your children guess. It might not always be a pleasant conversation, and the resolution may not always be to your liking, but if you get to the root of the problem early on, you will prevent unnecessary seeds of bitterness and resentment from being stored up and exploding later at unexpected moments.

If you reach an impasse, you can never lose by accepting the blame regardless of who's "right." With nothing left to fight about, you can get on with rebuilding the relationship. That's exactly what Jesus did when He took the blame for our sins on the cross even though He Himself was sinless (see 2 Corinthians 5:21) so we could have a relationship with Him.

Kingdom Key #3: When Communication Is In, Satan Is Out

"Do not give the devil an opportunity" (Ephesians 4:27). If I were to announce Satan's plan for your family, it would be simple: divide and conquer; destroy. His plan is to make sure your family is torn apart and God's destiny for each of you destroyed.

Satan is a schemer. He is conniving, always trying to bring something against you. He is looking for an opportunity to slip into your family relationships and ruin them. And one way he can do that is to cut off regular communication by making sure everyone is too busy running around, attending meetings, or distracted by other people to have time for each other.

A good way to thwart this plan is to intentionally covenant together as a family that you will communicate with each other every single day, no matter how busy the day has been. Never belittle the importance of frequency. When too much time elapses between communication, children or loved ones can feel devalued, dismissed, or taken for granted. While that may not be your intention, you are communicating that loudly and clearly through your actions. Remember our principle from an earlier chapter? Love *is* as love *does*. Nothing is more important in any relationship than consistent communication.

Out of sight doesn't have to mean out of mind. Maybe your children are grown, or perhaps you have a travel schedule similar to mine. No matter what, you must take it upon yourself to reach out to your family as much as possible. By maintaining a healthy esteem for each other, you may actually prevent future pain and lengthier, more difficult conversations caused by conflict. By modeling the importance of showing value to one another, when your children are grown and establishing their own families, they will have a benchmark to aim for.

You might want to say, "But Tony, I really do have a busy schedule, and in the evening I have a number of things I need to catch up on." My response is simple: "Friend, if you and your family don't get together for consistent time on a consistent basis, you aren't going to have a family for very much longer, or at least not a healthy one."

> *If you and your family don't get together for consistent time on a consistent basis, you aren't going to have a family for very much longer, or at least not a healthy one.*

A word of caution: Be careful not to spend that time complaining and venting. As a pastor, I know that if the only time you want to meet with me is when you have a problem, we're not communicating with one another. All we're doing is working through the negative stuff. The same thing applies in a family. Don't just talk about the problems and complaints. Minimize the complaining by keeping the communication flow open and ongoing. Deal with hurts and misunderstandings quickly and strive to enjoy more time complimenting and praising one another and making good memories.

Kingdom Key #4: Let Your Speech Edify

"Let no unwholesome word proceed from your mouth, but only such a word as is good for edification according to the need of the moment, so that it will give grace to those who hear" (Ephesians 4:29). This is a straightforward communication key. Don't talk badly or spread unkind words about anyone. Discuss only things that will lift somebody up. Make sure that good comes to those who hear you. As we examined in our chapter on the three pillars of parenting, encouragement is a necessary element of raising a child well. This encouragement should stem from an authentic heart full of love, seeing your children through God's eyes—as heirs to His throne with royal blood in their veins.

I often encourage parents to try an experiment with their family. For an entire week, don't say anything to your children or spouse unless it's wholesome and contributes to their personal and spiritual growth. For example, instead of asking, "When is dinner ready?" a spouse might say, "Can I help you with dinner?" That way you become part of the solution and not another part of the problem.

You may believe the task will be easy. But I think you might be surprised, as you become more conscious of your everyday speech, at how little purely positive communication comes out easily. You'll make mistakes. I know that. But after a while, you'll begin to reap the benefits.

Kingdom Key #5: Listen

Much has been written and preached over the years about the need to listen, but I have to mention it here because it's so important. Most of us are still lousy listeners. When someone else is talking, even if it's directly to us, our minds are on something entirely different—like what we want to say next or what we need from the other person. However, if you never listen to what the other person is saying, you will never get the message.

Yes, you have to work at listening. We all do. If our kids come to us with a question while we're busy on our tablet, we need to put it down long enough to make eye contact, listen closely, and respond. If we are watching television, we must look away from it so we can engage with them. Eye contact is crucial in listening.

If someone tells you something and you don't understand it completely, don't be too proud to ask for clarification. You can also repeat what someone said and ask the person to confirm that you have heard him or her correctly. This is all part of good listening skills, and without it real communication is impossible.

It's a good practice to establish a listening time with your kids where they are free to respectfully communicate with you about whatever is on their heart. Perhaps this is something you can set up as a routine occurrence each week; for example, every Wednesday your kids know they will have your undivided attention for anything they want to tell you—whether it's a complaint or something they are worried about. While daily and consistent communication is essential, it also helps to have this extra time set aside that your kids can count on so they will know they have access to you for anything deeper they may want to discuss.

There is no shortcut to communicating love to your children, and modeling for them the keys to kingdom communication. It takes commitment and effort. It takes being kind to our kids, recognizing that they often act up in order to seek our love and attention. It takes being patient with them when all we want is some peace and quiet. It takes forgiveness, patience, and love.

It takes talking.

It takes listening.

And it takes honoring our King by esteeming those He has entrusted to our care in all that we do.

10

TABLE TIME: GOD'S
WORD AND PRAYER

Four decades ago Congress set in motion a plan to increase the survival rate of
endangered species in our land. Millions of dollars and millions of hours have
gone toward the protection and growth of those species nearing extinction.
Their efforts have been highly successful, with more than 90 percent of the
protected species now on the pathway to recovery.[1] And while these successes
should not go unnoted, we face another endangered species in our country that
gets very little attention at all: the family.

We've already briefly examined the crisis of the family in our nation and
how that impacts our present, future, and ultimate stability of our land. But
let's take a look at an endangered subspecies within the family whose loss may
have triggered the beginning of the end of the family at large. This endangered
area resides at the table—the family meal.

A mushrooming of two-salary homes, working single moms, sports or
social commitments, and other activities that wreak havoc on schedules has
escalated our dependency on purchased meals, grab-and-go foods, or eating
out at restaurants. Not only has this negatively impacted our collective national
health, it has also reduced the opportunity for family connection, mentoring, discussion, fun, and prayer around the table. By reducing this time at the
table—a location where historically families have gathered and grown—we've
lessened our overall time together. Rarely do we redeem that time in another

place: technology, entertainment, our schedules, phones, activities, travels, and work scatter the members of our home in a variety of directions. We've traded the table for our tablets.

Returning to the lost art of the family table will strengthen our homes and better equip our children to raise kingdom kids when their time comes.

Making Mealtime Matter

When our children were still living at home, the table served as the centerpiece for family life. We gathered there every evening, unless I was traveling, to not only eat, but to also experience life together. We read and discussed God's Word, prayed, we talked, we told jokes. I used the table as the place where I would check in on whether the kids were keeping up their responsibilities and chores, or getting their homework done well and turned in on time.

> *We've traded the table for our tablets.*

Discussions revolved around the lesson taught in Sunday school that week, or read in that day's devotional, activities with peers, what they were learning in school, and whatever else was on their hearts—or ours—at the moment. Many times I would choose the devotional to be read and discussed ahead of time but then assign one of the children to lead the discussion. This gave my kids practice in teaching God's Word and facilitating spiritual dialogue. Other times, I'd have the kids pray for each other not only as an expression of caring for each other but also to hone the virtue of thinking of others, not just themselves, when they prayed.

Table time didn't consist simply of a lecture from the Bible on my part. Instead, the kids shared flannelgraph stories, performed skits, recited verses, or sang songs as we sat together after we were finished eating. There was never any rush to leave the table. It became our hub, and it remains so even to this day when the kids or grandkids stop by.

Above all else, I wanted our table time to be an enjoyable and fun experience for everyone. I saw my children respond best in that type of atmosphere when the more serious discussions would inevitably arise. I wanted to make them comfortable yet accountable, entertained yet interested. Sometimes I'd say, "Okay, everyone, let's go around the table and each person tell their very best joke, or do an impersonation." We also used the table as a place to teach etiquette: how a gentleman treats a lady at the table, how she is to respond, and the proper manners we should all have.

Table time in our home didn't include just us either. We were always intentional about hosting visiting missionaries or various ministry workers, not only to practice the gift of hospitality but also to strategically use the table as a way to reinforce our value system with our children. As our children heard stories about God's work from those in ministry or missions, they gained a greater appreciation for service. They also learned to cultivate their own gifts of hospitality, as we required them to pitch in with meal preparation, table setting, conversation, and cleaning up.

My philosophy on table talk grew out of my desire to create a centrally located place of discipleship in our home and take advantage of something we were already doing together naturally. But the theology behind table talk reaches much further back than that. The table often served as the meeting place for families in Jewish culture in biblical times. In fact, King David incorporated the table in my all-time favorite chapter of the Bible—the chapter that speaks about the kingdom family, Psalm 128:

> How blessed is everyone who fears the LORD, who walks in His ways. When you shall eat of the fruit of your hands, you will be happy and it will be well with you. Your wife shall be like a fruitful vine within your house, your children like olive plants *around your table*. Behold, for thus shall the man be blessed who fears the LORD. The LORD bless you from Zion, and may you see the prosperity of Jerusalem all the days of your life. Indeed, may you see your children's children. Peace be upon Israel!

In the third verse we read that the kingdom family will have "children like olive plants around" their table. We are to use the table as a major place for kingdom parenting, and in so doing, our children will receive the nurturing necessary for their growth. The olive plant takes on average fifteen years to become a tree, but it has to be nurtured properly during that time in order for it to grow into a strong tree. Kingdom parent, the table is not only the best place for physical nourishing of your children, but also for spiritual, relational, and moral nurturing to take place.

Now, I understand that circumstances don't allow for every family to gather around the table every night, but it's my hope that, as much as possible, we as a body of believers raising kingdom kids will make an intentional return to the table. Let's recognize it for the strategic place it plays in the life, health, and development of our homes.

> *Kingdom parent, the table is not only the best place for physical nourishing of your children, but also for spiritual, relational, and moral nurturing to take place.*

Your time at the table establishes rapport, openness, and familiarity within the family. These things contribute to your children's healthy maturing and provide the location for all other virtues and values to germinate. As you intentionally guide discussions, questions, and devotions, you can focus on areas needing the greatest improvement while offering encouragement and praise for those areas that have already been cultivated well.

But don't let the table become a formal time to check off your list. Instead, allow it to organically produce conversation guided along the lines of responsibility and growth. This creates an atmosphere for sharing and fun to occur, as well as an openness to learning.

Sanctified by God's Word

When writing to his protégé Timothy, Paul began a discussion about the day and time people would begin to fall away from the faith. Within that context, the subject of food was brought up, and Paul wrote, "For everything created by God is good, and nothing is to be rejected if it is received with gratitude; for it is sanctified by means of the word of God and prayer" (1 Timothy 4:4–5). Paul referenced more than just food in this passage, but the worldly wisdom and false ideologies he also spoke about are all topics for the table. And all these are to be sanctified by God's Word and prayer.

At the table, as well as in your home, a major component for cultivating a kingdom atmosphere is the value you place on God's Word and prayer. God's Word has the power to shape your children's character and guide their behavior more than anything else. It has the potential to be the single most impactful thing in a person's life.

Timothy tells us that Scripture is "inspired by God and profitable for teaching, for reproof, for correction, and for training in righteousness" (2 Timothy 3:16). In Hebrews we read that the Word of God is "living and active and sharper than any two-edged sword, and piercing as far as the division of soul and spirit, of both joints and marrow" (4:12).

God's Word contains within it everything necessary to guide, direct, and empower us to truly live a kingdom life. Yet this valuable treasure frequently goes unnoticed and unused by parents and children in our homes.

Understandably, many kids feel intimidated by the Bible. It's a huge book and it traverses about in a variety of directions. Add to that the numerous cultural nuances and contrasting literary styles, and young people can easily get confused or lost in the process of reading it.

Adults dedicate years to studying the Bible before they fully grasp how it flows contextually and thematically. I spent over a decade in my own personal studies, starting with graduating from Bible college, getting my master's degree, and then a doctorate in theology, and I still have a lot to learn. You can only imagine how a child or teenager who grew up on the Disney Channel, gaming, and texting might view this ancient, multifaceted, and, at times, complicated book.

That's why it's so important for you as a parent to search out and procure age-appropriate introductions to God's Word for your children. When they are young, get them a beginner's Bible that touches on the major stories. A colleague of mine has his eight-year-old reading through the entire Bible in a year, but he's doing it using a children's Bible. Of course that won't cover every verse, and it will probably have as many pages of pictures as it does text, but as that young boy experiences the joy and accomplishment of reading God's Word, it will develop in him a desire to know the Bible more and more as he continues to grow.

In addition, there are a number of books written for children that give an introductory overview, background, and breakdown of the Bible. It is a good idea to invest in a few of those and read them along with your children after mealtime while you are still at the table. You might commit to reading a chapter a week, or even a chapter a day, depending on the length, and you can use this time as an opportunity to discuss how to approach and study God's Word.

As you go about the process of creating an atmosphere of love for and dependence on God's Word in your home, there are three primary principles to pay special attention to. These principles, when applied, will make the most of your children's Bible-study experience. They include how we are to *receive* God's Word, how we *reflect* on it, and how we *respond* to it.

Receive the Word

James tells us how we are to receive the Word in this passage: "Therefore, putting aside all filthiness and all that remains of wickedness, in humility receive the word implanted, which is able to save your souls" (James 1:21).

Creating an atmosphere where God's Word is the ultimate authority on everything will go far in training your children how to value His truth.

Next, they are to receive the *implanted* word, which means "inborn," and can be best illustrated by comparing it to a fertilized egg in the womb of a woman.[2] Because of the position and connection of the implanted egg, it can now receive the nourishment that the mother provides in order for it to develop into a baby.

Just like the fertilized egg requires nourishment to grow and develop, the seed of God's Word implanted in us also requires nourishment. And similar to the baby who can receive the nourishment needed to grow only through the umbilical cord, God has supplied one way for the seed of His Word to expand within us, and that is through the Holy Spirit.

Keep in mind that it is possible to have the word implanted but still have not received it. The word *receive* means to "to receive favorably, give ear to, embrace, make one's own, approve, not to reject." It means more than just simply hearing something, having something, or knowing something. I interpret this word to mean "welcoming knowledge."[3]

> *You must train your children to allow God's Word to reach deep within them so it can take root and flourish.*

When you "welcome" someone who is standing at the door of your home, you invite that person in. The person walks through the door and enters your home. You don't just stand at the door and say, "You are welcome." You usher that person in, which enables your "welcome" to be experienced and lived out. When we "welcome" the word of God, it goes to work in our souls.

First and foremost, you must train your children to allow God's Word to reach deep within them so it can take root and flourish through their thoughts, feelings, and actions. This will require time to reflect on God's Word.

Reflect on the Word

As you read God's Word at the table, take time to allow each family member to reflect on what the passage is saying and then share their reflections with one another. Ultimately these reflections should produce responses to carry out. As James writes, "But prove yourselves doers of the word, and not merely hearers who delude themselves. For if anyone is a hearer of the word and not a doer, he is like a man who looks at his natural face in a mirror; for once he has looked at himself and gone away, he has immediately forgotten what kind of person he was" (James 1:22–24).

It's interesting that the word used for *man* in verse 23 is the specific term for the male gender.[4] This passage is dealing with men and mirrors, which is entirely different than dealing with women and mirrors. If it were dealing with women and mirrors, it would say, "Be a hearer and a doer of the word like a woman who looks at her natural or made-up face in a mirror; for once she has looked at herself, she does not go away, but rather grabs another mirror to look at the back of her hair, and another mirror to look at the close-up of her eyeliner and lipstick, and then walks to yet another mirror to get a full-length view. She will not forget what she looks like."

The Art of Listening
by Priscilla Shirer

I spent many hours as a kid sitting on the floor in the hallway of our home, listening intently to conversations happening just on the other side of the wall. Dad and Mom would often invite visiting preachers, singers, and missionaries over for a home-cooked meal. And when the conversation moved from the dining table to the comfort of the living room, I'd disappear to my perch in the hall just out of sight.

And I would listen.

I was out of place among these leaders, and I knew it. Great men of God would discuss the finer points of Scripture, dissecting various segments of theology with passion. Everything they said was interesting to me, even when all the people in the room were agreeing with each other's points. But what I loved the most was when they'd come to moments of dispute over some teaching or opinion. These were friendly bouts of arguing, of course. They were always kind and patient with each other. But whenever I could tell a good debate was starting up, I would press my ear directly against the wall and listen even more closely, hoping to understand.

I rarely did, of course. I was too young for understanding—but not for listening, eavesdropping, or looking up the scriptures I heard, pondering them for long periods of time after my parents' guests had left.

I still do.

The Word became alive to me as a child because *it was around me*.

Everywhere. My parents filled our ears and hands and hearts and minds with it. Praise music wafted through the air every day, not just on Sunday. They led us in devotions at dinnertime on regular occasions, and posted scriptures in strategic places throughout the house, creatively printed on artwork. They invited members of our church over and then purposefully turned the conversation toward spiritual things so my siblings and I could hear and learn, catching the crumbs of wisdom shared over cups of hot tea.

And then, of course, there was the flannelboard. Long before electronic options were available, that soft-faced, blackboard was always within arm's reach—tucked inside a closet just outside my bedroom door and ready to be used at a moment's notice. My mom would take it out, along with a bag filled with felt Bible characters, telling us stories of Jonah or David, Noah or Esther. We'd watch wide-eyed in wonder every single time she adhered that felt rock to Goliath's head and made him fall flat to the floor.

Every. Single. Time.

She loved telling us those stories. And we loved listening to them.

Because God's Word is a blessing. At that age; at every age. Even now, one of my deepest hopes as a parent is that I can pass along this blessing of loving God's Word to my children as well—the way it was passed along to me. At every opportunity.

Now that's an entirely different verse altogether. And that's actually how we are to reflect on God's Word—like a woman with a mirror, not like a man who looks once, leaves, and forgets to look again the rest of the day, likewise forgetting what he looks like. Men are satisfied with a glance in the mirror, while women need to gaze. Reflecting on God's Word is much more than a glance. It involves rolling it over in the mind until a person begins to see himself or herself as God says he or she really is. An excellent way to teach your children how to do this is to practice memorizing Scripture and then recite it at the table. This is one gift you can give your children on an ongoing basis that will stay with them into

We are to reflect on God's Word like a woman with a mirror, not like a man who looks once, leaves, and forgets to look again the rest of the day, likewise forgetting what he looks like.

adulthood. Once the Word takes root deep within their memory and soul, it will always be there for the Spirit to call up when they need it most. As our table time has evolved to include grandchildren, one of their favorite times by far is when they get to stand up on a chair or platform and recite their memory verses. I love to see their smiles as they receive everyone's undivided attention and applause for this important accomplishment in their lives.

Respond to the Word

Lastly, use your time in God's Word at the table to teach your children how to respond to it. God's blessing often depends on how we respond to what He says. In the parable of the soils, Jesus talks about four responses to the seed of His Word (see Luke 8:4–15). The first is actually a lack of response. The soil does not receive the seed at all.

Then there is the shallow response—those people who receive the Word but do not water and care for it, so it soon withers away. The third response Jesus talked about is what I call the inadequate response. These people are too much into the cares and worries of this world to give God the time and attention He deserves. As a result, their spiritual lives fall into a state of neglect.

The fourth response is the right response: The good soil absorbs the Word and produces fruit. It demonstrates in words, thoughts, and actions the precepts and principles of God's truth.

The Bible calls itself a law that liberates us (see James 1:25) when we respond to it correctly. That seems like a contradiction to a lot of us because we think of law as something that hinders and restricts, not liberates. But David said, "I will walk at liberty, for I seek Your precepts" (Psalm 119:45). The more he followed God's law, the freer he was because he was not bound by consequences of a life lived outside of the perfect will of God. Jesus tells us of this freedom when He says, "You will know the truth, and the truth will make you free" (John 8:32).

We can have rules and freedom at the same time because true freedom demands boundaries. Most people define freedom incorrectly. They think freedom is the absence of any rules, doing whatever they want whenever they want. But such "freedom" is actually the worst form of slavery. Jesus said, "Everyone who commits sin is the slave of sin" (John 8:34). Therefore, true freedom comes when we are set free from sin and become slaves to Christ.

One way we can speed up the process of responding to God's Word is through what James tells us in the first chapter: "Everyone must be quick to hear, slow to speak and slow to anger" (James 1:19).

You might be wondering, "Quick to hear what?" We are to be quick to hear God's viewpoint on a matter. You might also ask, "Slow to speak what?" We are to be slow to speak our own viewpoint on a matter. And when God's viewpoint on a matter differs from our viewpoint on a matter, then we are told to be slow to anger about it.

Parents, use your table time not only for fun and fellowship, but also use it to cultivate an atmosphere that knows and applies God's Word in the everyday situations of life.

Parents, use your table time not only for fun and fellowship, but also use it to cultivate an atmosphere that knows and applies God's Word in the everyday situations of life. By doing so, you will have placed within your children's spirits the seeds for a lasting legacy of truth. You will have positioned them for victorious kingdom living.

Sanctified by Prayer

In the passage we looked at earlier from 1 Timothy 4, Paul wrote that these things, including food, are sanctified by God's Word, but they are also sanctified by prayer. An atmosphere that encourages prayer as a normal and consistent occurrence will provide your children with the tools they need for spiritual growth in the home and on into adulthood. Mastering the art of prayer will start your children off on the right footing to face all that they need to in life.

Prayer is one of the most, if not the most, important things in the life of any believer.

Now, we Christians love to talk about prayer. We love to hear people tell us about answered prayer. We thrill to the stories of great Christians from the past who had unbelievable prayer lives and saw God do unbelievable things. We love everything about prayer—except, it seems, the actual discipline of praying.

Why do I say that? Only 38 percent of Protestants pray more than once a day. That means 62 percent pray only once a day or maybe only once a week or maybe not at all.[5] I shudder to imagine what the stats would look like if the researchers removed saying grace at mealtimes.

> *We love everything about prayer—except, it seems, the actual discipline of praying.*

If you want to know where you stand in your prayer life, let me suggest a test. Compare the time you spend complaining to the time you spend praying. Or compare the time you spend talking to people about other people to the time you spend talking to God about other people. Prayer is an area where many adults struggle. If you know how difficult it is for you to maintain a consistent prayer life, you can imagine how difficult it is for your child.

We all need to get better—a lot better—in prayer, children and adults alike. God has ordered His world in such a way that there are many things He will not do in the life of the Christian apart from prayer. Prayer is inviting heavenly intervention in history. It is pulling the supernatural into the natural—seeking the extraordinary to invade the ordinary.

The natural human tendency, even among Christians, is to think of prayer as a last resort. When we have a need or a problem, we consider what we can do and then work at it through our own power. Only when the situation seems hopeless do we decide that we need to pray about it. Yet if we were thinking straight, prayer would be our first response to a need.

Prayer is inviting heavenly intervention in history.

As parents, to create an atmosphere of prayer in your home, the best and most effective thing you can do is to pray for your children every day. Better than that is to pray *with* them while also *for* them every day. You can start by doing this at the table, but let it carry over to other locations and times in your family life. In fact, even when they move out of the house or are away at college, call them regularly to say a quick prayer with them—or a lengthy one if you can keep them on the line long enough. This will pour volumes of love and value into them while also seeking God's continual intervention and favor on their behalf. By doing this, you are training your children in the power of prayer by modeling your own value and use of it in front of them.

What are some of the things you should pray for with regard to your children? Let Luke 2:52, which describes the boyhood of Jesus, serve as your beginning guide. We read, "And Jesus kept increasing in wisdom and stature, and in favor with God and men."

Four areas of development are mentioned here, and they are all areas in which we would like to see our children mature. The first is wisdom—not just factual knowledge but the ability to apply spiritual truth to the practical issues of daily life. You can pray for your children that they will grow in wisdom. The book of Psalms tells us the fear of the Lord is the beginning of wisdom (see Psalm 111:10). As your children grow in their reverence for God, they will also be growing in wisdom.

"Increasing in . . . stature" refers to physical growth. Pray here for your children's safety and good health so that they can develop to the full extent of their God-given abilities. Pray that they will treat their bodies well by eating healthy, avoiding negative contaminants, getting enough rest, and practicing safety precautions, such as wearing their seat belts in the car.

"In favor with God" is a clear reference to spiritual growth. Pray that your children will always have tender hearts toward the Lord—that knowing Him, walking with Him, and serving Him will be their greatest desire. Pray that true Christlikeness will be developed in them as time goes by. And pray that the grace of God's favor will be given to them freely. Similar to the prayer that Jabez prayed when he asked for God's favor by expanding his borders of influence, ask God to expand your children's borders of influence as well through an abundance of His favor in their lives.

Finally, "in favor with . . . men" refers to social growth. Pray that your kids will learn how to get along with others, how to be true friends, and how to socialize without compromising their values. Pray that God will bring them good friends who will be a positive influence, and ask God to raise your children up as a positive influence in the lives of those around them. Ask God to give them a heart for His people and for taking His saving truth to those in need. And pray that, even while they are still young, God would be preparing the boy or girl who will grow up to one day be a godly mate for each one of your children.

Like any worthwhile endeavor, remember that prayer requires practice and persistence. There is no better place to engage in prayer than at your regular time at the family table. If you, your family, or your children have not been in the habit of talking with God and the concept seems unnatural or uncomfortable, make this the subject of your prayers. Be honest with God about wanting to develop a prayerful atmosphere in your home.

The bottom line is to pray. If you're tired, sick, or emotionally overwhelmed—pray. If you're on cloud nine and family life seems perfect—pray. If you lack direction for yourself or your kids—pray. If you doubt that prayer makes any difference—pray. If the circumstances of your home are out of your control—pray. If the circumstances of your home seem well within your control—pray even harder. Whatever you do—*pray*.

Don't let the enemy trick you or your children into giving up the priceless privilege and powerful position of communicating with our great God.

By incorporating the study of God's Word and prayer into your regular family meals, as well as adding fun activities, jokes, etiquette training, discussions about school and friends, and myriad other things, you will establish an atmosphere of spiritual health where your children will thrive as olive plants around your table.

The bottom line is to pray.

I want to introduce the next section of our time together by returning briefly to Luke 2:52 where we read that Jesus grew in wisdom, stature, and favor with God and man. Most of us believe passionately in our children's physical, social, and intellectual development. We make sure they have clothes and shelter. We see that they eat right and get enough sleep. We help them learn how to mix with other people so they don't feel odd and left out, and we monitor their friends so they aren't playing with the wrong kids. In addition, we keep a close eye on their grades and schooling so we know what they're learning.

God says we should take the same kind of care with our kids' spiritual development. We need to make sure we are giving them a regular diet of spiritual nourishment and training at home. Parents, this next section on instilling kingdom virtues outlines key biblical principles to nurture and encourage in your child's heart.

PART III

INSTILLING KINGDOM VIRTUES

11

~≈~

WISDOM

Life is full of decisions, and most of us are tired of making the wrong ones. As parents, some of us still feel the effects of poor choices we made in our youth, or even as adults. If you had the opportunity to relive your teen years, in light of what you know now, would you do anything differently? Would you make better choices?

While none of us have the opportunity to turn back the hands of time and make better decisions, as parents raising kingdom kids we can certainly do everything in our power and influence to instill the virtue of wisdom into our kids so they can live a life with the fewest possible regrets. No one will make the perfect decision every time simply because no one is perfect. But godly wisdom can enable a person to hit the mark more often than not, thus positioning oneself for security and positive accrual in the future.

The ability to make positive and productive decisions—to choose well—is what the Bible calls wisdom.

Choosing Well

I love Indiana Jones movies. I love the adventure, chase, intrigue, and ultimate conquests that show up in each one. Indiana Jones overcomes every obstacle and scales every wall in order to reach his ultimate goal. But victory doesn't come simply through brawn and resolve—most often it also requires wisdom for him to get what he wants.

One of my all-time favorite scenes in the movie *Indiana Jones and the Last*

Crusade is the one where he is chasing after the elusive Holy Grail, the cup that Jesus used during His Last Supper. Through many dangers, toils, and snares, Indiana Jones makes it safely to his final challenge—a challenge that will test every bit of his wisdom. We see Indiana Jones standing in the candle-lit Grail sanctuary in the Temple of the Sun, guarded continuously by the aged yet ageless Grail Knight. Dozens of chalices and bowls sit around the room, each having its own unique style and imprint. The final test to prove one's worthiness to discover the true treasured cup rests on a search through the various options to finally select the one, true Grail.

No one will make the perfect decision every time simply because no one is perfect. But godly wisdom can enable a person to hit the mark more often than not.

Whether that choice is correct or not will be revealed when the person takes his chosen cup, fills it from the fount of the chamber, and takes a sip. If he chooses the Holy Grail, he will live. If he chooses any other chalice, he will quickly experience a painful death.

As Indiana Jones and the other characters in the film first enter the Grail sanctuary, they are met by the Grail Knight who explains what they are to do and then adds these last words of warning: "Choose wisely, for as the true Grail will bring you life, the false grail shall take it from you."[1]

The antagonist in the film chooses first—and he chooses poorly, dying and decomposing before everyone's eyes. Indiana Jones chooses next. He chooses wisely, thus receiving not only life for himself but also the healing life he needs to give to his father, who has been injured and is near death.

The Indiana Jones films are meant to entertain us. But this scene echoes with the profound reality found in God's Word. God has given us His commandments, precepts, and principles to show us how we are to live a life of wisdom, but the choice is ultimately ours. The choice is ultimately our children's. You can parent your children, you can shelter them, and you can set boundaries for them while they are young, but eventually you will see that you cannot choose life's decisions for your children.

If your children choose wisely, the truth of God's Word will bring life to them and also to those around them. If they choose poorly, life can take them in a variety of less-than-desirable ways and likewise negatively affect those around them.

One of the areas I struggled with as a father was this balance between making choices for my kids or giving them the freedom to choose. This was especially true during the teen years, in particular with the choice of friends that both of my daughters, Chrystal and Priscilla, were making. They didn't always make the wisest choices about the kinds of friends to hang around.

It was difficult for me to determine how to either deny or limit the friendships my daughters valued while also helping them to make their own decisions about which friendships to develop, without my forcing them. Sometimes I would simply say, "No more," with regard to a particular friend. Other times, I'd ask my daughters to bring their friends to the house so we could spend time with them and then later have the opportunity to discuss positive or negative influences.

While wisdom is not something you can force on your kids, but rather something they need to learn for themselves, wisdom is the very heartbeat of life. Teaching your children wisdom and its value is critical to raising them as kingdom kids. Teaching your kids to choose wisely where relationships are concerned is

Teach your children to pick their friends based on their character, not their culture—based on ethics rather than ethnicity.

especially important. For example, it's important to teach your children to pick their friends based on their character, not their culture—based on ethics rather than ethnicity. Life is fragile; wisdom helps us to protect it, and one way is by whom we choose to surround ourselves with.

When your children apply God's wisdom to their lives, when they live in accordance with what He has outlined for them in Scripture, then they will experience being in God's will. Wisdom is the application of God's will to the practical areas of life.

Wisdom Versus Information

The book of Proverbs is an entire book about wisdom, and much of it is written from a parent to a child. In the first chapter we read, "The fear of the LORD is the beginning of knowledge; fools despise wisdom and instruction" (Proverbs 1:7). It is a fool who does not want to be wise. But those who seek wisdom will find it through knowing God and understanding His ways. "The fear of the LORD is the beginning of wisdom, and the knowledge of the Holy One is understanding" (Proverbs 9:10). Proverbs tells us how available wisdom is: "Wisdom shouts in the street, she lifts her voice in the square" (Proverbs 1:20). Wisdom is not elusive; rather, it offers help to anyone making a decision.

Ultimately, wisdom is the God-given ability to perceive the true nature of a thing and then implement the will of God concerning it. It is that special viewpoint that allows a person to intuit what is truly going on and then apply God's direction regarding that insight. Wisdom is spiritual truth applied to life's realities.

Because life is full of twists and turns, detours and drop-offs, being wise is critical. We constantly have to make decisions. Wisdom enables a person to clearly decipher what is going on, and then do the right thing with that information. But in order to perceive the true nature of a thing, you first have to know what's true. This is what the Bible calls knowledge: "The fear of the LORD is the beginning of knowledge."

Wisdom is spiritual truth applied to life's realities.

We live in a day of increased information but decreased knowledge. Information sits at our fingertips—on our tablets, in our phones, in our Google search boxes. It's there for us to access in a split second, even if it may not be entirely accurate. To a large degree, we have become a culture of great misinformation. Hoaxes go viral on the Internet and thousands of people believe them to be fact. Hearsay has become more valuable than fact, rumor more respected than reality.

Wisdom is more than information. It comes couched in the knowledge of the true nature of a thing because God at His core is truth—His Word is truth. Knowledge, though, in and of itself, isn't wisdom. There are a lot of people who have a great deal of knowledge about many things, but they don't know what to do with that knowledge. They can't apply it. Maybe you've met someone who is a genius, but he or she doesn't have much common sense. In essence, he or she is a brilliantly igno-

We live in a day of increased information but decreased knowledge.

rant person. For wisdom to be birthed, knowledge must be married to understanding (Proverbs 9:10). These two combined give us what we need to live kingdom lives and establish healthy homes.

Many of you reading this book have children in college, or will have in the future. They will spend four years or more acquiring the knowledge and skills necessary to develop a career. You hope this investment in information and training will pay off in the future. But one of the worst things a young adult can do is to acquire a bunch of knowledge without godly wisdom.

As soon as your child graduates and enters the real world as we know it, his or her decisions will begin to demonstrate how essential wisdom truly is. Perhaps your child will hop from one job to another, not understanding the importance of establishing a sound résumé. Maybe he or she will spend his or her newfound income on things that won't last, failing to invest in the future or, if need be, pay off the past. Maybe your child won't understand office nuances and the value of respect in relationships in work environments, suddenly finding himself or herself out of a job with little or no warning. Whatever the case, information without wisdom does little good in life.

The Benefits of Wisdom

Wisdom is life-giving because it comes from God, the author of life. It is in knowing God—His character, attributes, precepts, and desires—that we find the insight we need for kingdom living. Now, knowing God is not the same thing as knowing *about* God. Rather, it is an intimate, abiding fellowship with Him. That's why God referred to Abraham as His "friend." It's why He said David was a man after His own heart.

Many of your children, if they are preteens and older, "know" celebrities and athletes yet have never met them. You probably know them yourself. You can cite statistics of touchdowns or points scored. You can name which celebrity has recently divorced, who is in rehab, who wears what, shops where, and so on. Reality television has given us a glimpse into people's lives like never before. Hours and hours of individuals' lives are now displayed for the world to see. And after watching enough episodes, you might feel as if you actually know them.

> *Knowing God is not the same thing as knowing about God.*

Yet if you were to pass these athletes or celebrities on the street, they wouldn't even nod at you because they don't know you—and ultimately you don't know them. You just know *about* them.

I've been a pastor now for over three decades, and I've frequently seen something similar happen at church. People come to church, nod amen at the sermon, acquire book knowledge about God's Word, and then make disastrous decisions in their lives—ultimately revealing they don't know God very well at all. Knowing God requires two-way conversation and understanding, not just one-way information. It requires abiding in God's presence, allowing His Word to take root in the soul and bear fruit.

The blessing of knowing God deeply shows up in many ways. When you know God, you have a less problematic life, and you are victorious when problems do come. No matter how we slice it, life has problems and pain. To teach your children anything different is leading them astray. Many parents make the mistake of trying to shelter their children from life's pains or disappointments rather than teaching them how to face them confidently and victoriously. By isolating your children from the realities of life, you are simply delaying the inevitable. What's even worse, you will launch them into adulthood without the emotional and spiritual tools they need to navigate through life.

A member of our church once told me that when her third-grade daughter didn't make the elementary school choir tryouts, she was devastated. It broke this mom's heart to see her daughter's dreams crushed so early in life; it hurt to watch her daughter experience rejection at such a young age. But then she told me how a friend changed her viewpoint concerning the situation when she made the comment, "I'd much rather my children learn how to handle these tough life lessons in an affirmative environment of love while still in the home than never learn them at all until they become a young adult. It will be a rude surprise for them then, and they may not know how to receive it."

Even though we want to protect our children from disappointments and pain, we won't be able to do that forever. The wiser approach is not to try to cover up disappointment with a trip to the mall, a new toy, or some good food—by doing so you are actually teaching your child how to turn to vices rather than virtues, even if those vices seem innocent at the time. The wise approach is giving your child the tools to face disappointment in light of the wisdom of God's Word, which tells us He is sovereign and has a plan and destiny for each of us. There are many illustrations in Scripture where setbacks were simply setups for something better.

The benefit of wisdom is not that you won't have any problems. The benefit of wisdom is that the problems will not have you. In this world, we will have problems, but when you equip your children with wisdom, those problems do not have to consume them. They will know how to face them, and as a result, they will experience more of God's goodness in their lives.

Solomon writes in Proverbs, "For length of days and years of life and peace [wise choices] will add to you" (Proverbs 3:2). Wisdom brings peace. In verse 24 we read, "When you lie down, you will not be afraid, when you lie down, your sleep will be sweet." Basically, the fear and anxiety that plague so many of us today won't be your children's experience if you train them in this key virtue of wisdom.

The book of Colossians reveals another benefit of wisdom: a productive

The benefit of wisdom is not that you won't have any problems. The benefit of wisdom is that the problems will not have you.

life. "For this reason also, since the day we heard of it, we have not ceased to pray for you and to ask that you may be filled with the knowledge of His will in all spiritual wisdom and understanding, so that you will walk in a manner worthy of the Lord, to please Him in all respects, bearing fruit in every good work" (Colossians 1:9–10).

By learning to acquire and apply wisdom, your children will have the opportunity to make the most of their lives. They will be productive and fruitful in all that they do. What more could a parent hope for?

Different Kinds of Wisdom

God's Word teaches us that there are different types of wisdom arising out of two very different sources. We read about these two different types in the book of James:

> Who among you is wise and understanding? Let him show by his good behavior his deeds in the gentleness of wisdom. But if you have bitter jealousy and selfish ambition in your heart, do not be arrogant and so lie against the truth. This wisdom is not that which comes down from above, but is earthly, natural, demonic. For where jealousy and selfish ambition exist, there is disorder and every evil thing. But the wisdom from above is first pure, then peaceable, gentle, reasonable, full of mercy and good fruits, unwavering, without hypocrisy. And the seed whose fruit is righteousness is sown in peace by those who make peace. (James 3:13–18)

First, there is a form of wisdom that is not "from above, but is earthly, natural, demonic" (James 3:15). By contrast, "the wisdom from above is first pure, then peaceable, gentle, reasonable, full of mercy and good fruits, unwavering, without hypocrisy" (verse 17).

Look again at the wisdom that is not from God. It is "earthly," worldly, from below. In our society, people have become trapped by this way of thinking, which is not surprising. Yet what's unfortunate is the number of Christians who live by human wisdom rather than godly wisdom. These believers pay, and will continue to pay, a high price for following the world's wisdom. The Bible says, "There is a way which seems right to a man, but its end is the way of death" (Proverbs 14:12).

It is essential to train your children how to distinguish between these two types of wisdom. The Bible says, "How blessed is the man who does not walk in the counsel of the wicked, nor stand in the path of sinners, nor sit in the seat of scoffers! But his delight is in the law of the LORD" (Psalm 1:1–2).

Be an Eagle

by Anthony Evans Jr.

I've lived in Los Angeles for the past two years. I can honestly say that this city will challenge one's wisdom and conviction. The culture is impulsive and designed to move you toward adopting a lifestyle of doing whatever you feel is right in the moment.

I have learned the value of wisdom through the example of my parents. I watch them make calculated moves that have been checked against the truth of Scripture. As I navigate my way through this culture, trying to make good decisions, I constantly recall a story my dad used to tell me about a bald eagle that was raised on a turkey farm. Because of his environment, the eagle believed he was a turkey. He believed with all his heart that his potential was defined by the turkeys he had spent most of his life with—until one day he saw an eagle flying above his head. He looked up and noticed that this regal bird was extremely high and flying effortlessly. With his amazing vision he started to notice that he had similarities to this majestic creature. Out of curiosity the eagle began to flap his wings harder and harder until he left the ground and began to fly. He went higher and higher, enjoying his newfound ability. When he returned to the farmyard, his turkey brothers tried to make him feel odd because he was so different. This eagle now realized that he had always had this potential, but because of the turkeys he associated with, he had never reached it. My father would tell this story and then say, "Anthony, you are an eagle. Use wisdom and don't surround yourself with turkeys. They will limit your potential and keep you grounded."

When I talk about my parents, I often say, "I watched . . ." As a child of Christian parents, "watching" was the ingredient that made "hearing" translate into my adopting a belief system. As you encourage your children toward wisdom, it's so important that they not only hear what you say, but they also watch you do what you say.

Watching wisdom being lived out as a child is the reason why I want to be wise as an adult, no matter how unwise the culture around me might be.

You see, "the wisdom of this world is foolishness before God" (1 Corinthians 3:19). Human wisdom is worthless when it comes to doing what God expects. Apart from God we don't know where to find wisdom, since only God is all-wise.

We see much evidence around us of people following fleshly wisdom. Consider the often-asked question, "If it feels so good, how can it be so wrong?" I would ask in return, "If it is so right, how come your life is such a mess?" A fleshly approach to wisdom puts feelings on a higher level than faith. It allows emotion to overrule God's revelation. What human wisdom considers important is how I feel, not what God says.

We must adjust our feelings to our faith if we are going to be wise.

But godly wisdom says that our feelings must conform to God's truth. We must adjust our feelings to our faith if we are going to be wise. The Word of God coupled with knowing God intimately are the only sources of true wisdom from above. The Bible teaches us to "set your mind on the things above, not on the things that are on earth" (Colossians 3:2). Only those who are tapped into God's wisdom will experience God's power.

These days too many of our children are like the man from the rural country town who bought a chainsaw because the hardware store owner told him he could cut down more trees each day with a lot less effort. This guy had never seen a chainsaw before, but he went ahead and got one. He came back a week later, saying, "Give me my money back. This is a piece of junk. I used this thing all day long, and I only cut down one tree."

The clerk was surprised, so he took the saw from the man and pulled the cord. The chainsaw roared to life, and the man jumped back in astonishment. He never knew that he needed to turn it on for it to work.

Many youth—and many adults—think they have tried God's wisdom and have concluded it just doesn't work. They think that they have been living God's way—they've memorized Bible verses, attended Sunday school, checked off their list of dos and stayed away from their list of don'ts—but they're actually still stuck in the way they have been used to living. Instead of truly applying God's wisdom, they simply mix in a little bit of God with a lot of everything else, and then some. Yes, they've kept their religion's rules, but they've also kept the flesh. That doesn't work. We can compare this to rat poison. Did you know that a large percentage of rat bait is actually good food? It's not the food that kills the rats—it's the small percentage of poison that gets them. Even a little bit of earthly wisdom will cancel out godly wisdom, because you can't mix the truth with a lie.

That's why God wants our wholehearted, unmixed devotion. He wants all of us. Godly wisdom and worldly wisdom originate from vastly different, mutually exclusive sources.

Everyone has two choices on where to get wisdom—from above or below. Too many people today go to church on Sunday and then live their lives by hell's standards on Monday through Saturday because they are living according to the wisdom of this age. Most of our problems arise out of this combination of the two. As we see in James:

Too many people today go to church on Sunday and then live their lives by hell's standards on Monday through Saturday.

But if any of you lacks wisdom, let him ask of God, who gives to all generously and without reproach, and it will be given to him. But he must ask in faith without any doubting, for the one who doubts is like the surf of the sea, driven and tossed by the wind. For that man ought not to expect that he will receive anything from the Lord, being a double-minded man, unstable in all his ways. (James 1:5–8)

Burger King says to have it your way, but God says you can't have both. It's His way, or no way. When you don't seek wisdom from God in its entirety, you "ought not to expect that [you] will receive anything from the Lord." That's called double-mindedness.

When we seek to integrate wisdom from above with wisdom from below, God says we've made our choice—we want wisdom from below. He isn't going to integrate His ways, thoughts, and will with anything other than His ways, thoughts, and will. You can explain this to your children by using this example: Suppose your son has his driver's license and decides to drive 90 mph down the interstate. When the policeman pulls him over, your child decides to roll down his window and tell the policeman that his mom, or his friend, or even his boss (if he's working) said he could in fact go 90 mph. Ultimately, that would be an irrelevant conversation because a mom, friend, or boss is not the authority when it comes to the laws of the land.

> *Burger King says to have it your way, but God says you can't have both.*

Neither is earthly wisdom relevant as an authority when it comes to living under the King in the laws of His land. He rules over all.

The Spirit of Wisdom

Consider also the sharp contrast between the spirit behind earthly wisdom and the Spirit who energizes divine wisdom. As we saw in the passage from James, the spirit behind earthly wisdom stirs up jealousy and selfishness. This wisdom is from the devil, who became jealous of God and allowed his ambition to try to remove God from His throne.

But godly wisdom has the gentle and peaceable Holy Spirit behind it. This wisdom is characterized by mildness and calm, likewise producing the greatest results.

Scripture says that human wisdom produces "every evil thing" (James 3:16). Godly wisdom, on the other hand, is the source of "mercy and good fruits" (verse 17).

Earthly wisdom leads us to "lie against the truth" (verse 14)—to use the truth to satisfy ourselves and promote our own agendas. Human wisdom subordinates the truth to suit personal goals.

Godly wisdom, on the other hand, seeks to advance God's kingdom agenda on earth—"Thy kingdom come, Thy will be done"—through the knowledge, understanding, and application of God's nature and truth.

Train your children in godly wisdom and you will have prepared them to live their lives to the fullest, as well as experience eternity with the greatest rewards. When you give your child the gift of cultivating godly wisdom, you won't have to surround them with so many rules, because they will know how to make wise choices in the real world. Remember, kingdom parenting involves intentionally overseeing the generational transfer of the faith in such a way that children learn to consistently live all of life under God's divine authority.

One helpful way to train your children in the virtue of wisdom is to get them into the habit of attaching a spiritual principle to their choices and decisions. You can do this by allowing them to watch the

When you give your children the gift of cultivating godly wisdom, you won't have to surround them with so many rules, because they will know how to make wise choices in the real world.

way you apply spiritual principles to your life. You can also do this by offering them spiritual principles when decisions in their lives come up and discussing with them different ways to respond. Invite them to talk with you, and walk them through the decision-making process. This will give them an opportunity to interact with the principle and discern the direction themselves.

One way we did this with our children involved the area of stewardship and personal finances. We taught them that they could not wish their way into a kingdom economic way of life. We showed them where the Bible advises us to consider the ant that stores up for the future while things are good (Proverbs 6:6–11). We also taught them three words of wisdom to guide their money-making decisions.

The first word is *give*. We instructed our children to honor God with the "firstfruits" of their income. If they wanted God's blessing, they needed to honor Him first, because He is the Owner of it all. To help them with this when they were young, we had a shoebox in the kitchen where they placed 10 percent of their allowance every week. This amount was then given as an offering or to missions. We also taught them the spiritual principle that if a person robs God of His tithes to the church and offerings, thus not meeting the emergency needs of the poor, he or she can forget the rest that is promised (Malachi 3:8–9). We are meant to give God His portion first.

The second word is *save*. After our kids gave to the Lord, we taught them to save a portion of what they earned. They were never to spend everything. Lastly, the third word is *spend*. There's nothing wrong with spending. But it should come third in your financial priorities, not first. To help our children understand the value of money, we also encouraged all four kids to get jobs as soon as they were legally old enough to do so. They were far less willing to spend their hard-earned money—knowing how long it took them to get it—than ours. Finally, along with teaching our children wisdom in finances, we sought to model it as well in all that we did.

Another way you can instill wisdom in your children is to read the book of Proverbs together regularly in your home. Choose age-appropriate proverbs and take some time each day to go over a few, discussing the principles that are contained in them. You can do this as part of your normal mealtime activities, or it could be something you do before your children go to bed or when they wake up in the morning.

As you look at the book of Proverbs, or other scriptures, you'll note natural references to important subjects facing your children, such as their personal health or relationships. For example, much of the health crisis we are facing in our nation today is self-induced simply due to consuming cheaply produced, unhealthy synthetic, or genetically modified foods. One of the most important pieces of wisdom you can teach your child is how to discern healthy food choices. It is increasingly difficult these days to make healthy food choices, but the long-term cost of not doing so is debilitating, if not deadly (see Proverbs 23:8; 30:8; Daniel 1:8-14; 3 John 1:2).

In addition to what we put into our mouths, helping our children understand that the people they surround ourselves with will affect the choices they make in filling their time and their minds; their relationships will have a great impact on their future. The Bible is full of wisdom on relationships (Psalm 1:1–3; Proverbs 1:16; 4:14; 6:24; 24:1; 17:17; 27:6), and it serves as an excellent starting point for guiding your kids toward good choices in making friends. It has been said that you can predict where someone will be in ten years by the books they read and the friends they have. (That might need to be amended a bit these days to also include the apps and games they engage in on their tablets, smartphones, or computers.) Giving your children the foundation of wisdom in relationships will go a long way toward providing them with a solid footing for the future.

> *One of the most important pieces of wisdom you can teach your child is how to discern healthy food choices.*

However you choose to incorporate the teaching of wisdom in your home, make sure you are consistently teaching your children the principles behind the rules so they learn the value of wisdom and begin to apply it themselves.

12

❧

INTEGRITY

In 1980, I had the privilege of taking part in a trip to China as a Bible teacher with a number of NBA players, including Julius Erving, also known as Dr. J. The NBA players' presence in China attracted a lot of attention. People gathered wherever we went in order to check out these towering sports stars from the States. The players performed in exhibition games or put on clinics during most of our days.

The hype surrounding the players combined with other lively happenings on this trip made it one of my more interesting international visits. I marveled at the streets overflowing with the sheer volume of bicycles speeding around every which way. Having grown up in urban Baltimore, I wasn't accustomed to seeing that many people on bikes. The food wasn't quite what I had come to love in Baltimore either. Yet by far the most awe-inspiring occurrence on this trip to China took place during a visit to the Great Wall with our hosts one day.

Now, I had studied the Great Wall of China in school, but seeing that series of fortifications in photos or in old films did nothing to prepare me for what I witnessed when standing in front of it that day. The Great Wall commanded my attention, rising out of the earth as if it were alive, arching through the countryside in movements of formidable strength.

Our hosts wanted us to do more than simply see it. They wanted us to experience it. So they suggested that we climb it, which proved to be an adventure in itself. Something they didn't teach me in school about the Great Wall of China was the number of the steps. Never before had I lumbered up so many difficult and uneven steps. The construction of the Great Wall included intentionally making the spacing between the steps irregular in order to slow down enemies and prevent them from succeeding in taking over the wall.

Over time, the unaligned steps worked to slow down tourists like myself as well. Yet I eventually reached our lookout point, and I stood amazed, taking in the sheer magnitude of stone, brick, and other building materials that were solidly beneath me while stretching out as far as I could see. In a time and place where travel and battles remained limited to the ground, the Great Wall, by its sheer size, provided a high level of protection against military incursions and unwanted intrusions by nomadic neighbors.

But there was one thing the Great Wall of China could do nothing to defend against: the bribe.

After guarding its people securely for hundreds of years, the Great Wall was breached in 1644 by an invading group known as the Manchu, who bribed an influential general to open the gates and allow them into China.[1] Not even the magnificent Great Wall could defend itself against a significant lapse of integrity.

> *Boundaries, standards—call it what you will—integrity is an essential virtue to living out a full and victorious kingdom life.*

Like the Great Wall, integrity defines the boundaries placed in our lives that guide us, protect us, and secure us against the enemies' offenses. These boundaries will protect our children when Satan seeks to rob them of their destinies. Yet when these boundaries fail—for whatever reason—it becomes easy for the enemy to advance and overcome your children. Boundaries, standards—call it what you will—integrity is an essential virtue to living out a full and victorious kingdom life.

The Nature of Integrity

Integrity involves more than reputation. What other people think about you makes up your reputation, but integrity consists of that which resides inside of you—your thoughts and your personal code of conduct (your values). This moral code guides and governs your decisions. A person of integrity fears and reveres God while living authentically and according to his or her convictions. Integrity can be defined as being consistently honest and ethical in your speech, attitudes, and actions without compromising the truth. It means living consistently by your convictions—what you say and what you do are the same thing.

People of integrity are harder and harder to come by these days. Or perhaps they have always been hard to come by; in the Psalms we read, "O LORD, who may abide in Your tent? Who may dwell on Your holy hill? He who walks with integrity, and works righteousness, and speaks truth in his heart" (Psalm 15:1–2).

Integrity is about more than rules. It is not a checklist that you can mark off. Integrity resides in the heart, for out of the heart flow the springs of life (see Proverbs 4:23).

As parents, it would be a lot easier if we could somehow legislate integrity in our children. Raising them would be so much simpler if we could somehow create enough rules to control their decisions. But rules are not the essence of integrity. In fact, according to Paul, it's the law itself that arouses within us a temptation to break it (see Romans 7).

Raising kingdom kids goes deeper than managing how much time they spend texting on their smartphones, surfing the Internet, or spending time with their friends. It's more than choosing their wardrobe or deciding at what age they can wear makeup. Raising kingdom kids involves instilling an integrity deep within them so that your children are equipped to discern personal limits, standards, and boundaries for themselves in alignment with God's will.

Keep in mind that when your child grows up and leaves home, there won't be anyone there to make and enforce the rules he or she needs to live a productive and personally responsible life. Far too often, kids who have been highly sheltered, protected, or managed don't know what to do without external rules. Sometimes that leads to rebellion. Sometimes it leads to a mismanagement of time and resources at an age when it is very costly to do so.

Parenting through imposing and emphasizing rules rather than instilling integrity in your children has another downfall: A false security and pride can develop from keeping the rules simply for the sake of keeping them. After all, the Pharisees were excellent at keeping rules, yet Christ was not impressed. He was more interested in them cleaning the inside of the cup rather than the outside (Matthew 23:26). If the inside of the cup is clean, it will take care of the outside—but not the reverse.

In fact, as parents we can sometimes be fooled by how the outside of our kids' cups look. If you have more than one child, you have experienced the differences in personalities that show up between siblings. With some children, you know right away when they have done something wrong; it's obvious. But other children might be sneakier and look squeaky clean on the outside. Parents can easily get fooled and wind up not addressing a situation as they ought. This happened to us as parents from time to time, and one instance in particular involving our daughter, Priscilla, stands out the most to me.

As Priscilla already mentioned in one of her sidebar pieces, her mouth was the thing that caused her the most trouble. Whether she was being disrespectful, talking too much, or getting caught lying—her mouth was the issue. Now, as many of you know, Priscilla is a very persuasive speaker—so there were times when I would believe her right in the midst of a lie. One time I even went to her school to complain to her teacher about something Priscilla had told us about another student in her class. I found out that Priscilla had made up the whole thing—the other student had done nothing wrong at all. Not only did I have to go back and apologize to the teacher, I had to apologize to the student and the student's family as well. I learned an important lesson that day: Take the time to truly discern the heart of a matter. Integrity involves much more than outward actions—it involves the heart. And it isn't always easy to recognize when it's not there.

The process of sanctification in our children—the producing of spiritual growth, integrity, and godliness—is a complicated and ongoing development. Far too often busy parents can be tempted to reduce concepts of faith and integrity to a manageable list of dos and don'ts. But by focusing more on dos and don'ts rather than on the Lord Himself, the list itself can begin to eclipse God's proper place in your child's heart. The list becomes the god instead, which certainly makes it easier to follow when it's convenient—as well as easier to rationalize away when it's not.

We live in a world where integrity has fallen by the wayside, but when your children have integrity, it will protect them against irresponsibility, laziness, immorality, cheating, bullying, and many other temptations. I often compare integrity to going through security at the airport. The security equipment senses whether or not we have metals in our pockets or hidden on our persons. Yet that equipment must be programmed by someone who decides the proper sensitivity level. Some monitors easily pick up metals—sending a warning signal for keys and watches, while others rarely pick up anything at all.

Programming security equipment is akin to setting your children's conscience. By instilling the virtue of integrity, you provide your children with a heightened sensitivity to the things in this world that grieve God so their consciences enable them to live holy lives.

Daniel and His Lions

One of the greatest examples of integrity in Scripture comes to us through the life of Daniel. You'll remember from the first part of this book that Daniel had been taken captive in Jerusalem and sent to Babylon, where he was brought up in a secular environment. It's important to point out to your children that Daniel maintained his integrity in an environment that lacked it. In fact, the Bible mentions many people who also did this, such as Joseph, Esther, and Ruth. They did not succumb to the world's invitation to join them in compromise.

> It seemed good to Darius to appoint 120 satraps over the kingdom, that they would be in charge of the whole kingdom, and over them three commissioners (of whom Daniel was one), that these satraps might be accountable to them, and that the king might not suffer loss. Then this Daniel began distinguishing himself among the commissioners and satraps because he possessed an extraordinary spirit, and the king planned to appoint him over the entire kingdom. (Daniel 6:1–3)

By now Daniel was no longer a teen, and he had been working in a secular governmental environment. The 120 satraps were appointed to look out for the king's interests. They were divided into groups of three, each group with a commissioner over it. Basically this was an organizational structure for running the kingdom and protecting the king.

Because of Daniel's extraordinary spirit, the king ultimately had plans to appoint him over everything. In a matter of years, Daniel rose to the top. He had performed his jobs well, carried out his tasks exceptionally, managed his projects efficiently, and none of this had gone unnoticed.

But as is often the case when someone rises to the top, Daniel's favor created jealousy among the other leaders in the land, and they sought a way to accuse him somehow. After an exhaustive search, though, they realized that they could not find anything at all. No lack of integrity showed up in Daniel's work, no matter how deep his enemies dug (see verse 4).

Daniel's work stood the test of scrutiny in the discharge of his duty, as well as the attitude in which it was done. In other words, Daniel possessed integrity. Next his enemies sought to trap him instead. They tried to create a church-and-state conflict whereby the government would make it illegal for Daniel to carry out a certain law of God.

The first thing I find interesting about Daniel's story is that he possessed so much integrity that his enemies realized the only thing they could use against him was that very integrity. They assumed that, if they made a law against the laws of Daniel's God, Daniel would have enough integrity to still obey his God. They most likely remembered Daniel standing up against the Babylonian leaders when he was asked to eat the king's food as a youth. So, based on his integrity, they came up with a scheme to oust Daniel:

> Then these commissioners and satraps came by agreement to the king and spoke to him as follows: "King Darius, live forever! All the commissioners of the kingdom, the prefects and the satraps, the high officials and the governors have consulted together that the king should establish a statute and enforce an injunction that anyone who makes a petition to any god or man besides you, O king, for thirty days shall be cast into the lions' den." (Daniel 6:6–7)

This new law presented a spiritual conflict for Daniel: the Bible was clear on showing honor to others, but it was also clear that there was only one true God. Daniel had an employer, but that employer was not equal to God. Daniel's employer stepped over the line when he sought to claim his worship. Worship was for God alone, and on that principle, Daniel would not budge.

What happened next is a key point that I want you to catch as you raise your kids to have integrity: "Now when Daniel knew that the document was signed, he entered his house (now in his roof chamber he had windows opened toward Jerusalem); and he continued kneeling on his knees three times a day, praying and giving thanks before his God" (6:10).

The passage points out that Daniel had his window "opened toward Jerusalem." There are two critical pieces of information in that short phrase. First, it lets us know that despite the risks involved, Daniel chose to follow God publicly. Daniel didn't let fear of those in powerful positions cause him to hide his fear and reverence for the One who sits in the most powerful position of all.

Second, we see that Daniel kept his window open toward home. Jerusalem had been Daniel's home. It was where his parents had raised him, the place where he had first learned about God and had grown up as a young boy of character and integrity. By opening his window toward Jerusalem, Daniel had a continual reminder that the place where he lived was not the place where he was from. The place where he worked was not the place of his roots. The promises of God and the power of God originated from his home, so while Daniel may have lived in a foreign land, his mind was still at home.

Parents, as you raise your kids and instill godly virtues within them, you are doing this so that when they are grown and move out on their own into the secular environment we call our contemporary culture, they will always re-

Daniel had a continual reminder that the place where he lived was not the place where he was from.

member home. Their window will be opened toward home. They will not lose sight of the values, principles, and precepts they learned there.

In addition to Daniel praying publicly while facing Jerusalem, the passage also lets us know that he did it three times a day. This was Daniel's habit. This wasn't simply a fleeting thought toward heaven as he went about his plans. No, this was a position of concentrated, focused, and consistent prayer, demonstrating that God was at the center of his life.

No wonder the other leaders in the country despised him. He had risen to the top by gaining the king's trust. And by his behavior and work ethic, they didn't see him losing that trust anytime soon, so they trapped him.

Yet Daniel chose to trust God in the trap. And despite the king's love for Daniel (verse 14), he was unable to spare him from the punishment for breaking his law. Into the lions' den Daniel went. You know the story. God closed the mouths of the lions and the next morning this is what happened:

> The king arose at dawn, at the break of day, and went in haste to the lions' den. When he had come near the den to Daniel, he cried out with a troubled voice. The king spoke and said to Daniel, "Daniel, servant of the living God, has your God, whom you constantly serve, been able to deliver you from the lions?" Then Daniel spoke to the king, "O king, live forever! My God sent His angel and shut the lions' mouths and they have not harmed me, inasmuch as I was found innocent before Him; and also toward you, O king, I have committed no crime." Then the king was very pleased and gave orders for Daniel to be taken up out of the den. (Daniel 6:19–23)

Not only did the king have Daniel taken out of the den, but he had Daniel's enemies thrown into the lions' den as well. And this time God did not close the lions' mouths. God can take your enemies and make them your footstool when your life aligns under Him.

God can take your enemies and make them your footstool when your life aligns under Him.

I believe God never allows integrity to go overlooked. It may seem to be overlooked at the moment, but He will make a way for it to be brought to light or rewarded, even if that's in heaven. It is God who raises up or puts down kings. This reality needs to stand at the heart of your child's integrity—this ultimate trust that God is their source. Everyone else is just a resource. Whether that resource is providing them with entertainment, friendships, a job, or whatever—teach your children the principle that their needs will be met when they look to God and obey Him rather than man.

God is their source. Everyone else is just a resource.

When your children grow up, God may choose to place them in a Babylonian environment. They may face pressure on the job to compromise their values. But while their job might pay them, their job does not own them—they are owned by a bigger corporate entity called the kingdom of God. All through the Bible God had people tucked away in evil environments. He had a Daniel in evil Babylon, a Moses in evil Egypt, an Esther in evil Persia. He had men and women all throughout the Bible hidden away in order to rise up at just the right moment for eternal purposes.

Meeting the Standard
by Jonathan Evans

While I was growing up, my favorite sport was most definitely basketball. I was caught up in being like "Mike," just like everybody else at the time who loved to play the game. And even though I wasn't as good as Michael Jordan, I definitely was pretty athletic and did well at the game. In fact, the first time I dunked a basketball I was only eleven years old. If you have a hard time believing this, my father probably was thinking the same thing when I ran into his office and shouted, "I dunked, I dunked—come to the gym with me, Dad, so I can show you!" He knew I was pretty good at the game, but just like you he was very skeptical. I finally convinced him that what I was saying was true, so he got up and followed me to the gymnasium to see this incredible feat.

When we got inside the gym, I grabbed the basketball and told my dad to stand back. I vividly remember starting just above the three-point line to start my race toward the basket. I took a deep breath and then took off toward the basket. As I got close I put everything I had into leaping up as high as I could, and in the blink of an eye, BOOM!—at eleven years old I dunked with authority. I was extremely excited about what I had accomplished in front of my father.

However, when I looked at my father, he didn't seem to be quite as impressed as I thought he would be. He suddenly left the gym and came back a few seconds later with the head custodian and kindly asked him to raise the hoop from six feet to ten feet. Then he looked at me and said, "Son, don't be satisfied that you dunked at six feet, because that's not the standard. When you're ready to dunk at ten feet, which is the standard for professional basketball, come get me, because then I'll be ready to watch." I learned a valuable lesson that day: Just because you dunked doesn't mean you've met the standard.

Many people think they're doing well just because they're dunking at a cultural standard. However, living biblically and living culturally are two totally different levels of living. Just because the culture agrees with you doesn't mean that God does. Just because the culture applauds you doesn't mean that God does. As in the gym that day, my father and mother often impressed upon my siblings and me that even though we live in the culture, the culture is not the standard. However, if your goal is to make your heavenly Father proud, you must raise the goal and dunk at a biblical standard—even in a pagan culture.

Give your children a gift greater than simply the ability to follow the rules you've set for them. Develop in them a heart of integrity that will follow them into adulthood, enabling them to apply God's principles to whatever setting they are in.

Raise them so their window will always be open toward home.

13

~∾~

FAITH

I'll never forget the autumn day a few decades ago when we drove our oldest daughter, Chrystal, and a car full of her belongings to college. I know she was officially an adult at the time, but I still saw a young girl when I glanced at her in the rearview mirror as we drove. In many ways, it was exciting to see Chrystal transition into the independent life she had worked so hard to achieve, but it also gave me pause for a great deal of thought.

Is she really ready for all of this? I wondered. *Have we prepared her to be on her own? Will she make wise choices? Is the faith we have passed on to her strong enough to see her through any challenges and trials ahead?*

The answers to all of those questions, and more, would come soon enough. Some of the answers were good; some were not. But more than anything else I've ever experienced, watching Chrystal head out into her adult life underscored for me the utmost importance of instilling a living and strong faith in each of our children, as well as in our grandchildren.

Kingdom parent, once your children leave the nest, you will have only a limited effect on what happens to them—outside of offering advice, counsel, and assistance along the way. Therefore, one of the most important things you can do as a parent is to give your children their own faith—their own ability to go to God during trials and successes and learn how to handle life's situations well.

Chrystal writes about this in the book we coauthored, *Kingdom Woman,* but I wanted to share it here as well because it meant so much to me. Chrystal faced some pretty steep challenges as a young adult, and her faith was being tested on several fronts. She was a single mother, yet she was still in college, finances were difficult, time was tight, and her self-esteem had taken a pretty severe beating. On her own initiative, she wrote down some scriptures about how God felt about her. She didn't tell anyone about this at first; she just stuck them in a place where she could pull them out throughout the day and read them. She did this in order to remind herself who she was in Christ Jesus. Over time, these scriptures brought Chrystal back to a place of confidence in her position as a child of the King.

I couldn't have been more proud of Chrystal when I saw how she turned to her faith in God—even when that faith was at an all-time low—to pull her back up and set her on solid ground spiritually over the course of those few years.

As a parent, you can't make decisions for your children, even though you might often wish you could. Sometimes they will choose wisely, and sometimes they will choose poorly. Unfortunately, those poor choices will often bring unexpected and unwanted consequences they'll need to wrestle with. When that happens, you can only hope that your children will return to the Lord, at whatever level of faith they have, and rely on God to see them through.

When mistakes or sins and their accompanying consequences come, your kids will turn to their faith—at whatever level they can—to see them through.

Chrystal will tell you now that she didn't necessarily feel like the scripture verses she wrote down were true in her life. But she had been taught growing up that God's Word was something you could rely on. She had been taught to trust in it. So, in faith, she determined to put God's truth in her heart on a daily basis in hopes that it would eventually take root and bear fruit—which it did. Knowing that she did this during her deepest hour of need makes my heart full with both delight and satisfaction. What more could a father hope for than for his daughter's faith to be real during the trials and mistakes of life?

None of us will raise perfect children. We all have that in common. There is one thing every single parent will face—standing by while your child makes a mistake or a poor decision. This is simply because no human being is perfect. But what you can do as a parent is raise your child in such a way that when those mistakes or sins and their accompanying consequences come, they will turn to their faith—at whatever level they can—to see them through. This will produce an even greater level of spiritual growth in them as they mature.

Lessons in the Dark

I was born up north in Baltimore, Maryland, but Lois and I moved to Dallas so that I could attend seminary in the 1970s, and when we did, I discovered something I loved about Dallas—the heat. Another great thing about Dallas is the immensity of the Texas sky. Sometimes it seems as if you can look straight into eternity when you look at that sky.

An interesting thing happened one night as I looked at the sky around dusk. I saw one lone star in the enormous expanse, while the rest of the sky appeared empty. It was probably a planet. A few minutes later, I looked again. This time the sky had gotten a little darker, and so I saw a couple more stars. A few minutes later, I looked again. Even more were visible now.

The stars reminded me of a spiritual truth that relates to raising kingdom kids with a living faith: All the stars were already in place when I looked up that very first time. I just couldn't see them. My eyes didn't recognize them earlier, even though they had been there all along. It wasn't until the darkness settled in around me that I could see the stars clearly.

In the kingdom life, sometimes our greatest lessons of faith are learned in the dark. In our *own* dark. As parents, we wish our children could learn their lessons through the dark trials we have faced. We tell them things like, "Learn from my mistakes." But more often than not, each of us must learn our lessons on our own. Sometimes this is brought about by poor decisions we make, but other times it is the hand of God allowing difficulties in our lives that are not the result of anything we've done but simply designed to strengthen our faith.

The Virtue of Faith
by Anthony Evans Jr.

My faith was born out of watching my dad and mom follow the Lord. However, there was a time when I had to realize that God doesn't have grandkids. When I went to college, for the first time I became aware of the reality that my faith and my parents' faith were not synonymous. I found I had many questions about what I believed for myself. As the questions continued to come, my faith struggle grew, so much so that I no longer wanted to be at a Christian college. I dropped out for a semester to figure out what I wanted to do with my spiritual life. Full of turmoil, I wrestled with depression for months. I couldn't fathom that everything my life had been built on could possibly be something I no longer believed in. During this time of intense questioning, I inundated my father with phone calls. On one occasion he told me to read Psalm 128. I will never forget trying to internalize this passage for myself but only being able to think about how true this was for my grandfathers and father: "Blessed is everyone who fears the Lord . . . Your wife will be like a fruitful vine within your house" (Psalm 128:1, 3). I thought about how my grandfathers' and my father's faith in the Lord allowed them to see the promises in this psalm. I had watched them operate based on the truth of this passage. My dad frequently said, "Faith is acting like God is telling the truth. It is acting like it is so, even if it is not so, in order that it might be so, simply because God said so." (He's a master at those catchy concepts!) I, on the other hand, defined faith by my feelings, and that's why I was having such a hard time. Being able to see a faith that wasn't defined by emotions allowed me to start trusting, believing, and standing on my own two spiritual feet.

My encouragement to you is to create an environment where your children can see you exercising your faith and in turn experience the ripple effect of the promises of God. Then, as they grow and start their own spiritual journey, they will not only have your words—they will have your actual experience to lean on.

I often hear people say (maybe you have even said this yourself), "God will not put more on me than I can bear." Let me debunk that myth right now with a look at the life of Paul. In 2 Corinthians 1:8, Paul wrote, "For we do not want you to be unaware, brethren, of our affliction . . . that we were burdened excessively, beyond our strength, so that we despaired even of life."

If ever there was a hopeless situation, Paul was in it. Paul hadn't done anything to cause it. In fact, he had followed God's leading straight into it. And yet he writes that he was "burdened excessively"—beyond his strength. In fact, he wrote that he "despaired even of life."

God sometimes allows situations in life to appear hopeless because He wants to break us of our self-sufficiency and direct our focus onto Him. He sometimes lets us hit rock-bottom so we can discover that He is the Rock at the bottom. He allows these situations because He is after a greater good. He is trying to increase our faith. Some people may feel like giving up at that time because they can't seem to fix the situation that they are in, and no one they know can fix it either. All of the human resources have been depleted.

He sometimes lets us hit rock bottom so we can discover that He is the Rock at the bottom.

But it is precisely those times that Paul spoke about when he revealed a key principle about faith in his next statement: "We had the sentence of death within ourselves *so that we would not trust in ourselves, but in God* . . . He on whom we have set our hope" (2 Corinthians 1:9–10, emphasis added).

In order to take Paul deeper in his faith, God allowed a situation that his résumé, abilities, background, upbringing, and connections could not change. Why? So that Paul would grow in his faith and learn to trust God at a deeper level.

Was God being mean or cruel? It might have felt that way, but what He was really doing was trying to take Paul deeper. Ultimately it was in that hopeless scenario where Paul saw no way up, over, or out that God somehow delivered him. He restored a hopeless situation, and because Paul experienced it, God became even more real to him at a level he had not known before.

This is not to say that, as parents, we look for situations to create darkness in our children's lives. But the greatest gift you can give your children is a living faith so that when those dark times come—"in the world you have tribulation" (John 16:33)—either because of their own wrong choices or simply because God is seeking to grow and develop them, they will have the tools necessary to look to God and endure, rather than merely seek to escape.

To a large degree, living a victorious kingdom life comes down to how you learn to view life's situations through the lens of God's Word. It's all a matter of perspective. The clarity of your vision makes all of the difference. Will your children see the darkness, or will your children see the stars? Will they seek to live by their own lights, thus short-circuiting the lessons of faith and obedience God is teaching them? Remember, even the sinless Son of God grew spiritually in His humanity through the things He suffered.

Sure, Chrystal's faith wasn't at an all-time high when she penned those verses and carried them with her. But it takes faith only the size of a mustard seed to get that mountain moving. She knew enough to look for God in the midst of a dark situation. As a result, the Lord saw in her faith that His truth would make a difference in her life, and He saw her pull that paper out time and time again to read those verses. God then rewarded her actions by allowing His Word to take root and grow into something great within her.

The Race

The book of Hebrews is one of the most challenging books in the Bible, but it also teaches us some of the greatest lessons on faith. There is so much to discover about faith from this book alone. In fact, as I write this chapter, I'm preaching a sermon series on faith from the book of Hebrews at our church, and it's a series that will take a few months to complete! Faith is so important to the kingdom life that entire volumes have been written on it.

Before we close this chapter, I want to highlight some important principles you can take with you as you seek to raise kingdom kids of faith. Give your children these tools so they will have them available when they learn their own lessons in the dark.

We're not positive who the author of the book of Hebrews was, but many believe it was the apostle Paul. Paul seemed to have a fondness for communicating with athletic analogies, often using different sports situations to illustrate a spiritual truth. If you know me at all, then you know that Paul is a man after my own heart. I love seeing how spiritual truths come to life through sports.

In Hebrews chapter 12, we read one of the most powerful passages on faith, where the Christian life is compared to running a race:

> Therefore, since we have so great a cloud of witnesses surrounding us, let us also lay aside every encumbrance and the sin which so easily entangles us, and let us run with endurance the race that is set before us, fixing our eyes on Jesus, the author and perfecter of faith, who for the joy set before Him endured the cross, despising the shame, and has sat down at the right hand of the throne of God. (Hebrews 12:1–2)

When the writer says that we are to "run with endurance the race that is set before us," he isn't talking about a 100-yard dash. He isn't even talking about a lap around the track. Endurance implies that this is a long race—more like a marathon. To run a marathon, an athlete needs training and conditioning to work up to the level where he or she can even finish the race. Without the trial of training, there will be no race.

Raising kingdom kids with a living faith means raising them with the perspective that the Christian life isn't a short-term sprint. It isn't something that you can jump in and out of on Sunday and expect to live victoriously throughout the week. Kingdom living requires a day-in and day-out dependence on the character and attributes of God, as well as on His Word.

First and foremost, a living faith must be a daily faith. If it is not a daily faith, when the challenges of life come, your child will be too out of shape to take the next step.

Reading Scripture and memorizing Bible

Raising kingdom kids with a living faith means raising them with the perspective that the Christian life isn't a short-term sprint. A living faith must be a daily faith.

verses in our home when the children were growing up was a daily part of our faith. By doing this, we taught them that Scripture is to be depended upon. We demonstrated to them that the Bible is important enough that we immerse ourselves in it regularly—in the same way food is important enough for our bodies that we consume it regularly. Had the Bible simply been something we opened on Sundays when it came time for me to preach, we wouldn't have been teaching our children that kingdom life is a long-term commitment requiring ongoing exposure to God's Word. We would have been setting them up for a sprint when in reality they are each called to run a marathon.

Putting emphasis on God's Word will hopefully guide your children into their own personal faith as they mature into adulthood in the years to come.

As a result, when Chrystal came upon a time of personal crisis, she turned to what she had learned as a child would be the most effective way for her to overcome the negative emotions and realities she was facing.

Now that our children have children of their own, I've witnessed them pass this value down to our grandchildren. Every month we have a family lunch where all the children and grandchildren come together for a time of special bonding. The grandchildren take turns climbing up on a chair (if they are small) or simply standing in front of us and reciting the different Bible passages they have committed to memory over the previous month. It is this emphasis on God's Word that will hopefully guide them into their own personal faith as they mature into adulthood in the years to come.

Removing Encumbrances and Sin

As I'm writing this book, the winter Olympics have begun again for a time of global competition. One thing that never fails to impress me about the Olympics is the pageantry of the opening ceremony. Athletes from the participating countries take part in a parade wearing colorful, sometimes elaborate, costumes.

But when it comes time for them to compete, there is a noticeable change in their wardrobe. Jackets have been discarded. Skirts have been replaced with shorts. Flags have been rolled up, and hats have been stored away. Why? Because pageantry and props have never helped anyone win a race. Rather, they are an encumbrance—something keeping the athlete from moving forward at the fastest possible speed.

Encumbrances come in the kingdom life as well. One of the most critical things we need to teach our children is how to recognize them. So much of life is often wasted simply because we're tied up in distractions and encumbrances. Perhaps it is the wrong crowd—a group that seeks to bring about a negative influence or an ungodly lifestyle. Or it could be the encumbrances of past hurts or habits that paralyze your children's minds via a wrong thought pattern. Other encumbrances may not seem like encumbrances at all because they are fun—things like television, movies, tablets, and electronics. While there is nothing wrong with those things in and of themselves, they can become an encumbrance when they begin to dictate your children's thought life or dominate their time. There needs to be a balance between entertainment and personal responsibility and personal spiritual growth.

There is a simple scriptural prescription for dealing with encumbrances that you can teach your children. Hebrews 12:1 says to lay them aside. It doesn't say to pray about them, talk about them, or figure out a way to work things out. When something is recognized as an encumbrance—holding your children back from experiencing the full destiny God has for them—they are to lay it aside. It's as simple as that.

Many things can be considered encumbrances, and each needs to be dealt with in its own way and to whatever degree it proves to be a negative influence on your children's thoughts and time.

Now, as we progress through the passage we read earlier in Hebrews, you'll notice that while the author mentions a multitude of encumbrances, he mentions only one sin. Since only one sin is discussed, it is safe to assume that the writer is referring to the sin that stands at the root of all other sins—the sin of unbelief. Unbelief—a lack of faith—gives rise to all the other sins we commit. When we have faith and take God at His Word, we trust and obey Him, which keeps us from sin, for "whatever is not from faith is sin" (Romans 14:23).

It's like the college student who decided to do his laundry for the first time. He gathered all his dirty clothes and wrapped them up in his bedsheet. Since everything needed washing, he threw the entire bundle in the washing machine, only to discover later on that he had a clean sheet, but he also still had some dirty clothes. The clothes hadn't come clean because they were entangled in the sheet.

Show me your children's faith, and I'll show you their future.

The sin of unbelief entangles everything else in a person's life as well. That's why it is so important to train your children to have a living faith. It is important to train them to recognize the critical nature of trusting God, believing His Word, and committing their thoughts, words, and actions to Him in the realities of daily life. This faith will be the bedrock for their future. Show me your children's faith, and I'll show you their future.

Faith is acting like God is telling the truth. It is taking Him at His Word. Faith is acting like something is so even though it is not so in order for it to be so simply because God said so. Teach and model before your children that truth, and you will have positioned them for a victorious kingdom life.

14

RESILIENCY

When I was a young boy, we weren't allowed to watch much television in the home. On top of that, there really wasn't a large amount of television programming that appealed to me at that age. It was the 1950s, and radio served as our main source of entertainment. Without fail, my parents would listen to different preachers throughout the day, as well as music from time to time. I'm sure my love for preaching developed from my parents' insistence on having us listen to it on a regular basis. They were discipling my siblings and me in a way that would give us an ongoing thirst and hunger for God's Word.

I clearly remember, though, that occasionally a radio show would be interrupted by the announcement that the station was going to test the emergency broadcasting system, followed by a loud and very annoying noise that lasted for up to a minute.

I used to hate those tests because they always seemed to come at the worst time, just when I didn't want the programming interrupted. And since there was never any advance warning that the test was coming, there wasn't any way you could avoid it. The station just broke in and did its test.

Sometimes trials are like that. They come with no warning. They also come at the worst possible time. They are noisy, annoying, and always seem way too long. There's nothing to warn you that a test like this is on its way. I'm sure as a parent you've gone through your own trials and tests. And while that may be difficult for you, it can often be even more difficult to stand by and watch your children go through a test of their own, especially when you can't fix it for them. A kingdom virtue that every child needs when it comes to successfully navigating life's trials is resiliency. While tenacity is the deter-mination and ability to persevere through trials in such a way that the full manifestation of God's purpose is realized in life, resiliency is the ability to get on the front end of these challenges by cultivating strengths to face them when they first appear.

I know the importance of resiliency firsthand as I've seen my children go through their own trials from time to time—whether it's a trial they brought on themselves due to poor choices or a trial simply because life is often challenging. It's easy for kids to want to quit or throw in the towel, but our role as their parents is to encourage them to hold on and keep the faith. My father's heart often wanted to rush in and relieve them of their pain, but my mind and spirit reminded me that this was their opportunity to develop resiliency. While trials may not be fun, our children often need them—just as we do—in order to experience the full spiritual maturity that will allow them to live the abundant life. They need to learn how to grieve, particularly when they experience losses in life. They also need to learn how to forgive and be flexible in the face of unexpected change. They need to learn how to grow from their mistakes, learn from them, and move on.

> *Give them the wisdom and the tools they need to understand what life's challenges are and how to respond to them.*

My best advice to you as you train your children in the virtue of resiliency is to give them the wisdom and the tools they need to understand what life's challenges are and how to respond to them.

Our heavenly Father wants each of us to pass our tests, and your child is no exception. And like a good teacher, He doesn't mind retesting. Equipping your child with the spiritual insight and strength to overcome life's tests is ben-eficial, because the sooner your child grows in whatever area the test is aimed to strengthen, the less often they may have to retake it. Let's review the nature and purpose of trials in this chapter so you have what you need to teach your children how to both view and approach them.

Trials Are Unavoidable

We see throughout Scripture that trials are an inevitable reality in life, and we read imperatives like "Consider it all joy, my brethren, when you encounter various trials" (James 1:2). Notice the Bible does not say "if" you encounter trials; it talks instead about "when" they come. Trials are inescapable. Job said, "Man is born for trouble, as sparks fly upward" (5:7). The only way to exit trouble is to exit life. Jesus said, "In the world you have tribulation" (John 16:33); you can count on it.

One of the worst things a parent can do in raising a child is to shield him or her from every struggle, especially early on when the consequences and depth of those struggles are limited. I would much rather have a child of mine learn life's lessons in the controlled context of elementary school than in the chaos that can occur when he or she becomes a teen.

When I was in junior high, I stole a cinnamon roll from the cafeteria line. It's my only recollection of stealing anything. I can't say that I was starving or needed it in any way. It just looked good and I wanted it, so I took it. Fortunately, one of the cafeteria workers saw what I did. I say "fortunately" because I'm grateful to have learned a lesson on stealing in this manner rather than by shoplifting as an older teen and possibly spending some time down at the police station.

When the cafeteria worker saw what I did, she came straight over to me and told me that she had seen what I had done. My face grew hot with guilt, and I could picture myself in the basement standing in front of my father who was about to make me remember never to do that again. But instead, she could see that I was truly sorry for what I had done, and she realized that getting caught by her was causing me enough pain to learn my lesson. She told me never to do it again, and I didn't.

Had she looked the other way and chosen not to go through the difficulty of confronting me, I would have learned that I could get away with things like that, and perhaps I would have done it again, and again—until the consequences were more severe. But because she lovingly corrected me and allowed me to experience the pain and embarrassment of that situation—as well as the fear of possibly having to face my father if she had chosen to tell him—I grew through that experience.

Far too often, as parents we want to relieve our children of pain, so we overlook prime teaching opportunities by failing to confront them. But keeping them from life's realities—making their lives too comfortable—simply sets them up to experience greater trials as they get older. Ultimately they will need to learn the lessons that come from living in a less-than-perfect world. Whether these are lessons from their own wrong choices (like mine with the cinnamon roll) or whether they are lessons about the difficulties of life regardless of whether they deserve those difficulties or not—these are truths that we all must learn if we are to overcome trials, put the past behind us, and move on.

My story of the cinnamon roll is an example of a small trial. But in our family we have had our fair share of large challenges as well. While I was still young in the ministry, our older daughter, Chrystal, called us from college to tell us she was pregnant. She was not married, and I'll never forget the utter feeling of disappointment and failure that flooded my emotions. Thoughts of stepping down from the pastorate flashed through my head as I considered how I would tell our congregation. I soon realized that most of what I was thinking revolved around how I felt other people would view our family rather than how God wanted us to respond to this situation. It wasn't until my assistant pastor encouraged me to look to God for how He wanted all of us to grow through this that my focus changed. That year was a difficult one for us as we worked through various emotions, but ultimately God used that time to teach us a great deal about compassion, grace, forgiveness, and flexibility. These are lessons we could then share more fully with the other members of our home, as well as with our congregation.

The Reason for Trials

There is a reason for trials. God is very open about why He puts them in our path. How you respond to the trials in your life models to your children how they are to respond to their own trials. If you are constantly complaining, blaming others, or feeling sorry for yourself, you are showing your children that you do not trust in the sovereign hand of God. You are teaching them that there is no reason for trials.

Tenacity

by Chrystal Evans Hurst

I used to sneak out of my room at night and tiptoe quietly to the kitchen table where I'd be sure to find my dad with his books open—studying. Many times he'd be preparing for the Sunday sermon. Other times he studied for school. He finished up his doctorate when I was ten years old, which means I spent the first half of my childhood watching him balance quite a load. With a growing family, a growing local church, and a growing national ministry, I witnessed my dad work hard. I learned what tenacity looked like by watching him.

I've also watched my mother wear many hats. She always juggled many responsibilities over the years, and she looked good while doing it, too! I know now that keeping up with a busy husband and four active kids was no easy task. I know now that keeping our home while working in ministry or being in the workplace was probably exhausting. But she did it. My mother was and is an immaculate housekeeper. Our house, while furnished comfortably enough for us to feel at home, was also managed well enough for people to drop by—and wonder how she kept it all together. One morning, I vividly recall my mother coming into Priscilla's and my room to make our beds. She was crying. To this day, I don't know what caused those tears. But here's what I do know. She was making my bed. She wasn't in her own bed, under the covers, watching soap operas and eating bonbons. She was working diligently despite a difficult moment. And I now know that motherhood, marriage, and ministry have the potential for lots of difficult moments. I witnessed my mom work hard. I learned what tenacity looked like by watching her.

My prayer is that my children see me pressing through difficult times with the same tenacity my parents have. Doing hard things and continuing despite cloudy days is what lives worth living are made of. I've had my fair share of rough roads, but with the onset of trying terrain, my tendency is to keep going—because that's what I observed my mom and dad do.

Knowing there is a reason for our trials is critical. If your child is facing a trial and he or she cannot connect the experience with biblical truth, your child will be discouraged and overwhelmed rather than "consider[ing] it all joy" (James 1:2). That joy comes when, in the midst of trials, your child realizes that God is up to something great with him. And that realization is the key to enduring and overcoming trials.

The problem is not so much that your child will undergo trials—the real problem is if your child doesn't understand why. God wants your children to know that trials have three important purposes: to test their faith, to increase their tenacity, and to grow spiritually.

To Test Your Children's Faith

When your children experience hard times, God is putting their faith to the test. Anyone can say "I love you" to God when things are going well. But the test of that love comes when things are rocky. When God allows trials to touch your children, He does so for a specific purpose. Trials test the heart and reveal what is truly there. They show whether faith is young and still has a long way to grow, and they reveal where there has been growth already. Trials are designed to call faith to the witness stand to validate in experience what a person declares as a believer.

Trials are designed to call faith to the witness stand to validate in experience what a person declares as a believer.

The apostle Peter tells us that you and your child are "protected by the power of God" in terms of eternal salvation. But in the meantime, Peter says, you are distressed by "various trials, so that the proof of [your] faith . . . may be found to result in praise and glory and honor at the revelation of Jesus Christ" (1 Peter 1:6–7).

I'm sure you remember what it was like to be tested in school. A good teacher tests students only on information that has already been taught. A good teacher also wants the students to pass the test. This doesn't mean that trials don't hurt; they do. One of the worst things you can do to a child who is experiencing a trial is to minimize the reality of their pain. Yes, the pain is real. Yes, it ought to be validated. Overcoming a trial does not mean ignoring its presence. The essence of overcoming a trial means accepting the pain, learning from it, and discovering how to move on without diminishing one's faith.

To Increase Your Children's Tenacity

A second reason for trials is to increase your child's tenacity (see James 1:3). Again, it's an issue of maturing their faith. In Scripture, the word *endurance* is used. This word is comprised of two Greek words that mean "to remain under," or to stay put in a trial until its purpose has been accomplished.[1]

The Bible says we should not run from trials. Instead we are to run *in* them to develop our endurance and tenacity. Every so often, I get a painful, firsthand lesson in the importance of tenacity during trials. This occurs when I decide once again to start getting up early and going to the gym. I begin a weightlifting program on the very first day—curls, bench presses, the whole bit. Without fail, twenty-four hours later, I am experiencing a trial! I can't walk easily. In fact, I have sometimes been in so much pain that I had to have help buttoning my shirt. I can assure you, when I am in the first stages of that trial, I often want to run from it. I want it to stop. But because I have set my focus on the end goal, I remain in it even in the midst of the pain.

I'll never forget the year when my son Anthony dropped out of college. I was immediately frustrated when I sensed that he was quitting rather than simply wrestling through some adjustments. There were times that I didn't feel like talking with Anthony about his decision because I was too focused on my own disappointment. That's one way we "run from a trial"—we simply avoid addressing it. In the end, though, I had to swallow my own concerns and re-place them with an acknowledgment that he needed me to walk him through this period in his life. In the beginning I tried to force him to stay in school, but had I stayed in that mindset, I would have not modeled flexibility and resiliency when he did sit out a semester.

In the trials of life, God will put weights on your child, but He will also say, "Keep lifting. Don't quit, even though it will hurt for a while." Even if your child pushes pause on a project, a goal, or a decision in life—try not to label it as quitting, but instead look for the way God might be redirecting him or her. We often learn our greatest lessons in life during these times of adjustment. Just as in lifting weights, we sometimes have to adjust our grip or position to lift better. And if you keep on lifting weights, pretty soon you'll see spiritual muscles appear where only flab had been before.

To Grow Your Children Spiritually

Why does God test your children's faith in order to increase their tenacity in trials? So that "endurance [can] have its perfect result, so that you may be perfect and complete, lacking in nothing" (James 1:4).

God's goal for your children's trials is their growth into spiritual adulthood. That won't happen without some pain and effort. Imagine a young person announcing, "I want to be a doctor, but I don't want to spend all those years in medical school!" We know that's a ridiculous statement, but we often do the same when it comes to trials. We try to avoid them, and we distract ourselves from the pain rather than embrace it and allow it to strengthen our spiritual muscles. God wants to mature your children through trials, not just make them comfortable. He is too kind and too wise to allow your children to remain spiritually immature, whining whenever things don't go their way and demanding what they want when they want it. God's goal for your children is that they might "become conformed to the image of His Son" (Romans 8:29). And He will not be satisfied until your children get there.

> *God's goal for your children is that they might "become conformed to the image of His Son" (Romans 8:29).*

How to Respond to a Trial

What is the best way to respond to a trial? James first says that we are to respond with joy (James 1:2). Now, doesn't that sound a little far-fetched? How in the world can a person be joyful if his or her world is falling apart? This is exactly the question your children will ask you when you sit down to talk through this virtue with them. The answer comes in understanding that we cannot confuse joy with happiness. The Bible doesn't tell us to consider it all happiness when we encounter trials. It says to consider it all as joy. There's a big difference.

Happiness is triggered by circumstances. It describes that warm and excited feeling you get inside when everything is going your way. If you were to hand your child a million dollars in cash, there is no doubt that he or she would feel happy. But the happiest person alive doesn't necessarily have joy. Joy is more than an emotion; it is a life-changing mindset. Joy is a deep, abiding sense of well-being that can sustain your child even if he or she were to lose that million dollars.

The Declaration of Independence asserts our right to life, liberty, and the "pursuit of happiness." But being free to pursue happiness is no guarantee that we will find it. Finding it is no guarantee that we will keep it. Keeping it is no guarantee that we will appreciate it. Why? Because emotions are transient, unpredictable, and undependable. God wants to give us more than a "reasonable facsimile" of satisfaction. He wants us to have joy.

When trials come, teach your children to realize that God is up to something even greater. Help them to see that everything must first pass through God's hand before reaching them. There is nothing that happens to them in life where God says, "Oops, I didn't see that one coming." If God allowed it, then He has a purpose for it. Help your children to look for God's purpose in the pain—His treasure in the trial.

That doesn't mean teaching your children to avoid the pain or pretend they are happy when they aren't. Scripture doesn't tell us to *feel* joyful during trials; rather, we are to "consider" that trial as joy. The Greek word for *consider* is actually a term used in accounting that means "to evaluate," or "add it up."[2] That's what James is asking each of us to do during a trial. The trial and the pain may not make sense on their own, but we are to add it all up and evaluate it from an overall spiritual perspective and, in so doing, recognize that good will come. We are meant to recognize that there is a greater purpose for everything.

Your children's outlook will determine their outcome. Showing them that a right response to a trial sometimes hastens its ending is another way of teaching them to look at the greater good as being more valuable than the temporary loss or pain. This joy is a decision, not an emotion. When we consider it joy in trials, it demonstrates our faith in God's sovereignty. Secondly, because life has pain and none of us can avoid it, it is important to know how to approach that pain so a "root of bitterness" (Hebrews 12:15) does not spring up and choke out the abundant life.

Jesus is the great example here. The Bible says He endured the cross because He foresaw the joy of His resurrection, exaltation, and redemption of humanity (Hebrews 12:2). He wasn't happy about going to the cross. He prayed for His cup of suffering to pass if there was any way it could.

But He considered it all joy because He was accomplishing His Father's will by redeeming us from sin. Think about a mother in labor with her child. There is plenty of pain, but there is also plenty of joy. It's not a hopeless pain because she is focused on the greater good that will soon come.

Similarly, God uses trials in our lives to bring us to a greater good. When we teach our children to keep their eyes on Christ and the hope of His glory and goodness, we are teaching them how to respond to life's pain.

> *When we teach our children to keep their eyes on Christ and the hope of His glory and goodness, we are teaching them how to respond to life's pain.*

Another thing God instructs us to do in the face of trials is to ask for His help. James tells us that if we go to God for wisdom, He will freely and generously give it to us (1:5). What is the wisdom we need to ask God for? Wisdom to know how to handle the trial. Teach your children to pray for God's wisdom—but not halfheartedly. As James says, "But he must ask in faith without any doubting, for the one who doubts is like the surf of the sea, driven and tossed by the wind. For that man ought not to expect that he will receive anything from the Lord, being a double-minded man, unstable in all his ways" (1:6–8).

Wisdom, as we have already seen, is the ability to apply spiritual truth to life situations. A knowledgeable person has stored away a lot of information, but a wise person knows how to draw on that information to apply it to life. God freely gives wisdom when we ask.

Trials Bring About a Perfect Result

We read in James 1:4 that trials produce endurance and endurance brings about God's intended result: "And let endurance have its perfect result, that you may be perfect and complete, lacking in nothing."

One day a young boy discovered a cocoon in a backyard tree. He studied the cocoon carefully, seeking some sign of life. At last, several days later, the boy saw what he had been waiting for. Inside the filmy shell, a newly formed butterfly was struggling to get out. Filled with compassion for the tiny creature, the boy used his pocketknife to enlarge the hole.

Exhausted, the butterfly tumbled out and lay there. What the boy didn't know was that the struggle to escape was designed to strengthen the butterfly's muscle system and prepare it for flight. His act of "compassion" had inadvertently crippled and ultimately doomed the butterfly.

The night before He was crucified, Jesus prayed to His Father, asking Him not to take us out of the world, but to keep us safe *in* the world. The goal, Jesus realized, was not to steer us around trials, but to help us navigate safely through them. That concept may seem troublesome to both you as a parent and your children, because many of us have the mistaken idea that kingdom life should be trial-free. But that's just not true. Imagine a basketball player stumbling to the sidelines saying, "Well, coach, I would have scored. But every time I went up to make a shot, some guy from the other team had his hand in front of my face." It doesn't take a veteran coach to arrive at an answer: "The guy from the other team is supposed to have his hand in your face; that's the way the game is played. It is his job to do everything he can to prevent your success." In basketball, as in life, obstacles are inevitable.

God understands that the process of overcoming trials is just as important as the result. That's why He sometimes elects not to deliver us from certain situations. I remember taking my son Anthony to the doctor when he was young. When the diagnosis was rendered, a shot was prescribed. "No, Daddy," he yelled. "Don't let him stick me!" Tears welled up in his eyes. He couldn't understand why I was holding him down to get a painful shot. He thought that, as his father, I was his deliverer. I was definitely bigger than the doctor. Yet I allowed the doctor to give him the shot because I knew that he needed that shot to get well.

God will do the same with each of us in a trial if He knows that trial is producing a greater result. Knowing this, one of the greatest gifts you can give your child is the wisdom to understand the sovereignty of God and what trials are all about. Remember, parents, in helping your children to grow through their trials, God may be simultaneously growing you as well.

15

PURITY

To say that God puts a very high value on sexual purity is an understatement. The reason so many people give sex away so easily is that they don't know how valuable sexual purity is in God's eyes. Stuff you think is cheap, you throw away. Stuff you think is expensive, you hold on to.

A great tragedy today is that, if your kids are in public school, they are most likely getting some harmful, incorrect information about sex. Even if your school does not dispense condoms, the "safe sex" mentality still permeates a lot of what is taught. And this mentality often creeps into Christian schools as well. It's definitely prevalent in mainstream entertainment. So whether you want to address this topic with your children or not, giving them the tools to face this challenge and maintain their sexual purity is one of the most important things you can give them. You can't ignore it, because their bodies won't ignore it, however much you wish they would.

Sex is a legitimate and lawful passion given to us by God. As your children become teenagers, they will experience hormones that God placed there to serve His purposes of family, procreation, and pleasure at the appropriate time. Instead of pretending this reality doesn't exist, pray with and for your children that they will not be mastered by their legitimate and lawful sexual desires. Sex is a part of our God-given DNA, but it was never designed to be our master.

Sex is like a fire. Contained in the fireplace, a fire keeps everybody warm. Set the fire free, though, and the whole house burns. You don't want the fire in your house to have free rein. You want it contained so it can generate warmth but not destruction. Freedom does not mean doing whatever we *want* to do.

Freedom is doing what we *ought* to do—and not doing what we ought not to do.

Yes, Sex Is a Spiritual Issue

The body and the spirit are closely linked. For the Christian, sex is a spiritual issue. A person cannot worship God on Sunday and enter into sexual immorality on Monday and keep those separate, because the body—not just the spirit—is for the Lord. In fact, anytime a Christian engages in sexual activities, whether physically or even mentally, Christ is right there too. So is the Holy Spirit, and He is grieved.

One of the first things to teach your children regarding sexual purity is the primary reason behind it, which is that they have been bought with a very high price—the death and blood of Jesus Christ. They no longer belong to themselves; now Jesus Christ owns them. As a result, decisions they make with their body—whether it's piercings, substances they consume, or sexual activity—all should be considered in light of whether or not it glorifies the One to whom they belong. Paul wrote, "For you have been bought with a price: therefore glorify God in your body" (1 Corinthians 6:20). That's the bottom line question regarding multiple issues that relate to the body, because the body is the temple of the Holy Spirit.

In 1 Corinthians 6:18, Paul underscores the spiritual nature of sex: "Every other sin that a man commits is outside the body, but the immoral man sins against his own body." Sexual immorality is unlike any other sin because its destructive nature leaves lasting damage in one's own body.

Neither drugs nor crime can compare to sex in its destructiveness because sexual sin carries its own built-in, self-deteriorating issues. This stems from the reality that sex uniquely combines the physical and the spiritual.

The act of sex means that a spiritual relationship has taken place, a covenantal bond, which is designed to occur only within marriage. So in an illegitimate spiritual relationship (such as premarital sex), when one person backs out of it, he or she backs out with spiritual as well as physical and emotional scars. Oftentimes these then carry over into that person's next relationship, also affecting his or her personal self-esteem—which then impacts future decisions and dreams. Premarital sex robs youth of their future in more ways than just the risk of an unplanned pregnancy. It reshapes the way they think about others, themselves, and God. God places a great deal of value on virginity and sexual purity.

This is not a message your child will likely hear from his or her peers at school. Because of this, it is utterly important that you get in front of this area of temptation in his or her life by establishing a kingdom mindset toward sexual purity early on.

> *Sexual immorality is unlike any other sin because its destructive nature leaves lasting damage in one's own body.*

Sexual purity involves more than just staying away from the actual act of intercourse. In his letter to the church at Corinth, Paul addressed this issue head-on when he wrote, "It is good for a man not to touch a woman" (1 Corinthians 7:1). The word *touch* means "to light a fire," which came to be understood as a euphemism for sexual passion.[1] Paul tells us that it is good to not even light the fire.

The passionate love treatise found in the Song of Solomon speaks directly to the way to approach sexual purity with our youth. Protection in the form of supervision is needed in order to maintain sexual purity; it just doesn't happen by chance. As parents, we have to be intentional in this area that carries so much potential to run wild. As the Song of Solomon puts it, "We have a little sister, and she has no breasts; what shall we do for our sister on the day when she is spoken for? If she is a wall, we will build on her a battlement of silver; but if she is a door, we will barricade her with planks of cedar" (8:8).

These older siblings knew that when their younger sister was "spoken for," when that young man chose her as the object of his affection, the battle would begin. They spoke in terms of war and defense measures—barricading and creating a battlement. Sexual purity is to be guarded at all costs because of its extreme value.

God's idea is that the sexual relationship is to be preserved for one man and one woman in the context of marriage. Sex is not a way to say thank you for a nice evening. Sex was not given for people to release tension or explore a hobby. Sex is not just so people can feel good. God gave us sex to express a total commitment and covenantal surrender to another person.

Teach your children to wait until God gives them the person they are to marry. Pray with them for that person. Remind your children of their value, purity, and esteem on a regular basis. Remember that it is a very serious thing to unleash one's sexuality outside the safety of a lifelong, one-flesh marriage.

Sex Is Also a Chemical Issue

The sex act creates a covenantal and spiritual bond between two people and God. But sexual activity of any kind (not just intercourse) also creates a physiological bond between two people. Sex doesn't necessarily take place in the bedroom. Rather, it takes place in the chemical connections occurring in the limbic portion of the brain.[2]

There is a part of the brain called the diencephalon, which contains two other parts called the thalamus and hypothalamus. This might sound overly scientific, but within those areas of the brain, chemical reactions occur from the actions of viewing, hearing, smelling, seeing, cuddling, and arousal at any level, and the reactions are even greater when coupled with attraction. This is a highly complex mixture of chemicals, designed by God to bring about an intended response within our marriages. These chemicals are not contingent upon a marriage vow, however; they come about as a response to these different activities. As you can see, there is no such thing as safe sex. All arousal, at any level, produces a response that then alters the pathways of our brains. It can literally be called a chemical romance.

In marriage, this is all good. Outside of marriage, it's not. These chemical bonds can leave lasting scars, cravings, holes, and even symptoms of withdrawal. They can cause young adults to make impetuous decisions about marriage or getting engaged before they are adequately ready and prepared. Deeper heartbreak often results when a relationship falls apart, sometimes leaving the residual effects of excruciating pain due to the chemical cementing without commitment.

The Key to a Holy Sex Life
by Jonathan Evans

When I was seventeen years old, my father took me out for lunch so we could have a serious, one-on-one conversation about purity. He wanted me to clearly understand God's expectations as I was getting closer to leaving home and going off to college. He explained that God has called me to sanctification—to live and walk as one who believes. He continued explaining that God had not called me to sexual immorality and that impurity was the opposite of being sanctified. He told me that God had a world of living for me to access called godliness, but using the keys of impurity and immorality would not unlock that world. When the conversation was over, he pulled out a little box and slid it across the table for me to open. Inside was a gold necklace with a charm attached to it in the shape of a key. My initial response was certainly that of a typical seventeen–year-old young man. "Dad, this necklace looks like it's for a girl—do you really want me to wear this?"

Fortunately for me, my dad responded by letting me know that it was indeed for a girl. "It's for the girl that God has ordained for you to marry," he explained. He went on to reiterate to me that the key represented access, and had been designed for a specific lock. He explained that this key was to be given only to the woman that I would marry; she would be the God-created lock for my key. He ended our lunch by saying, "Take this key and access the kingdom of godliness rather than breaking into a world of impurity."

Not waiting for the spouse waiting for you in God's kingdom is simply gaining access to a place where you're not welcome. Like a burglar, you may have gotten in, but you won't be there long, and there are always consequences.

Our culture has decided not to use the key of purity, and all these unlawful break-ins have caused chaos in society today. Sexually-transmitted diseases, teenage pregnancies, single parenting, poverty, depression, suicide, and the breakdown of the family—which is the nucleus of the culture—have all been the result. In order to minimize the chaos, we must first minimize the break-ins. It's time for us to teach the next generation the importance of the kingdom key of purity.

Because chemicals are connected to the fluctuating ups and downs of broken relationships, they can be compared to stopping an addiction to heroin cold turkey. The desire, attachment, and withdrawal cravings remain simply due to the chemical impression made on the brain. If the decision to stop using heroin remained, another addictive chemical-producer would be required to satiate the craving and numb the pain. Thus, a cycle of addictive behaviors, or the symptoms related to trying to stop addictive behaviors—depression, confusion, and irritability—would occur.

In essence, heroin will have made a lasting impression, or groove, in the brain that doesn't go away simply because it is no longer around. A similar thing happens during premarital sexual activity. Pile up enough pain from the cementing and tearing apart, and the result is countless teens turning to sex again to alleviate the pain or fill the emptiness, or resorting to other forms of coping.

Scientific studies have enlightened us to the truth God's Word has taught us all along. When accompanied by physical attraction, these chemicals can be produced through something as seemingly innocent as engaged eye contact or subtle touching and hugs. This can be good—when appropriate. Oxytocin is a positive chemical God gave us to bring happiness and solidify connections in our lives and relationships.[3] It is only when high levels of oxytocin are associated with an illegitimate attachment with someone outside of marriage that they become damaging, especially when that relationship either ends or dissipates over time. Once that chemical is present and cemented on the brain, it is difficult to forget it, dismiss it, or satisfy it legitimately.

When Paul wrote to the citizens of Corinth at the height of the moral and spiritual decay in that society, it was as if he already knew about these chemical bonds. He said, "Or do you not know that the one who *joins* himself to a prostitute is one body with her?" (1 Corinthians 6:16).

Paul used the word *join,* which in the original language means "to glue together, cement."[4] Under the inspiration of the Holy Spirit, Paul's letter to the Corinthians was as scientifically sound as any article or study in the most recent medical and psychological journals of our day.

Sexual activity and the subsequent release of brain-imprinting, binding chemicals literally "glue" or "cement" people together. When those two people decide to part ways, a painful physiological reality occurs—primarily among females, whose limbic systems that house these chemical stores and grooves are generally larger than those of males.

When such a strong physiological reaction occurs in the brain, stopping the action is a challenge. And once stopped, going back to it happens more easily and more frequently. We might compare this to removing an alcoholic's favorite brand of beer, but then sending him back into a bar with countless other brands to choose from. Would he have stopped drinking his favorite brand of beer? Yes. But would he have the emotional, physical, and spiritual tools necessary to turn down the opportunity to try a different brand? Probably not.

I can't overemphasize the importance for kingdom parents to help their children grasp the spiritual need for sexual purity. This is an area where an ounce of prevention will be worth a lot more than just a pound of cure.

God's teaching on the sacredness of sex and the essential nature of keeping the sexual relationship pure, reserved for two married people joined by a covenantal commitment, is nothing to take lightly. Knowing how deeply addictive and cementing the sexual relationship is, God makes His warning clear: "Flee immorality. Every other sin that a man commits is outside the body, but the immoral man sins against his own body" (1 Corinthians 6:18). We actually sin against our own brains, let alone against our own bodies in light of all the potential diseases and the damage that can be done physically or spiritually.

When sex is kept sacred, it opens up the pathway toward true intimacy and knowing. But when sex is casually misused, it creates cemented bonds that, when broken, leave lingering symptoms of insecurity, pain, abandonment, disrespect for both self and others, and increased

Marriage is God's only method for safe sex.

neediness for another attachment—making personal relational boundaries less secure in future relationships as well.

In order to raise your kids according to the kingdom principle of sexual purity, you must encourage them to aim for the standard God has given us in His Word. Marriage is God's only method for safe sex. Parents, don't let the culture provide your children's sex education. Rather, educate them with age-appropriate skills and the wisdom necessary to live victoriously in this area of life.

16

SERVICE

It's hard to find full-service gas stations anymore unless you are in the Pacific Northwest; most stations throughout the US offer self-service only. I remember the days when someone would come out to pump the gas, wash the windows, and check the oil and the tires. Not anymore—in fact, these days you rarely see anyone at all. You just swipe your credit card, fill up your tank, and head on your way.

Unfortunately, what is true for filling stations nowadays is also true for God's people in many ways. Instead of individuals coming to worship service, they now show up to "worship selfish" . . . because it's all about them. They want the benefits and blessings of the kingdom without investing and serving in the kingdom. While there is nothing wrong with benefits or blessings in and of themselves, I find nothing in the Bible that says a blessing is ever to stop with the one being blessed. A blessing is always meant to go through—not just to—someone in order to benefit others as well. Our kids are growing up in a "me generation" like never before. Social media and easy access to so many things have cultivated in them a spirit that seeks to be instantly gratified as if that were normal.

Many parents raise children with the mindset that everyone around them is there to serve them. Returning to our Magic Kingdom metaphor from the beginning of this book, when you walk into the Magic Kingdom, you are greeted with ongoing smiles, employees helping you along the way, fun activities, tasty food, characters dressed up in costumes waving and giving hugs—and these days many of our children think all of life should operate that way.

Far too many of our children have been raised with a distorted prince and princess mentality that causes them to believe that the world in which they walk rotates around them. Upon reaching adulthood, though, they will receive a rude awakening. Not only does the real world not operate that way, neither does God's kingdom. We are royalty in God's kingdom, but His kingdom is not the Magic Kingdom—in God's kingdom Christ has called us to roll up our shirtsleeves and serve.

> *A blessing is always meant to go through— not just to—someone in order to benefit others as well.*

The Jesus who came to give us life abundantly is the same Jesus who asks us to take up our cross, and do so daily. Service ought to be a way of life—a service mindset in both you and your children because we were created to serve. We read in Ephesians, "For we are His workmanship, created in Christ Jesus for good works, which God prepared beforehand so that we would walk in them" (2:10). Good works involve actions or activities that benefit others while bringing glory to God. Essentially, good works mean service.

Whether that service involves a one-time action such as passing out additional Christmas presents to needy families or giving the mailman a bottle of water when he comes to your door in the summer, or whether it is a long-term commitment to the betterment of others, all service matters to God. When service is both a mindset and a virtue, your children will look for ways to serve on an ongoing basis throughout their lives.

In Galatians we read, "For you were called to freedom, brethren; only do not turn your freedom into an opportunity for the flesh, but through love serve one another" (5:13). One way we express our identity in Christ is through service. The freedom Jesus purchased for us on the cross is meant to be the catalyst for our service. A non-serving Christian is a contradiction.

When your children reach a certain age, you expect them to get a job. Up until then, you are more than happy to feed, clothe, and buy things for your children. After a certain age, though, it's your child's responsibility to get those new clothes they are wanting. The same holds true for us as children of the

King. There comes a time in our spiritual development and maturity when we are expected to serve. We must become contributors to God's kingdom agenda rather than merely takers.

A non-serving believer cannot fully receive all God has in store for him. If it's all about him, God loses interest in continuing to bless him. Yes, He still loves him, but if he is not furthering God's program and plan, God will look for someone else to bless. God saves a sinner so that sinner can then serve.

The freedom Jesus purchased for us on the cross is meant to be the catalyst for our service

What would you do with a refrigerator that didn't feel like getting cold, or a stove that didn't feel like getting hot, or a can opener that didn't feel like opening any cans? You would probably replace them with appliances that would work the way they were designed to work. You would have to conclude that the refrigerator, stove, and can opener simply didn't understand the reason why they had been chosen to be in your kitchen.

Christmas Service

by Priscilla Shirer

Christmas.

That one word conjures up a flurry of nostalgia for the Evans family. My mother, whom we affectionately call "Mrs. Claus" during the month of December, adores this holiday. She always has. The turkey from Thanksgiving would barely have been digested before she'd begin planning and prepping for the merriest time of the year. And part of that plan would leave an indelible imprint on my life, searing its life-lesson on my soul like a branding iron hot off the coals.

We *gave* gifts at Christmas.

Oh, we got them, too. Our tree hid a good number of treats under its branches, waiting for us to rush in and open them when the morning dawned on the twenty-fifth. But *before* that day, we'd already delivered gifts to someone else's home as well. We'd taken Christmas outside the walls of our own house.

Every year, my parents sought out a family whose children were similar in age to us who needed help with the holidays. Together, we'd purchase (or make) gifts, wrap them, and then go out to meet our new friends, spend time together, and share the goodies.

I remember it all so well, so clearly. As soon as we'd ring the doorbell and walk across the threshold into their home, it was like unwrapping a gift of our own. The eyes and countenance of the children would brighten, the shoulders of the weary mom would relax, the strained temples of the exhausted father would ease, and the home would pulse with an excitement and peace that bounded through the air like electricity on a live wire. Oh, what a joy it was! We walked away empty-handed—but far from empty-hearted.

It was one of the best Christmas presents any of us ever received, from then until now. We received a generous heart toward others. The gift of giving. The satisfaction of serving. And all because my parents made it a priority each year to strategically plan this family activity.

We've done the same thing in our own family so that our children also can know this unparalleled pleasure. Each December I take the boys shopping. They lay their too-long Christmas lists aside and walk down the store aisles in search of fulfilling someone else's wishes. I don't do the shopping for them lest I rob them of the pure delight that spills into their hearts when generosity dismantles the wall of self-centered hubris, brick by brick. *They* pray for the kids whose photos I tape to their bedroom door as we consider which gifts might suit which person. *They* pick out the gifts they most desire, resisting the urge to keep the best ones for themselves. And then *they* go with my husband and me to the family's home, so that *they* can know the joy of giving during a season known for receiving.

The surrender of service. It's not just a Christmas tradition. It's a kingdom family's legacy that the generations never need to outgrow.

Each of us as a child in the kingdom of God has been created with a purpose, and that purpose is to serve God. Yet far too many of us don't understand that purpose.

King David's epitaph ought to be the aim for each one of us, including our children: "For David, after he had served the purpose of God in his own generation, fell asleep, and was laid among his fathers" (Acts 13:36).

On the cross, Jesus Christ paid the price to purchase your children's salvation, but He didn't purchase it just so your children could sit, soak, and sour. Neither did He purchase it for your children to simply be the recipients of His blessings. He purchased it so that your children might glorify Him in all that they do (see 1 Corinthians 6:20). Like David, your children are called to do no less than serve the purpose of God in their own generation. Keep in mind that each of your children is called to serve "the purpose of God" in his or her life, not *your* purpose for them. Instead of telling them what *you* think they should be doing, help them to discover God's calling of service on their lives. One of my greatest struggles and areas of failure as a father was pushing my kids too hard, especially early on. I wanted them to be involved in areas of the church that had absolutely no interest to them. For instance, a couple of my kids enjoyed the youth choir, but others didn't. Forcing them to participate created a frustration for them rather than a desire in them to serve in the church. Thankfully Lois helped me to recognize this, and I learned not to "cookie-cutter" my kids into serving. Instead I sought to encourage them to plug in where they fit best.

Greatness Through Service

In Mark 10, we read about the time when Jesus dealt with His disciples with regard to their attitude toward greatness. Two of His disciples, James and John, had asked Jesus if they might be positioned to sit on his right and left side in the kingdom of God. They sought for their own greatness. And while there is nothing wrong with greatness itself—in fact, Jesus did not correct His disciples for their desire to be great—it's how a person is to go about becoming great that Jesus clarified:

Hearing this, the ten began to feel indignant with James and John. Calling them to Himself, Jesus said to them, "You know that those who are recognized as rulers of the Gentiles lord it over them; and their great men exercise authority over them. But it is not this way among you, but whoever wishes to become great among you shall be your servant; and whoever wishes to be first among you shall be slave of all. For even the Son of Man did not come to be served, but to serve, and to give His life a ransom for many." (Mark 10:41–45)

Jesus didn't say, "Don't have a desire to be great." He said, "If you want to become great, serve." That's how you do it. Instill in your children a desire for greatness, but also instruct them that this is achieved through the virtue of service. In God's kingdom, the way up the ladder is down.

When your children stand before Jesus at the judgment seat of Christ someday in order to receive rewards for their works, nowhere in the Bible does it say that God is going to check the Sunday school attendance sheet (although Sunday school is important for instilling godly virtues). But what is going to be checked is where and in what spirit your children served—how well they loved one another. How many glasses of cold water did your children give in Jesus' name (see Mark 9:41)?

Instill in your children a desire for greatness, but also instruct them that this is achieved through the virtue of service. In God's kingdom, the way up the ladder is down.

There's a careful distinction that must be made concerning service. Service that is done with the right heart attitude is service that is done expecting nothing in return. It is offered that Christ might be glorified. Doing something for someone else and then expecting them to do something for you in return is called business, not service. And while there is nothing wrong with doing business, we want our children to understand that it is service only when it is done simply to glorify God and help someone else. No matter how small the action, when accompanied by the right spirit of service, God takes notice. The Lord has called your child to a life of greatness, and that greatness comes by walking the pathway of service.

Humility

For service to truly be God-honoring, it must be cradled in a heart of humility. We read in Philippians:

> Do nothing from selfishness or empty conceit, but with humility of mind regard one another as more important than yourselves; do not merely look out for your own personal interests, but also for the interests of others. Have this attitude in yourselves which was also in Christ Jesus, who although He existed in the form of God, did not regard equality with God a thing to be grasped, but emptied Himself, taking the form of a bond-servant, and being made in the likeness of men. Being found in appearance as a man, He humbled Himself by becoming obedient to the point of death, even death on a cross. (Philippians 2:3–8)

Jesus existed in the form of God, but He did not regard that form as something to hold onto tightly. He denied that form; He just didn't embrace it so tightly that He couldn't lower Himself enough to serve someone else. Rather, He emptied Himself in order to pour Himself into others. The Greek word used for *bond-servant* in this passage is the word *doulos*, which means "slave."[1]

In Roman culture when Jesus lived, a slave was as low as you could go. We learn from this that Jesus wasn't content just to stick some extra cash or bags of food in His car in order to dole it out to a homeless person as He drove here or there. That's called charity, not service. Rather, He took on the form of a servant—in fact, the lowest form of a servant, that of being a slave. And as heirs and heiresses with Christ, we are to do no less. Your children are to do no less.

Parents, as you teach your children the essential virtue of servanthood, give them a heart of service. Give them a heart of sacrifice for their Savior and compassion for their neighbor. Let them witness you serving others, because it is in modeling this heart before them that you will be their greatest tutor. And let compassion be their guide.

Compassion

Scripture teaches us that authentic faith shows itself in compassion. But it's not just feeling compassion; we are called to have compassion in action—to be compassionate. It's visiting "orphans and widows in their distress" (James 1:27). The Greek word for *visit* in this verse doesn't mean to drop by once in a while to see how things are going. The word means "to care for people" and meet their needs.[2] True religion is not selfish. It helps those who can do nothing for us in return.

In the economy of the first-century world, orphans and widows were the most helpless people in society. They were the poorest of the poor. They often needed help, but they could offer those who helped them nothing in return. And because widows and orphans were basically powerless, they were often the victims of injustice. God warned His people to make sure they defend the helpless.

In Isaiah 1:11–17, God has some biting words for Israel. He begins by asking:

> "What are your multiplied sacrifices to Me?" says the LORD. "I have had
> enough of burnt offerings of rams and the fat of fed cattle; And I take
> no pleasure in the blood of bulls, lambs, or goats . . . Yes, even though
> you multiply prayers, I will not listen." (verses 11, 15)

What had Israel done to cause God to despise their sacrifices and prayers? Scripture goes on to tell the story: "Your hands are covered with blood" (verse 15).

In other words, Israel was a place where injustice flourished. The helpless were mistreated by the powerful. Things were so bad that the people's hypocritical acts of religious observance made God's stomach turn.

This is what He asked them to do in order to remedy the situation: "Wash yourselves, make yourselves clean; remove the evil of your deeds from My sight.

Cease to do evil, learn to do good; seek justice, reprove the ruthless, defend the orphan, plead for the widow" (verses 16–17).

To live out a faith that is valuable to God, we must reach out to those who cannot help themselves. That's what our heavenly Father did for us. When we were sinners and could do nothing for God in return, God in Christ became sin for us that we might become the righteousness of God in Him. God wants us to raise kingdom kids who will see to the needs of the helpless in the kingdom. It is in this way that our children will truly be image bearers of our King.

Compassion through service, though, not only motivates us to help those in need, it also encourages us to take ongoing responsibility for doing so. This is one place where the body of Christ has dropped a critical ball. We have turned over to the government our spiritual responsibility to care for the needy among us. Scripture asks the question, "What use is it, my brethren, if someone says he has faith, but he has no works? Can that faith save him?" (James 2:14). In other words, what good is a religion that is all talk? The call to serve the helpless and needy is a strong theme throughout Scripture and particularly in the New Testament. In 1 John we read:

> We know love by this, that He laid down His life for us; and we ought
> to lay down our lives for the brethren. But whoever has the world's
> goods, and sees his brother in need and closes his heart against him, how
> does the love of God abide in him? Little children, let us not love with
> word or with tongue, but in deed and truth. (1 John 3:16–18)

John says our faith must include both conviction and service. It's not a matter of one or the other; it's both. In Matthew 25:31–46, Jesus said the sheep saw Him hungry and thirsty and naked and a stranger and in prison—and met His needs. The goats saw Jesus in need but did nothing. The sheep will ask, "Lord, when did we see You [in need and serve You?]" Jesus will answer, "To the extent that you did it to one of these brothers of Mine, even the least of them, you did it to Me" (verse 40).

In other words, Jesus credits your account in heaven when you help people in need. In His day, widows and orphans were at the top of the "least of these" list. When you raise your kids with a heart to help the helpless, you set them up to reap God's blessings in their lives.

One way I modeled this mindset for my kids was to reach out to a young boy from a single-parent home whose father wasn't around. I'd often invite him to join us at family devotions and meals, or I'd make sure he sat with us as a family in church. This kind of lifestyle-mentoring can be done simply by including those around you in your normal activities.

We've encouraged members of our church to be intentional about mentoring through our church-school partnership outreach. Every year we send hundreds of mentors into the public schools to share life, give advice, and impact those who are at risk for poor decisions due to a broken or unstable home. We also mentor youth through our church sports program, with over a thousand kids participating each year on our church campus, as well as in other ways. Our church has been doing this for over twenty-five years, and we continue to see the fruit as non-college-bound kids get a glimpse of hope that alters their course, ultimately ushering in their God-given destinies.[3] Many of our mentors cultivate relationships that run deeper than a program because they are birthed in a spirit of authentic service and love.

Paul, who modeled servanthood at great personal cost, asks us to have Christ's mind when we serve as well. This is not a mindset of charity, where we give out of our excess to meet someone in want. Serving is giving of yourself to meet the needs of those around you on an ongoing basis. While Christ is the King of Kings, He humbled Himself to the point of death. What He gave cost Him dearly. Jesus served because He possessed a worldview that looked beyond the present. He didn't see only the cross, He also saw the victory the cross and resurrection would secure. He didn't see only the pain; He also saw you and me living in salvation. He saw your children.

We have been given a great and wonderful gift through Christ's service on the cross: eternal life. All He asks in return is that we have the same mindset He was willing to have Himself—a mindset of service.

Parents, servanthood is a powerful tool for a kingdom kid. It can take them far because God gives grace to the humble and exalts those who serve, as He exalted Jesus. Yes, God desires to bless your children, but He also desires this blessing to extend beyond your children to others. He desires that, as a result of having been saved and subsequently blessed, your children will have this spirit within them—the very mindset of Christ—in order to serve others.

I enjoy old Westerns from time to time, and one of my favorites is *The Hanging Tree* starring Gary Cooper. In it, Cooper plays a young doctor who, at one point in the film, comes across a young cowboy who has been shot. Cooper takes out his knife, cuts the man open, and removes the bullet, thus saving the man's life. After the doctor cares for the cowboy during his recovery, the cowboy eventually recovers and is healthy again.

The cowboy asks the doctor what he can do to repay the doctor for saving his life. The doctor replies that the cowboy can be his assistant.

The cowboy then wonders how long the doctor might want him to do this service in exchange for him saving his life. To this, the doctor replies that he wants the cowboy to serve him for the rest of his life, since that's precisely how long he would have been dead.[4]

Jesus Christ has paid the price for the salvation of your children for all eternity. When your children trust Him for their salvation, they receive that gift. Serving Christ for a gift of that length shouldn't be a struggle. God shouldn't have to beg those He has saved to serve Him in return. These days He does have to beg, though, because we have raised a generation that has forgotten what He did for them, and we have raised them with the mindset that God owes them something in return for whatever they do.

This concept reminds me of a young boy who wrote his mom a note one day before heading off to school. After he left, his mom found the note lying on the counter in the kitchen. It read:

Dear Mom,
For cleaning my room, you can pay me $5.00.
For cleaning the garage, $5.00.
For raking the leaves, $5.00.
For taking the stuff to the attic, $5.00.
For babysitting my little brother, $5.00.
Mom, you owe me $25.

The next morning when it was time for the young boy to leave for school, he found a note in the same place he had left his own. It read:

Dear Son,
For carrying you in my womb nine months, no charge.
For staying up with you all night when you were sick, no charge.
For losing money to take off from work to be with you when you got in trouble, no charge.
For working overtime in order to get the money you needed to buy the sports uniform so you could play the sport you wanted to, no charge.
For all of this, and more, no charge.
Son, you owe me nothing, because I love you.

As we saw earlier in Galatians, we have been justified freely by God's grace. God shouldn't have to pay us to serve—He has given us an eternity of grace already. God shouldn't have to plead with us to serve, either.

Kingdom parents, train your children in this virtue so they will actively search out opportunities to serve out of gratitude for what God has already done. It is this heart that will truly propel your children into a life of greatness.

For the kingdom of God belongs to such as these.

17

USING ALL
YOUR ARROWS

Because I'm a pastor, parents facing difficult situations in their homes or marriages regularly ask me how God is going to show up and transform whatever challenge they are in. My answer is always the same: "I don't know. But what I do know is this: When God tells you to cross the Jordan, you'd better start walking, and let Him work it out."

God rarely starts working things out until He sees you respond to what He has asked you to do. God responds when you walk by faith, not when you wish by faith. You can't exercise faith in a rocking chair. A rocking chair makes you comfortable, but it doesn't take you anywhere. Far too many parents are satisfied with comfortable homes at the expense of creating families who will carry out God's agenda and advance His kingdom on earth.

God has as many methods for restoring or strengthening your home and your children as there are stars in the sky. He is the great "unfigureoutable" God. He knows how to fix things, tweak things, and turn things that are upside down right-side up again. He can turn kid situations around on a dime, stabilize your marriage, and heal wounds that have festered for years, or even decades. The problem comes when we try to figure out *how* He's going to do it—or when we resist how He is doing it.

God may lead you one way in a situation and a totally different way in another very similar situation. When David fought the Philistines in the Valley of Rephaim the first time, God told him to go directly up against them and He would give them into his hands (see 2 Samuel 5:17–21).

Yet in the very next battle, which took place when the Philistines once again invaded the very same Valley of Rephaim, God told David, "You shall not go directly up," but rather he was to, "circle around behind them and come at them in front of the balsam trees." God instructed David that when he heard "the sound of the marching in the tops of the balsam trees, then you shall act promptly, for then the LORD will have gone out before you to strike the army of the Philistines" (2 Samuel 5:23–24).

> *God responds when you walk by faith, not when you wish by faith.*

In the first battle, David was to engage the enemy head-on. In the second battle, David was to wait until he heard the breeze blowing in the trees. I imagine that is not something David would have learned at the Holy Land Battle Academy. I'm pretty sure David never attended a combat-strategy class on "Breeze Blowing in the Trees."

God's ways are not our ways. Yet within the constancy of change remains one element that never changes: God will respond to your faith. God will frequently either increase or limit what He does in response to what you do.

Arrows in the Quiver

As you begin your journey of parenting, continue it, or perhaps are ready to launch your children out on their own, I want to leave you with one last thought. The calling of parenthood is a high one. To do it well takes more than what you have to offer on your own. But never lose sight of the fact that when God called people to do something spectacular in the Bible, the thing He called them to do was typically larger than themselves. He called Abraham to be the father of a mighty nation. He called David to single-handedly defeat someone twice his size with one small stone. He called Moses to part the Red Sea.

And He is calling you to raise kingdom kids.

You will often know that it is God asking you to do something if it is something you cannot do on your own. You cannot discover how big God is unless you need Him for something bigger than you can handle. Raising kingdom kids in today's culture of mayhem and mess is something bigger than any of us can handle on our own. It will be done well only through a spirit and heart of humility that knowingly depends on God and follows His ways and precepts.

As individuals, we often can do great things in terms of our human abilities, but only God gets the glory when He pulls off what you could have never done on your own. And frequently He pulls it off in response to your forward movement in faith. To parent well is a joint venture with God.

Shortly before the prophet Elisha died, King Joash of Israel came to him in panic. He was under attack by the Arameans, and he grew terrified that he was not prepared to win the battle. The scent of defeat and disaster wafted on the winds from a distance. A pure analysis of the numbers told Joash quickly that he was on the losing side

Never lose sight of the fact that when God called people to do something spectacular in the Bible, the thing He called them to do was typically larger than themselves.

of this battle. Everything that was available to him was not enough to win this war. So, in desperation, the king went to Elisha for help. Even though the king was facing a physical, tangible military crisis, he sought a spiritual solution.

Elisha responded by telling the king to take his bow and arrows and place his hands on them. When he did, Elisha then placed his own hands on top of the king's. By doing so, he merged the spiritual with the physical, inviting heaven's viewpoint to impact earth.

Next, Elisha instructed the king to open the window that faced toward the east—where his enemy waited—and shoot an arrow out of it. When the king did, Elisha said, "The LORD's arrow of victory, even the arrow of victory over Aram; for you will defeat the Arameans at Aphek until you have destroyed them" (2 Kings 13:17).

In this passage Elisha gave the king a prophetic word. He gave him exactly what he needed in the midst of a crisis: the ability to see the spiritual side of the issue. If all you see is the issue itself, you will inevitably see defeat. But when you are able to see what God sees, it gives you the opportunity to conduct yourself in light of that truth. Keep in mind that it is only an opportunity, though, because God never forces you to have faith. If He did, it would negate the very faith He forced you to have.

After this, Elisha told the king to take his remaining arrows, which he did. Elisha instructed him to "strike the ground," which the king also did (see 2 Kings 13:18). But then came the problem. In the king's fear-induced haste, or out of self-preservation—we don't know the reason—he did not act on the prophetic word Elisha had just given him, which declared his victory. Rather, the text tells us that "he struck it three times and stopped" (2 Kings 13:18).

This made Elisha very angry, and he rebuked Joash by saying, "You should have struck five or six times, then you would have struck Aram until you would have destroyed it. But now you shall strike Aram only three times" (2 Kings 13:19).

Kingdom parent, the lesson of King Joash teaches us this: Most of the time God's promises are in your reach. They are not in your hand. Like Joshua, who had been promised every place the sole of his foot touched, and like this king, you have to go and get them. God's promises for your family, future, your kids, and more don't come by you simply sitting around waiting for them. They require you to act in faith, to live out the principles taught in this book, and more—to diligently train your children in God's truth.

> *God's promises for your family, future, your kids, and more don't come by you simply sitting around waiting for them. They require you to act in faith.*

With the first arrow that Elisha called "the LORD's arrow of victory," the promise of victory for King Joash had been established. Yet the king was told to shoot more arrows out the window. We know that at a minimum he had at least six arrows in his quiver because of what Elisha said to him. But the king chose to shoot only three. Maybe he wanted to save his remaining arrows for the upcoming battle. Maybe he didn't want them damaged, or maybe he didn't want to have to retrieve them or lose them altogether. The king was obviously covering himself in keeping back a few of his arrows. Yet for whatever reason, the prophet gave him an instruction, and he held back. He quit long before he should have.

Passing the Baton
by Tony Evans

In any relay race, the outcome depends entirely upon the passing of the baton. Miss this, and everything else is a waste of time. In parenting, passing the baton to your children includes the transference of kingdom values. In this way, you prepare the next generation to run and continue the kingdom race well. It is to be part of the inheritance that parents are to leave to not only their children but also to their grandchildren (Proverbs 13:22).

We hope you'll consider intentionally discipling your children throughout their growing-up years. A good way to do that is by using materials such as puzzles, games, devotionals, magazines, and workbooks, such as our *Kingdom Quest* strategy guides.

Children are a blessing from the Lord, but as I said earlier in the book, they are the one blessing we often seek to limit. However, when we view the great call and purpose of parenting through the kingdom lens of dominion and advancement of the glory of Christ, we will see the blessing for all it truly is and can be.

It is my prayer that as you have read the words of Lois and my four kids, you have been inspired to see and hear your own children one day saying similar things of you, and to live lives rooted in the solid foundation of God's Word. There is nothing more satisfying than to experience your children walking with the Lord. May you pass the baton well.

All of us as parents, to one degree or another, can identify with this king. After all, children are described as arrows in our quiver in the Bible:

> Behold, children are a gift of the LORD, the fruit of the womb is a reward. Like arrows in the hand of a warrior, so are the children of one's youth. How blessed is the man whose quiver is full of them; they will not be ashamed when they speak with their enemies in the gate. (Psalm 127:3–5)

At some point we all have found ourselves under attack—overwhelmed by circumstances and situations coming against our families and our homes, and even our kids, with no earthly solution in sight. There has never been a time like this in our nation when so many parents feel so helpless and defeated. In myriad ways, many families today are mirroring this king, concerned about the attacks they are facing.

Yet many parents are quitting way too early as well.

They are trying to mix "God's way" by shooting a few arrows out the window with "their way" by making sure they have enough arrows remaining should they need to figure it out for themselves. These parents, like the king, are too afraid to empty their quiver in faith. When it comes down to whether or not parents will, few do.

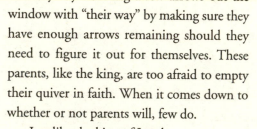

What God makes legal through His covenantal chesed love, you must make literal. You must bring its reality from heaven to earth.

Just like the king of Israel.

We want a little bit of God.

And a little bit of us.

Just in case.

But God rarely drops His promises into our laps. What God makes legal through His covenantal *chesed*[1] love, you must make literal. You must bring its reality from heaven to earth. You must usher in what God has promised with regard to your children by participating in the grand drama called *movement*.

Because the king chose to use only part of what he had, he received only part of what had been promised. Don't let that happen to you as you raise your kids.

The promises for your children are true, and the promises are complete. But rarely do these promises come without your participation. You must raise kingdom kids, not just birth them. Oftentimes, the level of your participation in how they are raised affects how they will experience God's promises for their lives in His kingdom. God does not negate His promises, yet neither does He force your participation in order to receive their full manifestation.

When you attended high school or college, you were promised a degree when you completed your course of study. However, your participation in the process was what ushered in the reality of the promise.

If you buy a toaster and bring it home, the marketing verbiage surrounding that toaster promises to supply you with toasted bread. But you still must plug it in. You still must put the bread in. You still must push it down for it to start toasting. There are things you must do to fully benefit from the promise of the toaster.

King Joash's problem was real. His problem was big. I know that whatever you might be facing as a parent is real as well, and that it is also big. But don't quit. Don't throw in the towel. Don't let the failures of yesterday negate your tomorrows. God can hit a bull's-eye with a crooked stick. When God gives you His perspective on what He would have you do, go ahead. Do it. Don't merge what He says with what your friends say, what you hear on TV, or what your kids say—or even with what you think. You already have the answer.

Don't let the failures of yesterday negate your tomorrows.

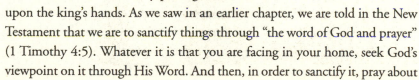

But if you have not made a spiritual connection to everything you do in your role of parenting, then you will not see God's ways. Elisha sanctified the arrows by placing his hands upon the king's hands. As we saw in an earlier chapter, we are told in the New Testament that we are to sanctify things through "the word of God and prayer" (1 Timothy 4:5). Whatever it is that you are facing in your home, seek God's viewpoint on it through His Word. And then, in order to sanctify it, pray about how to apply it—and then do it. Maybe that means studying God's Word for yourself, or in the context of other believers, but know that God will guide you and direct you if you seek Him with your whole heart.

Parents, we can no longer be satisfied with halfhearted measures. If we have six arrows and God wants six arrows, then that means we shoot six arrows. As parents, we must be all in when it comes to parenting. We must parent on purpose by fulfilling all that God has created us to do in order to replicate His image on earth in our children as we send them out in His name. We must empty our quivers well.

God is not going to force kingdom kids on you. You have to diligently raise them based on what He has revealed to you through His Word and through the confirmation of His Spirit. That is, unless you are satisfied with having a half-victorious kind of home.

A lot of people talk about a victory kind of life for themselves and their families. They can wax eloquent on the omnipotence and power of God. Depending on where you are on a Sunday morning, they can even shout it. But too few homes have ever experienced God's ongoing victory as more than a theoretical concept or a theological axiom. Too few parents have ever laid claim to their legitimate authority and destiny as leaders in their home. Too few parents wholeheartedly embrace God's promises combined with fulfilling their own responsibilities. Too few families dare to empty their quivers in faith. Most parents keep an arrow or two of worldly wisdom nearby, which is exactly why many children end up living empty and defeated lives, often camouflaged by erroneous definitions of success given to them by our culture.

We must empty our quivers well.

It takes faith to raise a kingdom family. It takes complete and total dedication to God's Word and His ways. It takes intimacy with Christ and fellowship with the Holy Spirit. It takes the intentional training and discipleship of your children and keeping them ever before God in a heart of prayer. No parent will ever do this perfectly. I know I didn't—I made many mistakes. But that's the great thing about God. When you commit your ways to Him and make His will and glory the desire of your heart, He makes up the difference in all the places you lack. If your kids have gone off course and you have done all that God has asked you to do, then pray for a strong wind from heaven to blow them back to Him. Make sure you keep the light on so they will always know that home eagerly awaits their return (Luke 15:11–32).

May you apply the truths in this book to your parenting adventure and receive God's favor and hand of blessing as you do. That is my prayer for you. And may you truly raise kingdom kids who will serve their King with such hearts of faith that they will one day also be able to empty their own quivers well.

CONCLUSION

If you are a responsible adult, most likely you have a will. In your will, you have taken the initiative to let people know what should happen to your belongings and your finances once you are no longer here. This preplanning on your part will prevent confusion, chaos, and conflict when it comes time for you to pass on what you are leaving behind on earth.

Just as adults make physical wills letting others know what should be passed on to the next generation, we as parents are to live our lives in light of a spiritual will. We are to focus on those attributes, qualities, and principles we want to pass on to the next generation. We must put forth effort to secure these spiritual treasures for ourselves and make sure they are passed down to our children and grandchildren.

In a physical will, you are not free to pass on something you yourself do not own. You don't include other people's things in your will. Similarly, as parents raising kingdom kids, the most important thing you can do is to maintain and grow in your own faith so you have something authentic to pass down to your kids. By doing this, you are willing them a living faith. You are giving them something they can possess internally and take with them for the rest of their lives.

Parents, don't merely leave something *to* your children; leave something *in* them.

Whatever else you pass on to your children, if you miss passing on the spiritual legacy of a living faith—everything else is in trouble. In the book of Judges, we discover what it looks like when a living faith is not passed down: "All that generation also were gathered to their fathers; and there arose another generation after them who did not know the LORD, nor yet the work which He had done for Israel" (2:10).

Throughout the remainder of the book of Judges, we see the devolution of a nation, communities, families, and individuals due to the fact that the next generation "did not know the LORD." The next generation did not know

God, His ways, or His works, and the result was chaos in the culture. That is why kingdom parenting is so important. Like a water filter in your home, your job as parents is to filter out that which leads your children away from the Lord in order to instill the purity of His Word in their hearts and minds. As the psalmist records: "I will sing of the lovingkindness of the LORD forever; to all generations I will make known your faithfulness with my mouth" (89:1).

> *Parents, don't merely leave something to your children; leave something in them.*

In making His faithfulness known through all that you do as a parent, you will be giving your children the greatest gift—a spiritual will—the legacy of a living faith. You will, in fact, be raising kingdom kids.

APPENDIX 1:
THE URBAN ALTERNATIVE

Dr. Tony Evans and The Urban Alternative (TUA) *equips, empowers,* and *unites* Christians to impact *individuals, families, churches,* and *communities* through a thoroughly kingdom agenda worldview. In teaching truth, we seek to transform lives.

The core cause of the problems we face in our personal lives, homes, churches, and societies is a spiritual one; therefore, the only way to address it is spiritually. We've tried a political, social, economic, and even a religious agenda.

It's time for a *Kingdom agenda.*

The Kingdom agenda can be defined as the visible manifestation of the comprehensive rule of God over every area of life.

The unifying central theme throughout the Bible is the glory of God and the advancement of His kingdom. The conjoining thread from Genesis to Revelation—from beginning to end—is focused on one thing: God's glory through advancing God's kingdom.

When you do not have that theme, the Bible becomes disconnected stories that are great for inspiration but seem to be unrelated in purpose and direction. The Bible exists to share God's movement in history toward the establishment and expansion of His kingdom highlighting the connectivity throughout which is the kingdom. Understanding that increases the relevancy of this several-thousand-year-old manuscript to your day-to-day living, because the Kingdom is not only then, it is now.

The absence of the kingdom's influence in our personal and family lives, churches, and communities has led to a deterioration in our world of immense proportions:

- People live segmented, compartmentalized lives because they lack God's Kingdom worldview.
- Families disintegrate because they exist for their own satisfaction rather than for the Kingdom.
- Churches are limited in the scope of their impact because they fail to comprehend that the goal of the church is not the church itself, but the Kingdom.
- Communities have nowhere to turn to find real solutions for real people who have real problems, because the church has become divided, ingrown, and unable to transform the cultural landscape in any relevant way.

The kingdom agenda offers us a way to see and live life with a solid hope by optimizing the solutions of heaven. When God, and His rule, is no longer the final and authoritative standard under which all else falls, order and hope leaves with Him. But the reverse of that is true as well: As long as you have God, you have hope. If God is still in the picture, and as long as His agenda is still on the table, it's not over.

Even if relationships collapse, God will sustain you. Even if finances dwindle, God will keep you. Even if dreams die, God will revive you. As long as God, and His rule, is still the overarching rule in your life, family, church, and community, there is always hope.

Our world needs the King's agenda. Our churches need the King's agenda. Our families need the King's agenda.

In many major cities, there is a loop that drivers can take when they want to get somewhere on the other side of the city, but don't necessarily want to head straight through downtown. This loop will take you close enough to the city so that you can see its towering buildings and skyline, but not close enough to actually experience it.

This is precisely what we, as a culture, have done with God. We have put Him on the "loop" of our personal, family, church, and community lives. He's close enough to be at hand should we need Him in an emergency, but far enough away that He can't be the center of who we are.

We want God on the "loop," not the King of the Bible who comes downtown into the very heart of our ways. Leaving God on the "loop" brings about dire consequences, as we have seen in our own lives and with others. But when we make God, and His rule, the centerpiece of all we think, do, or say, it is then that we will experience Him in the way He longs to be experienced by us.

He wants us to be kingdom people with kingdom minds set on fulfilling His kingdom's purposes. He wants us to pray, as Jesus did, "Not my will, but Thy will be done." Because His is the kingdom, the power, and the glory.

There is only one God, and we are not Him. As King and Creator, God calls the shots. It is only when we align ourselves underneath His comprehensive hand that we will access His full power and authority in all spheres of life: personal, familial, church, and community.

As we learn how to govern ourselves under God, we then transform the institutions of family, church, and society from a biblically based kingdom worldview.

Under Him, we touch heaven and change earth.

To achieve our goal we use a variety of strategies, approaches, and resources for reaching and equipping as many people as possible.

Broadcast Media

Millions of individuals experience *The Alternative with Dr. Tony Evans* through the daily radio broadcast playing on nearly one thousand radio outlets and in over one hundred countries. The broadcast can also be seen on several television networks and is viewable online at TonyEvans.org. You can also listen to or view the daily broadcast by downloading the Tony Evans app for free in the App store. Over four million message downloads occur each year.

Leadership Training

The *Tony Evans Training Center* (TETC) facilitates educational programming that embodies the ministry philosophy of Dr. Tony Evans as expressed through the kingdom agenda. The training courses focus on leadership development and discipleship in the following five tracks:

- Bible and Theology
- Personal Growth
- Family and Relationships
- Church Health and Leadership Development
- Society and Community Impact Strategies

The TETC program includes courses for both local and online students. Furthermore, TETC programming includes course work for non-student attendees. Pastors, Christian leaders, and Christian laity, both local and at a distance, can seek out The Kingdom Agenda Certificate for personal, spiritual, and professional development. Some courses are valued for CEU (Continuing Education Unit) credit as well as viable in transferring for college credit with our partner school(s).

Kingdom Agenda Pastors (KAP) provides a viable network for like-minded pastors who embrace the Kingdom agenda philosophy. Pastors have the opportunity to go deeper with Dr. Tony Evans as they are given greater biblical knowledge, practical applications, and resources to impact individuals, families, churches, and communities. KAP welcomes senior and associate pastors of all churches. KAP also offers an annual Summit held each year in Dallas with intensive seminars, workshops, and resources.

Pastors' Wives Ministry, founded by Dr. Lois Evans, provides counsel, encouragement, and spiritual resources for pastors' wives as they serve with their husbands in the ministry. A primary focus of the ministry is the KAP Summit that offers senior pastors' wives a safe place to reflect, renew, and relax along with training in personal development, spiritual growth, and care for their emotional and physical well-being.

Community Impact

National Church Adopt-A-School Initiative (NCAASI) prepares churches across the country to impact communities by using public schools as the primary vehicle for effecting positive social change in urban youth and families. Leaders of churches, school districts, faith-based organizations, and other nonprofit organizations are equipped with the knowledge and tools to forge partnerships and build strong social service delivery systems. This training is based on the comprehensive church-based community impact strategy conducted by Oak Cliff Bible Fellowship. It addresses such areas as economic development, education, housing, health revitalization, family renewal, and racial reconciliation. We assist churches in tailoring the model to meet specific needs of their communities while simultaneously addressing the spiritual and moral frame of reference. Training events are held annually in the Dallas area at Oak Cliff Bible Fellowship.

Athlete's Impact (AI) exists as an outreach both into and through the sports arena. Coaches are often the most influential factor in young people's lives, even ahead of their parents. With the growing rise of fatherlessness in our culture, more young people are looking to their coaches for guidance, character development, practical needs, and hope. Athletes are next on the influencer scale after coaches. Athletes (whether professional or amateur) influence younger athletes and kids within their spheres of impact. Knowing this, we have made it our aim to equip and train coaches and athletes on how to live out and utilize their God-given roles for the benefit of the Kingdom. We aim to do this through our iCoach App and weCoach Football Conference as well as resources such as *The Playbook: A Life Strategy Guide for Athletes*.

Resource Development

We are fostering lifelong learning partnerships with the people we serve by providing a variety of published materials. Dr. Evans has published more than one hundred unique titles based on over forty years of preaching, whether that is in booklet, book, or Bible study format. The goal is to strengthen individuals in their walk with God and service to others.

* * *

For more information
and a complimentary copy of Dr. Evans's devotional newsletter,
call (800) 800-3222;
or write TUA at PO Box 4000, Dallas, TX 75208;
or visit us online at www.TonyEvans.org.

APPENDIX 2:
A MESSAGE TO SINGLE PARENTS

The story of Hagar has some real-life lessons for single parents.[1] We first meet Hagar in Genesis 16, where she was the servant of Sarai, who, along with her husband, Abram (this was just before their names were changed), was unable to have children.

In the custom of their day, barren women in Sarai's situation would bring in another woman who would bear the husband's child and thus act as a surrogate. Hagar became a surrogate for Sarai.

When Hagar got pregnant Sarai became jealous and drove Hagar out of the house. Pregnant and alone, with no Abram or any other male to support and protect her, she found herself wandering in the wilderness. Hagar was about to become a single parent because she got caught in someone else's plan.

But then the Angel of the Lord (Jesus preincarnate) went out to the wilderness for the benefit of this single mother-to-be. In other words, Jesus showed up. That was good news for Hagar.

If you are a single parent, that's also good news for you. When you have been rejected, when the father or mother of your child is nowhere to be found, God knows the situation you are in, and He knows where to find you. He loves you and has great compassion on you. When you hurt, He feels it. He knows your loneliness, stigma, and pain. After all, He experienced the fullness of all three on the cross.

When God showed up He told Hagar to name her son Ishmael, which meant "God hears and God knows." Every time she would use that name, she would remember something about God. That's the beauty of the grace of God for a single parent. Hagar is out on her own with no help, but God says, "I know."

In verse 13 Hagar responded. Giving God the name *El Roi*[2] she declared, "Thou art a God who sees."

Do you know that God sees you? That He sees the circumstances you are in, out there in the desert all alone with no one to provide for you, give you spiritual and emotional covering, and protection? He is not unaware of what you are going through. No matter what you are going through, God says, "I see. I hear. I know."

The saga of Hagar does not end here. In Genesis 21 we see that Hagar, instructed by the Lord, has gone back to Sarah. By now Sarah has had Isaac, the son God had promised her and Abraham (their names had been changed by then also).

One day when Sarah saw Ishmael making fun of Isaac (see verse 9), she said in effect, "Not in my house you won't!" She had Abraham send them away. Hagar, along with her son, was homeless again and left to wander in the wilderness alone. Now, she was a bona fide single mother.

This is a classic single-parent scenario—one that, with a few changes of detail and geography, could easily be repeated today. Hagar lost her home, she had a teenage son to take care of, and she was on the streets, so to speak, with no money in her pockets. She was thirsty and probably hungry. She feared that her boy would die. In despair she sat down and cried.

When the Son of God showed up again, He asked Hagar, "What is the matter with you?" (verse 17). He was in effect saying, "Hagar, have you forgotten what I did for you earlier? How I found you out in the wilderness when you were pregnant and Sarah had chased you away? Do you think I am going to remember you one minute and forget you the next? You yourself said I am the God who sees. Do you think that now I have gone blind?"

Single parent, God has not gone blind. He sees, He hears, and He knows. You may be in a far-from-ideal situation, but you have an ideal God.

Single mother, the greatest thing you can do is have a passion for God, because when you have a passion for God, you have Someone who will be a Father to your child and a Husband and protector to you. Single father, when you know God, you have Someone to lean on who understands a father's heart and desires for his children.

As He was with Hagar, so is He with you . . . the God who sees and knows and cares.

ACKNOWLEDGMENTS

I want to express my heartfelt gratitude to Focus on the Family and Tyndale House Publishers for the support, commitment, and excellence they have given to this work.

SCRIPTURE INDEX

NOTES

Chapter 1: This Isn't the Magic Kingdom

1. Mike Devlin, "10 Real-Life Disney Deaths," Listverse.com, March 27, 2013, http://listverse.com/2013/03/27/10-real-life-disney-deaths/.

2. *Education Week*, "Dropouts," August 2, 2004, updated June 16, 2011, http://www.edweek.org/ew/issues/dropouts/; for an easy-to-read chart summarizing the *Education Week* data, see Statistic Brain, "High School Dropout Statistics," January 1, 2014, http://www.statisticbrain.com/high-school-dropout-statistics/.

3. The National Campaign to Prevent Teen and Unplanned Pregnancy, "Counting It Up: The Public Costs of Teen Childbearing," accessed May 13, 2014, http://thenationalcampaign.org/why-it-matters/public-cost#.

4. Steve McSwain, "Why Nobody Wants to Go to Church Anymore," *The Huffington Post*, October 14, 2013, http://www.huffington post.com/steve-mcswain/why-nobody-wants-to-go-to_b_4086016.html.

5. Byron Pitts, "Hidden America: Heroin Use Has Doubled, Spreading to Suburbs," *ABC News*, July 31, 2013, http://abcnews.go.com/blogs/headlines/2013/07/hidden-america-heroin-use-has-doubled-spreading-to-suburbs/.

6. Centers for Disease Control and Prevention, National Center for Injury Prevention and Control, Web-based Injury Statistics Query and Reporting System (WISQARS) (2010), cited in "Youth Violence: Facts at a Glance, 2012 Report from the National Center for Injury Prevention and Control Division of Violence Prevention," http://www.cdc.gov/violenceprevention/pdf/yv-datasheet-a.pdf.

7. Katherine Sharpe, "The Medicine Generation," *Wall Street Journal*, June 29, 2012, http://online.wsj.com/news/articles/SB10001424052702303649504577493112618709108.

8. *Strong's Greek Lexicon*, s.v. "G0932, *basileia*," accessed May 13, 2014, http://www.biblestudytools.com/lexicons/greek/nas/basileia.html.

Chapter 2: Asher and the Elephant

1. Dr. Seuss, *Horton Hatches the Egg* (New York: Random House, 1940), 1.
2. Seuss, *Horton Hatches the Egg*, 16.
3. *CBSnews.com* Staff, "The Delinquents: A Spate of Rhino Killings," *60 Minutes*, August 22, 2000, http://www.cbsnews.com/news/the -delinquents/.
4. *Strong's Hebrew Lexicon*, s.v. "H836, *Asher*," accessed May 13, 2014, http://www.blueletterbible.org/lang/lexicon/lexicon.cfm?Strongs=H 836&t=KJV.

Chapter 4: Life Outside the Palace Walls

1. American Gaming Association, "Casino Alcohol Policies," © 2013, http://www.americangaming.org/industry-resources/research/fact -sheets/casino-alcohol-policies.
2. The character Romeo utters these words in Act II, Scene II. See *Romeo and Juliet*, Bartleby.com, accessed May 14, 2014, http://www.bartleby. com/70/3822.html.

Chapter 5: Transferring the Royal Blessing

1. Ragnhild Sleire Oyen, "King Olav 5," *Store Norske*, December 30, 2004, http://www.nrk.no/underholdning/store_norske/4356194 .html; "King Olav Named Century Norwegian," *VG Nyheter*, December 17, 2005, http://www.vg.no/nyheter/innenriks/kongehuset /kong-olav-kaaret-til-aarhundrets-nordmann/a/299446/.
2. *Wikipedia*, s.v. "Coronations in Norway," accessed May 22, 2014, http://en.wikipedia.org/wiki/Coronations_in_Norway#cite_note-5.
3. Jan Sjåvik, *The A to Z of Norway* (Lanham, MD: Scarecrow Press, 2008), 154, http://books.google.com/books?id=_lNV6AnqTl4C&pri ntsec=frontcover&dq=the+A+to+z+of+norway&hl=en&sa=X&ei=Nc WEU_zFF8KkyATNsIKAAg&ved=0CC0Q6AEwAA#v=onepage& q=the%.

4. Vince Lombardi, *What It Takes to Be Number One* (Nashville: Thomas Nelson, 2012), 91.

5. "A Football Life: Vince Lombardi," NFL Network, December 24, 2013, http://www.nfl.com/videos/a-football-life/0ap2000000303829 /A-Football-Life-Vince-Lombardi-Football-is-his-mistress.

Chapter 7: Three Pillars of Parenting

1. *Strong's Greek Lexicon*, s.v. "G3962, *patr*," accessed May 15, 2014, http://www.blueletterbible.org/lang/lexicon/lexicon.cfm?strongs =G3962

2. Kyla Boyse, "Television and Children," University of Michigan Health System, last updated August 2010, http://www.med.umich.edu/your child/topics/tv.htm.

3. Harold Taylor and Geraldine Taylor, *Hudson Taylor in Early Years: The Growth of a Soul* (Philadelphia: China Inland Mission, 1912) chapter 4, "Nurture and Admonition." See http://www.worldinvisible.com /library/hudsontaylor/hudsontaylorv1/hudsontaylorv104.htm.

Chapter 8: Honor and Respect

1. *Strong's Greek Lexicon*, s.v. "G5091, *tima*," accessed May 19, 2014, http://www.blueletterbible.org/lang/lexicon/lexicon.cfm?Strongs =G5091&t=KJV.

Chapter 9: LOL, SMHS, and CC (Cultivating Communication)

1. Kevin Eikenberry, "What the Best Leaders Will Learn from Peyton Manning (But Most Will Ignore)," *Leadership and Learning with Kevin Eikenberry* (blog), January 27, 2014, http://blog.kevineiken-berry.com /leadership/what-the-best-leaders-will-learn-from-peyton-manning -but-most-will-ignore/.

2. *Unguarded with Rachel Nichols*, "Interview with Seahawks' Russell Wilson," January 10, 2014, http://transcripts.cnn.com/TRAN SCRIPTS/1401/10/rnu.01.html.

Chapter 10: Table Time: God's Word and Prayer

1. Environment News Service, "Celebrating 40 Years of Endangered Species Act Success," December 31, 2013, http://ens-newswire.com/2013/12/31/celebrating-40-years-of-endangered-species-act-success/.

2. *Strong's Greek Lexicon*, s.v. "G1721, *emphytos*," accessed May 21, 2014, http://www.blueletterbible.org/lang/lexicon/lexicon.cfm?strongs=G1721.

3. *Strong's Greek Lexicon*, s.v. "G1209, *dechomai*," accessed May 21, 2014, http://www.blueletterbible.org/lang/lexicon/lexicon.cfm?Strongs=G1209&t=KJV.

4. *Strong's Greek Lexicon*, s.v. "G435, *Aner*," accessed May 21, 2014, http://www.blueletterbible.org/lang/lexicon/lexicon.cfm?Strongs=G435&t=.

5. *General Social Survey 2010*, cited in The ARDA: Association of Religion Data Archives, "Frequency of prayer by religion," accessed May 22, 2014, http://www.thearda.com/quickstats/qs_104_p.asp.

Chapter 11: Wisdom

1. IMDb.com, *Indiana Jones and the Last Crusade* (1989): Quotes, accessed May 22, 2014, http://www.imdb.com/title/tt0097576/quotes.

Chapter 12: Integrity

1. Julia Lovell, *The Great Wall: China Against the World, 1000 BC-AD 2000*, (New York: Grove/Atlantic, 2006), 252–254, http://books.google.com/books?id=IWS53cuiuVgC&printsec=frontcover&dq=The+great+wall:+china+against+the+world&hl=en&sa=X&ei=0MSEU9z8LIWGyAS_IYGYDQ&ved=0CC0Q6AEwAA#v=onepage&q=The%20great%20wall%3A%20.

Chapter 14: Resiliency

1. *Strong's Greek Lexicon*, s.v. "G5281, *hypomon*," accessed May 21, 2014, http://www.blueletterbible.org/lang/lexicon/lexicon.cfm?Strongs=G5281&t=KJV.

2. *Strong's Greek Lexicon*, s.v. "G2233, *hgeomai*," accessed May 21, 2014, http://www.blueletterbible.org/lang/lexicon/lexicon.cfm?Strongs =G2233&t=KJV.

Chapter 15: Purity

1. *Strong's Greek Lexicon*, s.v. "G680, *haptomai*," accessed May 21, 2014, http://www.blueletterbible.org/lang/lexicon/Lexicon.cfm?Strongs =G680.

2. Rand S. Swenson, "Review of Clinical and Functional Neuroscience," Dartmouth Medical School, accessed May 22, 2014, https://www .dartmouth.edu/~rswenson/NeuroSci/index.html.

3. Dirk Scheele, Andrea Wille, Keith M. Kendrick, Birgit Stoffel-Wagner, Benjamin Becker, Onur Güntürkün, Wolfgang Maier, and René Hurlemann, "Oxytocin Enhances Brain Reward System Responses in Men Viewing the Face of Their Female Partner," *Proceedings of the National Academy of Sciences of the United States of America* (*PNAS*), 110 (50) 20308–20313, November 25, 2013, http://www.pnas.org /content/110/50/20308.full?sid=74396885-99fc-4bfc-b8d4-bd01ece 3514a, cited in Brenda Goodman, "How the 'Love Hormone' Works Its Magic," WebMD from HealthDay, November 25, 2013, http:// www.webmd.com/sex-relationships/news/20131125/how-the-love -hormone-works-its-magic.

4. *Strong's Greek Lexicon*, s.v. "G2853, *kolla*," accessed May 21, 2014, http://www.blueletterbible.org/lang/lexicon/lexicon.cfm?Strongs =G2853.

Chapter 16: Service

1. *Strong's Greek Lexicon*, s.v. "G1401, *doulos*" accessed May 21, 2014, http://www.blueletterbible.org/lang/lexicon/lexicon.cfm?Strongs =G1401.

2. *Strong's Greek Lexicon*, s.v. "G1980, *episkeptomai*" accessed May 21, 2014, http://www.blueletterbible.org/lang/lexicon/lexicon.cfm?Strongs =G1980&t=KJV.

3. To learn more on how you can implement a church-school outreach in your area, visit us online at www.ChurchAdoptaSchool.org or call 800–800–3222.

4. IMDb.com, *The Hanging Tree* (1959), accessed May 26, 2014, http://www.imdb.com/title/tt0052876/?ref_=nv_sr_1.

Chapter 17: Using All Your Arrows

1. This word means "mercy." *Strong's Concordance*, s.v. "H1136, *Ben-chesed*," accessed May 22, 2014, http://biblesuite.com/hebrew/1136.htm.

Appendix 2: A Message to Single Parents

1. This material was adapted from Dr. Evans's book *Help and Hope for the Single Parent* (Chicago: Moody, 2014). Used with permission.

2. *Strong's Hebrew Lexicon*, s.v. "H7210, *ro'iy*" accessed May 22, 2014, http://www.blueletterbible.org/lang/lexicon/lexicon.cfm?Strongs=H7210&t=KJV.

ABOUT THE AUTHOR

Dr. Tony Evans is founder and senior pastor of the 9,500-member Oak Cliff Bible Fellowship in Dallas, founder and president of The Urban Alternative, former chaplain of the NFL's Dallas Cowboys, and longstanding chaplain of the NBA's Dallas Mavericks. His radio broadcast, *The Alternative with Dr. Tony Evans*, can be heard on nearly 1,000 US radio outlets daily and in more than 130 countries.

Dr. Evans is a prolific author of more than seventy books, including the best-selling *Kingdom Man* and *Kingdom Woman* (written with his daughter Chrystal Evans Hurst).

Dr. Evans has received many honors over the years but two that he especially treasures are the Father of the Year award voted by the Dallas Father of the Year Committee and the Marian Pfister Anschutz Award for "dedication to protecting, encouraging, and strengthening the American family" from the Family Research Center.

Dr. Tony Evans is married to Lois, his wife and ministry partner of over forty years. They are the proud parents of four children, all of whom serve in ministry: Chrystal Hurst, Priscilla Shirer, Anthony, and Jonathan. They are also the proud grandparents of eleven: Kariss, Jessica, Jackson, Jesse III, Jerry Jr., Kanaan, Jude, Joel, Kelsey, Jonathan II, and Kamden. For more information, visit TonyEvans.org.

THE ADVICE YOU NEED FOR
RAISING KINGDOM KIDS
FROM DR. TONY EVANS

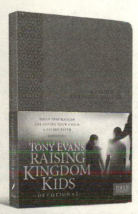

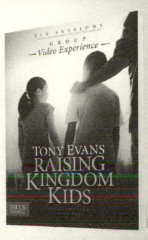

RAISING KINGDOM KIDS
DEVOTIONAL
978-1-62405-409-9

RAISING KINGDOM KIDS
VIDEO STUDY
978-1-62405-407-5

KINGDOM QUEST
STRATEGY GUIDE – AGES 7-10
978-1-58997-807-2

KINGDOM QUEST
STRATEGY GUIDE – AGES 11-13
978-1-58997-808-9

KINGDOM QUEST
STRATEGY GUIDE – AGES 14+
978-1-58997-809-6

Meet the rest of the family

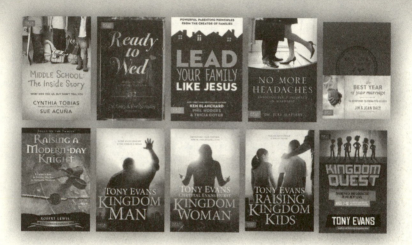

**Expert advice on parenting and marriage . . .
spiritual growth . . . powerful personal stories . . .**

Focus on the Family's collection of inspiring, practical resources can help your family grow closer to God—and each other—than ever before. Whichever format you need—video, audio, book or eBook—we have something for you. Visit our online Family Store and discover how we can help your family thrive at **FocusOnTheFamily.com/resources**.

More Resources to Help You Thrive in Marriage and Life

Starting now, this could be your best day, week, month, or year! Discover ways to express your needs, embrace your purpose, and love more fully. We offer life-transforming books, e-books, videos, devotionals, study guides, audiobooks, and audio dramas to equip you for God's calling on your life. Visit your favorite retailer, or go to FocusOnTheFamily.com/resources.